H. Wiley Hitchcock, editor

Prentice-Hall
History of Music Series

MUSIC IN THE MEDIEVAL WORLD, *Albert Seay*

RENAISSANCE MUSIC, *Joel Newman*

BAROQUE MUSIC, *Claude V. Palisca*

MUSIC IN THE CLASSIC PERIOD, *Reinhard G. Pauly*

NINETEENTH-CENTURY ROMANTICISM IN MUSIC, *Rey M. Longyear*

TWENTIETH-CENTURY MUSIC: AN INTRODUCTION, *Eric Salzman*

FOLK AND TRADITIONAL MUSIC OF THE WESTERN CONTINENTS, *Bruno Nettl*

MUSIC CULTURES OF THE PACIFIC, THE NEAR EAST, AND ASIA, *William P. Malm*

MUSIC OF LATIN AMERICA, *Gilbert Chase*

MUSIC IN THE UNITED STATES: A HISTORICAL INTRODUCTION, *H. Wiley Hitchcock*

TWO HUNDRED YEARS OF RUSSIAN MUSIC, 1770–1970, *Boris Schwarz*

Nineteenth-Century Romanticism in Music

REY M. LONGYEAR
Department of Music
University of Kentucky

PRENTICE-HALL, INC., ENGLEWOOD CLIFFS, NEW JERSEY

PRENTICE-HALL INTERNATIONAL, INC., *London*
PRENTICE-HALL OF AUSTRALIA, PTY. LTD., *Sydney*
PRENTICE-HALL OF CANADA, LTD., *Toronto*
PRENTICE-HALL OF INDIA (PRIVATE), LTD., *New Delhi*
PRENTICE-HALL OF JAPAN, INC., *Tokyo*

to my former students
serving in the armed forces in Vietnam

*M*usic *is the most* Romantic *of all the arts, as its subject is only the Infinite, the secret Sanskrit of Nature expressed in tones which fill the human heart with endless longing, and only in music does one understand the songs of the trees, flowers, animals, stones, floods!*

Kreisleriana, E. T. A. Hoffmann

Foreword

Students and informed amateurs of the history of music have long needed a series of books that are comprehensive, authoritative, and engagingly written. They have needed books written by specialists—but specialists interested in communicating vividly. The Prentice-Hall History of Music Series aims at filling these needs.

Six books in the series present a panoramic view of the history of Western music, divided among the major historical periods—Medieval, Renaissance, Baroque, Classic, Romantic, and Contemporary. The musical cultures of the United States, Latin America, and Russia, viewed historically as independent developments within the larger Western tradition, are discussed in three other books. In yet another pair, the rich yet neglected folk and traditional music of

Foreword continued

both hemispheres is treated. Taken together, the eleven volumes of the series are a distinctive and, we hope, distinguished contribution to the history of the music of the world's peoples. Each volume, moreover, may be read singly as a substantial account of the music of its period or area.

The authors of the series are scholars of national and international repute—musicologists, critics, and teachers of acknowledged stature in their respective fields of specialization. In their contributions to the Prentice-Hall History of Music Series their goal has been to present works of solid scholarship that are eminently readable, with significant insights into music as a part of the general intellectual and culture life of man.

H. WILEY HITCHCOCK, *Editor*

Preface

The spectrum of nineteenth-century music is characterized by a number of familiar, if not overly familiar, compositions; a larger number of worthy compositions that have fallen into neglect; and an enormous mass of music still awaiting classification and evaluation. To the general observer, the history of music in the nineteenth century resembles a panorama of mountains, some in shadow, separated by mist-shrouded valleys; in the limited space of this volume, an author studying this period can only direct the reader's attention to various aspects of the peaks, tell him something about their shadowy portions, and point out some of the salient features of the valleys.

Some of the procedures I have followed and some of the priori-

Preface continued

ties I have assigned require explanation. Most of the bibliographical references are to works in English; those who desire further information about a given composer should consult the entries in *Grove's Dictionary of Music and Musicians* (the second edition often gives more detailed information about nineteenth-century composers than the fifth), *Die Musik in Geschichte und Gegenwart*, and *The Music Index* as well as the bibliographies in the books and articles I have cited.

The principal complaint about most of the general histories of music and the few scholarly handbooks dealing with nineteenth-century music is that they are organized around genres rather than composers, in defiance of the period's emphasis on individualism. Thus, I make no apology for writing what the late Manfred Bukofzer called a "portrait gallery of composers"; a few of the loose ends which are not amenable to such an organization are hopefully tied together in the final chapter.

Since no handbook in English deals adequately with the music written between 1790 and 1830, I have devoted what some may think a disproportionate amount of the limited space available to composers active then. Since this is not a comprehensive history of nineteenth-century music, I have had to omit several composers whose influence did not extend beyond the single medium in which they were active; I apologize to cellists, violinists, and organists for thus excluding Duport and Grützmacher, Vieuxtemps and Wieniawski, Boëly and Karg-Elert. Chapter 8 presented a special problem since by 1900 virtually every European people had its own "nationalist" art music; the lack of a sufficient number of important composers to justify separate subject headings precluded discussion of Spain (Albéniz), Poland (Moniuszko), Belgium (Benoît), or the Baltic States (Ciurlionis, Wihtol). The brief treatment of music in the

Preface continued

United States will be more than compensated for by H. Wiley Hitchcock's *Music in the United States: A Historical Introduction* in this series, and is included chiefly to provide a historical perspective.

Wherever feasible, I have used the English titles of compositions when they have common currency, even at the risk of such incongruities as "Siegfried's Rhine Journey" from *Die Götterdämmerung*, or to translate titles not known to English-speaking readers in their original language, *e.g.*, *Wallenstein's Camp* for *Valdštynuv Tábor*. At the risk of "didacticism," I have endeavored to follow current practices in transliterating Russian proper names rather than to perpetuate the Franco-German versions which still clutter concert programs.

Space does not permit my listing all of those whose help was so valuable in preparing this book. I would, however, like to give special thanks to Almonte C. Howell, Jr., Gordon J. Kinney, György Króo, and Wasley S. Krogdahl, and to commend Aimo Kiviniemi, acting chairman of the Department of Music at the University of Kentucky, for kindly arranging my teaching schedule to permit blocks of uninterrupted time for study and writing. Summer research grants provided by the University of Kentucky Research Foundation substantially assisted the completion of this volume. I am grateful to the staffs of the Sibley Music Library and the music divisions of the Library of Congress and the Newberry Library, and especially to Norma Jean Gibson, Vivian MacQuown, and Adelle Dailey of the University of Kentucky Libraries. I wish also to acknowledge the editorial assistance of H. Wiley Hitchcock and the help rendered in so many wonderful ways by my wife.

R. M. L.

Ɪ

Contents

1   The Romantics and Music   1

2   Beethoven and His Predecessors   10
Precursors of Romanticism, 11   Ludwig van Beethoven: His Apprenticeship, 13   Influences on Beethoven's First Period, 15   Beethoven's First Period, 19   Beethoven's Second Period, 21   Beethoven's Final Period, 28   Beethoven's Legacy, 32

3   Beethoven's Contemporaries   35
Louis Spohr, 36   Carl Maria von Weber, 39   Franz Schubert, 43   Lesser Composers, Mostly Pianists, 54

4   The German Romantic Efflorescence   59
Felix Mendelssohn-Bartholdy, 60   Robert Schumann, 66   The German Romantic Legacy, 74

5 *Italian and French Romanticism* *76*
Italian Opera, 1813–1853, 76   French Operatic Genres, 84   Fryderyk
Chopin, 88   Hector Berlioz, 94

6 *The Music of the Future* *102*
Ferenc Liszt, 104   Richard Wagner, 116   Other Composers, 128

7 *The Rebirth of Absolute Music* *130*
Anton Bruckner, 131   Johannes Brahms, 135   The "French Musical
Renaissance," 145

8 *Nineteenth-Century Nationalism in Music* *154*
Russia, 158   Bohemia, 167   Scandinavia, 172   Hungary, 175
England, 179   United States, 180

9 *The Twilight of Romanticism* *184*
Italian Opera after *La Traviata*, 185   Central Europe, 188   France,
197

10 *Nineteenth-Century Musical Romanticism and Its Audience* *208*
Sociology of Musical Romanticism, 208   Romantic Performance Practice, 212

Index *215*

I

The Romantics
and Music

The very term "Romanticism" has conjured up, as Arthur
Lovejoy has remarked, "one of the most complicated, fascinating,
and instructive of all problems in semantics." Some writers have
called for the abolition of this "rubber band" term, yet what word
could replace it?

Any period term, like Baroque, Classic, or Romantic, can be
used pejoratively, neutrally, or as a term of praise; as a convenient
substitute for citing dates; or can be used to mean what its users
intend it to mean. To writers on music, Romanticism means music
between 1828 and 1880 in its narrowest and 1789 to 1914 in its
broadest sense. Some consider Romanticism, in opposition to Classi-

cism, a phenomenon which recurs throughout artistic and intellectual history: J. S. Bach, Monteverdi, the troubadours, St. Paul, and Plato have been called "Romantics" by various writers. Others wish to limit the term drastically to those German writers of the 1790's and those French writers of the 1830's who called themselves Romantics. The present fashion is to consider Classicism and Romanticism as opposite sides of the same coin current between 1740 and 1830 (at its most limited) and 1910 (at its broadest); this eliminates searches for precursors or survivals or the jumble of "pre-," "post-," and "neo-" prefixes, but on the other hand does not fully take into account the changing clusters of musical and other ideas during the 90 to 170 years included in this period. All period terms are conveniences, and their usefulness declines in proportion to the effort made to define them or to postulate relationships among their cultural, intellectual, social, and historical components. A period term does imply that certain norms exist which at least tenuously link the personages and ideas subsumed under this heading, that other persons and configurations of thought are excluded, and also that a certain chronology exists even though the terminal dates at each end cannot be fixed with much precision and considerable overlapping occurs with adjacent periods.

Romanticism is a difficult period term to define because its protagonists, as opposed to their rationalistic predecessors, were so wary of definitions. Victor Hugo's statement that Romanticism was "a certain vague and indefinable fantasy" is as close to the mark as any attempt at a concrete definition. Examination of salient characteristics will serve us better.

First of all, this movement was an international manifestation, strongest in Germany, quite influential in England, France, and Russia, but also evident in Bohemia, Poland, Spain, and Italy. Secondly, the nineteenth century was a period of extreme contrasts, and any idea expressed was certain to elicit its exact opposite. In religious thought, for example, one may compare the diverse ideas of Joseph Smith, Pope Pius IX, Ernst Haeckel, and Mary Baker Eddy and recall that religious martyrdom occurred not only in Uganda and Indo-China during this period but also in Paris under the Commune of 1871. This diversity explains why we can subsume under the heading of Romanticism such contradictory composers as Bruckner and Offenbach, Donizetti and Brahms, Chopin and Sousa. Thirdly, Romanticism repudiated Classic emphases on harmonious adjustment, discipline, moderation, and adaptation whereas it valued striving rather than achieving, becoming rather than being, emotional and inspired rather than rational expression. Classic "uniformitarianism," on the other hand, considered differences in opinion and taste to be evidences of erroneous deviation from the "rationalist collectivism" which taught that the artist should try to communicate not the unique but the views and sentiments common to an idealized mankind. Finally, none of the past seven centuries has ended without a significant change in musical style during its last decade. In the 1790's a new musical language became evident, albeit well-prepared by significant forerunners, and it existed side by side with the old musical language (Haydn, Pleyel, Rossini) for a few decades; a similar co-existence took place during the period from 1890 to 1914 (Debussy, Stravinsky, and subsequently Schoenberg as opposed to d'Indy, Elgar, and Mahler), the new idiom becoming, around 1910, what is loosely called "contemporary" music.

Are we justified in calling the musical language which became discernible as a new idiom around 1790 and declined during the first decade of the twentieth century Romantic? Ernst Theodor Amadeus Hoffmann (1776–1822), a writer with unimpeachable Romantic credentials, considered J. S. Bach, Haydn, Mozart, and especially Beethoven to be Romantics, and Théophile Gautier (1811–1872), a charter member of the Romantic movement, bestowed a similar accolade on Berlioz and Chopin. Hoffmann remarked on several occasions that music, particularly instrumental music, was the most Romantic of the arts, and instrumental music was at least intellectually dominant between 1790 and 1910; it may also be noted that during the nineteenth century both opera and art-song had increasingly active instrumental accompaniments. Parallels, some more tenuous than others, can be drawn between the new expressive melody, the rhythmic experimentation, the coloristic use of harmony and instrumental timbres, the relaxation of and uncertainty about formal canons, the veneration and occasional misuse of the legacy of the past mingled with a sense of writing for the future, and the new tendencies in poetry, the drama, the novel, the pictorial arts, and architecture which are customarily called Romantic. Whereas Classicism was an international movement, as witness the careers of Hasse, Gluck, Haydn, and Mozart, or such international figures as Voltaire, Casanova, and Benjamin Franklin, Romanticism and nationalism are closely intertwined, and the lands which produced Pushkin, Mickiewicz, Palacký, and Ibsen were the homelands of Glinka, Chopin, Smetana, and Grieg. It is furthermore indisputable that the musical languages of Richard Strauss, MacDowell, Elgar, and Delius have more in common with those of Beethoven and Schubert than with those of Stravinsky, Milhaud, or Webern in the 1920's. In short, there is a musical entity whose approximate points of chronological demarcation are 1790 and 1910 and which can justifiably be termed Romantic not just because other writers have done so, but because there are unified musical and cultural traits which were recognized as Romantic then and are identifiable as such today.

The seeds for the interpenetration of the arts which was such a salient characteristic of the nineteenth century were sown by Jean-Jacques Rousseau (1712–1778), known chiefly as a social and educational philosopher and novelist but also gifted in music, musical criticism, and sketching. To him, and to a lesser extent the writers of the French *Encyclopédie* (28 vols., 1751–1772), can be credited the virtual mania for writing about music that arose around 1770.

During most of the eighteenth century, writings about music were by musicians for musicians, and the musical interests of the nonprofessional authors of the time were directed to such practical topics as the use of incidental music in the drama. After 1770 a greater interest in music is a hallmark of German literature, as seen, for example, in the frequent use of music as a literary effect, such as the expressive clavichord playing by Lotte in Goethe's novel *Werther* (1774) or Lady Caroline in Klinger's drama *Sturm und Drang* (1776), which gave its name to an entire if brief literary epoch. "Romantic" musicians as literary figures begin to appear in the mid-1770's and culminate in the incarnation of the Romantic musician, Kreisler, in the stories and novels of E. T. A. Hoffmann.

The writers associated with the movement known as Weimar Classicism—Christoph Martin Wieland (1733–1813), Johann Wolfgang von Goethe (1749–1832), Johann Gottfried Herder (1744–1803), and Friedrich Schiller (1759–1805)—had a lively and often Romantic interest in music. Herder collaborated with J. C. F. Bach, one of J. S. Bach's sons, translated the texts of Handel's *Messiah* and *Alexander's Feast*, and collected folk songs. Schiller distrusted the effect of music because of its appeal to sensuous natures, yet precisely because of its power he used incidental music extensively in most of his dramas, musical metaphors and characterizations in many of his literary works, and musical ideas as an ancillary but not insignificant part of his aesthetic system. Among Goethe's many other activities in Weimar, he also wrote texts for *Singspiele* for amateur court productions and later served as director of the court theatre, where most of the significant operas of the 1780's and 1790's were performed. Yet the musical tastes of these writers were inherently conservative: Schiller ranked Gluck above Haydn and Mozart, Herder considered vocal music superior to "empty" instrumental music and disliked the dominance of music over text in Mozart's operas, and Goethe, though a champion of Mozart's music, rejected the settings of his songs by Beethoven and especially Schubert, preferring the simple tunes of Carl Friedrich Zelter (1758–1832).

Other interesting personages of the time with intense musical activities were C. D. F. Schubart (1739–1791), an organist and composer as well as a poet, aesthetician, and journalist who was imprisoned for his libertarian ideas, and Johann Friedrich Reichardt (1752–1814), a composer and journalist whose activities on behalf of the French Revolution involved him in a celebrated literary feud with Goethe and Schiller.

The role of music in the thought of the German Romantics who came to maturity in the 1790's remains fully to be investigated. One can credit the increasing interest in music partially to the novels of J. J. W. Heinse (1746–1803), but the most influential of the early Romantic writers on music seems to have been Wilhelm Heinrich Wackenroder (1773–1798), who influenced both Hoffmann and Ludwig Tieck (1773–1853). With both Wackenroder and Jean Paul (J. P. Friedrich Richter, 1763–1825), one senses the idea of music as a drug or balm; Wackenroder could listen to music attentively for only an hour, but found that music, apart from the particular mood created by a given composition, would stimulate his thought and imagination (Schiller similarly liked to have music played in an adjoining room while he wrote). "In the mirror of tones the human heart learns to know itself; it is how we learn to feel feelings," Wackenroder wrote, and his fictional musician Josef Berglinger heard "sounds that seem to be words" in music. Jean Paul's ideas on music were Romantic in their contradictions: he once compared music's effect to a lion's tongue licking at the heart "which tickles and scratches until the blood flows," yet later called music, rather than poetry, the "happy art." He preferred the "simple souls" of Haydn and Mozart to composers with great self-possession like Reichardt, and his description of Walt's hearing a Haydn symphony is so rhapsodic, colorful, and impassioned that one would suspect that Beethoven or Schumann was the real composer.

Though Tieck was a musical amateur, Hoffmann spent five years as Kapellmeister (musical director) in Bamberg and directed an opera troupe for a year; composed sonatas, chamber music, and several operas of which *Undine* (1816) is considered a landmark in German Romantic opera; wrote reviews for the *Allgemeine musikalische Zeitung*, the leading musical journal of the time; and created in Kreisler one of the greatest fictional musicians.

Tieck and Hoffmann both agreed that instrumental music was superior to vocal music. In his essay "Symphonien," published in 1814, Tieck regarded the "symphony," as he understood it, as the highest form of art and considered sonatas and chamber music merely as preliminary studies for it, yet he seems to be discussing Reichardt's music for *Macbeth* and Beethoven's music to *Egmont*. Despite his activity as an opera composer and conductor, Hoffmann gave instrumental, and particularly orchestral music, the palm. His statement "Music is the most Romantic of all the arts" recurs constantly throughout his writings, but in his essay "Beethovens Instrumental-Musik" he qualified this statement to refer to instrumental music. Other Romantic writers placed a primary emphasis on music; among them, Jean Paul stated that "no color is as Romantic as a tone," and Heinrich von Kleist (1777–1811) considered music the root of all the other arts.

Hoffmann tended to view all his musical heroes—Beethoven, Mozart, Haydn, even J. S. Bach and Palestrina—as Romantics. Though he esteemed Haydn for perceiving "the human in human life Romantically," he was among the first to appreciate the daemonic element in Mozart's music and compared Bach's eight-part motets to the "daring, wonderful, Romantic" construction of the Strasbourg cathedral. Hoffmann mocked the shallow appeal of virtuosos and repeatedly portrayed the dualism between the Romantic artist and the pseudo-cultured "Philistine," a favorite topic of later Romantic writers on music like Berlioz and Schumann.

All of the German Romantic writers, as well as such later poets as Baudelaire (1821–1867) and Verlaine (1844–1896) and musicians like Skryabin and Ciurlionis, and even the historian Oswald Spengler (1880–1936), perceived music as part of a glorious synaesthesia, *audition colorée*, in which words were tones and tones colors.

Heinse called music a "speech without consonants." Tieck asked, "Isn't it permitted and possible to think in tones and to make music in words and thoughts?" And Hoffmann described how, in a delirious condition preceding sleep, especially after hearing much music, he felt a synaesthesia of colors, tones, and odors. Space precludes further discussion of German Romantic ideas on music, but it should be mentioned that these ideas were expressed before 1825.

Music played a less significant role in the writings of the French Romantics; it was not a major force until the 1880's, with the symbolist poets and the *Révue Wagnerienne*. French Romanticism was later than its German counterpart and, except for Rousseau and Chateaubriand (1768–1848), was not a major force until 1830. Henri Beyle (1783–1842), writing under the pen name of Stendhal, was the French writer most interested in music; although his biographies of Mozart and Haydn were at least partially plagiarized, his *Life of Rossini* (1824) is still a valuable document. Yet Stendhal disliked Weber's music. Although Honoré de Balzac (1799–1850) gave lip service to Beethoven and Alfred de Musset (1810–1857) to Schubert, their chief delights were Italian opera and French Grand Opera; Balzac's two musical novellas, *Massimilla Doni* and *Gambara*, are rhapsodic analyses of, respectively, Rossini's *Mosé in Egitto* and Meyerbeer's *Robert le Diable*. The lady writers of the French Romantic period found the musicians of the time most interesting as amatory partners. Théophile Gautier discussed only three composers in his *History of Romanticism* (1874): Berlioz, Chopin, and the insignificant Hippolyte Monpou (1804–1841). He admitted to intimate friends that he preferred silence to music. The French Romantic novelists chiefly used music to portray social milieux, and their works are excellent sources for a sociological history of music.

In conclusion, the influence of Romantic writers on composers was greater than the influence of composers, even in Germany, on the writers. Romantic literature is echoed through the music of the nineteenth century far more than Romantic music was discussed or even mentioned in the writings of the time. It is also important to recall that most nineteenth-century musicians had strong interests and capabilities in other fields, in contrast to the preceding century when such versatile figures as Rousseau, Schubart, and Reichardt were rarities. Berlioz and Wagner were significant literary figures apart from their music; Weber, Schumann, and d'Indy had more than a common competence as authors; and many composers wrote their memoirs or a series of essays on music. Spohr, Mendelssohn, and especially Mikolajus Ciurlionis (1875–1911) were gifted painters, and the latter's paintings with musical titles, e.g., "Serpent Sonata," represent a high point of Romantic synaesthesia. Many Romantic musicians were musical journalists, and such composers as Brahms, Chaikovsky, Saint-Saëns, and d'Indy edited early music. Most Romantic composers were well-read and literarily sensitive to a degree unprecedented in the history of music, and only a few musical figures, like Bruckner and Dvořák, displayed the exclusive concentration on music characteristic of most eighteenth-century composers.

Literary historians date the end of Romanticism between 1843, when Victor Hugo's drama *Les Burgraves* failed, and 1849, when the last of the unsuccessful revolutions which had convulsed continental Europe was suppressed. Such literary genres as realism, naturalism, symbolism, and *fin de siècle* decadence followed in succession, but parallels between these literary styles and later nineteenth-century music can be at best tenuously drawn in only limited instances; Romanticism in music is unified stylistically and is an historical entity. One can speak best of generations of musical Romanticism, beginning with its precursors in Baroque Venice and concluding with those composers who reached musical maturity in the late 1880's and 1890's.

Bibliography

The literature on Romanticism is extremely copious; I have found the following to be valuable because of their divergent ideas about Romanticism: Frederick B. Artz, *From the Renaissance to Romanticism* (Chicago, 1962); Irving Babbitt, *Rousseau and Romanticism* (New York, 1919); Friedrich Blume, article "Romantik" in *Die Musik in Geschichte und Gegenwart* (Kassel, 1951–   ), XI, cols. 785–845; Howard E. Hugo (ed.), *The Portable Romantic Reader* (New York, 1957); Arthur O. Lovejoy, "On the Discrimination of Romanticisms" in *Essays in the History of Ideas* (Baltimore, 1948); and René Wellek's articles on Romanticism in his *Concepts of Criticism* (New Haven, 1962), which includes a survey of recent writings on this topic. The methodology of W. T. Jones's *The Romantic Syndrome* (The Hague, 1961) is not readily applicable to music.

The principal sources for the study of the relationship of the literary figures of Romanticism to music are: Wilhelm Bode, *Die Tonkunst in Goethes Leben* (Berlin, 1912); R. M. Longyear, *Schiller and Music* (Chapel Hill, 1966); Willi Reich, *Musik in romantischer Schau* (2 vols., Basel, 1946), a selection of excerpts from Romantic writers; Ronald Taylor, *Hoffmann* (New York, 1963); Julien Tiersot, *La Musique aux temps romantiques* (Paris, 1930), and Walter Wiora, "Herders und Heinses Beiträge zum Thema 'Was ist Musik?'" *Die Musikforschung* XIII (1960), 385–95.

Among the general histories of music, the best treatments of the nineteenth century are in Donald J. Grout, *A History of Western Music* (New York, 1960); Albert Smijers, *Algemene Muziekgeschiedenis* (Amsterdam, 1940); Karl H. Wörner, *Geschichte der Musik* (3rd ed., Göttingen, 1961), Jules Combarieu, *Histoire de la musique* (3 vols., Paris, 1913–1919), and the nineteenth-century sections in Guido Adler (ed.), *Handbuch der Musikgeschichte* (1924; reprint, Tutzing, 1961). The best book wholly devoted to nineteenth-century music is Ernst Bücken's *Musik des XIX. Jahrhundert bis zur Moderne* (Potsdam, 1932); other important works are Gerald Abraham, *A Hundred Years of Music* (3rd ed., London, 1963), the best book in English but dealing with music only since 1830; Alfred Einstein, *Music in the Romantic Era* (New York, 1947); Georg Knepler, *Musikgeschichte des XIX. Jahrhunderts* (2 vols., Berlin, 1960–1961), with a sociological emphasis from the viewpoint of left-wing Marxism; and Hugo Riemann, *Geschichte der Musik seit Beethoven* (Berlin, 1901).

Among the histories of individual genres or stylistic traits, those with significant and important sections on the nineteenth century are: Donald J. Grout, *A Short History of Opera* (1st ed., New York, 1947; 2nd ed., New York, 1965, both valuable); Ernst Kurth, *Romantische Harmonie und ihre Krise in Wagners Tristan* (Bern, 1920); Robert U. Nelson, *The Technique of Variation* (Berkeley and Los Angeles, 1948); William S. Newman, *The Sonata in the Classic Era* (Chapel Hill, 1965) and *The Sonata Since Beethoven* (in preparation); Curt Sachs, *Rhythm and Tempo* (New York, 1953); Bence Szabolcsi, *Bausteine zu einer Geschichte der Melodie* (Budapest, 1959); D. G. Tovey, *Essays in Musical Analysis* (6 vols., London, 1935–1945) and *The Forms of Music* (reprint, New York, 1956), Homer Ulrich, *Chamber Music* (2nd ed., New York, 1966), R. M. Longyear, "Music, Sacred: Romanticism," *New Catholic Encyclopaedia* (New York, 1967) and Fritz Egon Paner, "Das deutsche Lied im 19. Jahrhundert" in Guido Adler (ed.), *Handbuch der Musikgeschichte* (reprint, Tutzing, 1961), pp. 939–955.

2

Beethoven
and His Predecessors

Whereas the *galant* style of the eighteenth century arose first in Paris and Naples, the ultimate source of musical Romanticism was the Venice of the seventeenth and early eighteenth centuries. Personal expression and subjective feeling make a work like Monteverdi's *L'Incoronazione di Poppea* (1642) sound surprisingly "modern," and the subsequent Venetian operas, with their expressive arias and highly organized ritornelli, led directly to the Venetian concertos of Tomaso Albinoni (1671–1750), Alessandro (*ca.* 1684–*ca.* 1750) and Benedetto (1686–1739) Marcello, and especially Antonio Vivaldi (*ca.* 1669–1741). In Vivaldi's music the future is discernible in such passages as the long melodic lines of his slow movements

(Concerto for Three Violins, F major), the dotted unison ritornelli in other slow movements (C minor Violin Concerto, Fanna No. 92), and the dramatic syncopations, drumming basses, slow harmonic rhythm, and emotional turbulence of the Concerto for the Dresden Orchestra. The Vivaldian style was brought to Germany (especially Saxony-Thuringia) by his pupil J. G. Pisendel (1687–1755), J. S. Bach, and finally G. B. Platti (1690–1753), one of the major keyboard composers of the early Classic period.

Precursors of Romanticism

There are two basic styles in Classic music, the light, airy *galant* and the emotional, subjective *empfindsamer Stil*, the latter best seen in the music of two of J. S. Bach's sons, Wilhelm Friedemann (1710–1784) and Carl Philipp Emanuel (1714–1788). Wilhelm Friedemann was an extremely expressive composer whose output was small, more from laziness than from a supposed fondness for the bottle, and his subsequent influence was slight. On the other hand, C. P. E. Bach can be justly called the most original and one of the most influential composers of the Classic period. Geiringer has admirably described his musical style as

> a daring harmonic language with incisive dissonances and stunning chord-combinations; dramatic pauses, unexpected rests, alterations in tempo, and sudden changes in major and minor modes, an effect often increased by varying dynamics and the use of different registers.[1]

C. P. E. Bach sincerely believed that music should touch the heart, which, as he said, could not be done through "running, rattling, drumming, or arpeggios." His music is surpassed during the eighteenth century only by major works of Gluck, Haydn, and Mozart, and his yearning appoggiaturas and strange, distant modulations were only tentatively approached by his more timid successors. His Sinfonia in E minor (1756) contains virtually all the effects Haydn later employed in his *"Sturm und Drang"* symphonies of the 1770's, and his use of instrumental recitative (first "Prussian" sonata) looks ahead to Beethoven, Spohr, and Weber; some of the appoggiaturas and modulations of his later fantasies are positively Wagnerian.

[1] Karl Geiringer, *The Bach Family* (New York, 1954), p. 355.

Although C. P. E. Bach may be called the first "Romantic" composer, his influence is most immediately important in its effect on Mozart and Haydn. As a young man, Haydn diligently studied Bach's "Prussian" and "Württemberg" sonatas, and their strong influence is the chief difference between Haydn's best sonatas and the more brilliant and fluent keyboard works of Mozart. Mozart knew Bach's sonatas and their imitations written by German composers residing in France, but was most affected by Bach's symphonies, which he heard at Baron van Swieten's academies in Vienna in the early 1780's and which brought about the increased depth and richness of his last five symphonies.

The *"Sturm und Drang"* movement of the 1770's, so evident in Haydn's symphonies and sonatas of this period, had little direct effect on the Romantic musical style. Haydn ceased to compose in this idiom because his patron, Prince Esterházy, disliked it, and his attempts to recapture this mood in his later symphonies (nos. 83, 95) were not successful. The spirit of the dawning Romanticism is most pronounced in Haydn's slow symphonic introductions, the slow movements of his later symphonies and string quartets, and especially the "Representation of Chaos" in *The Creation* (1798). Mozart, on the other hand, more successfully sublimated and assimilated the *"Sturm und Drang";* even during what his biographers Wyzewa and Saint-Foix call his "crise romantique" of the early 1770's, Mozart balanced tragic works like his early G minor Symphony (K. 183) with sunny, *galant* works like the motet *Exsultate, Jubilate,* and in later years paired his intensely personal and tragic or daemonic works in the keys of C minor, G minor, and D minor with contrasting gayer compositions, often for the same or similar media. These contrasts are best seen in the opposition of D Minor and D major in his opera *Don Giovanni* or in the second and closing theme-groups of his sonata-form movements in the minor mode, stated in mediant major in the exposition but given an air of poignancy and even high tragedy through their recapitulation in tonic minor.

Mozart's influence on Beethoven was immense: one need only compare two of their C minor piano sonatas, Mozart's K. 457 and Beethoven's Op. 13, or "Pathétique." Mozart's ventures into chromatic harmony, most evident in his E-flat String Quartet, K. 428, and his *Requiem,* influenced Beethoven's contemporaries like Hummel and Spohr, who regarded themselves as Mozart's legitimate heirs.

Ludwig van Beethoven (1770–1827): his apprenticeship

Beethoven is the most important composer of the nineteenth century, for all his successors were influenced or even intimidated by his works, which became the touchstone for Romantic critics from E. T. A. Hoffmann onward. Beethoven's music is the culmination of the "Viennese Classic" tradition, yet it furnished the impetus for virtually all instrumental and much vocal composition of the nineteenth century; not a single major composer of this period could wholly escape his influence.

Many writers have attempted to organize Beethoven's compositions according to "periods:" from two to as many as five have been postulated, with three the most commonly agreed upon number. Beethoven's compositions written before the publication of his Opus 1 in 1795, however, constitute a separate period of apprenticeship, and groups of transitional works separate his first and second and third periods. Demarcations between periods can only be approximate, and there is some chronological overlapping between periods, since Beethoven frequently had several compositions in progress at the same time.

Beethoven lived in Bonn until 1792 and during his stay there wrote works which reveal in embryo many of the salient traits of his style. The two most important of these early pieces, the 24 variations on the arietta "Vieni, amore" by Vincenzo Righini (1756–1812), WoO (without opus number) 65, and the Cantata on the Death of the Emperor Joseph II, were written in 1790, although the variations were revised in 1802.

The cantata is an excellent illustration of Beethoven's "noble" style, seen at its best in his later hymn-like slow movements; it not only anticipates his *Missa Solemnis* but also Brahms's works for chorus and orchestra. The influence of the Mannheim symphonist and opera composer Ignaz Holzbauer (1711–1783) has been found in this work; equally important influences are the styles of Gluck and his most important successor, Luigi Cherubini. It was this cantata which induced Haydn to accept Beethoven as a pupil.

EXAMPLE 2-1. Beethoven, Cantata on the Death of Joseph II, WoO 87.

The Righini variations display several characteristics of Beethoven's style: aggressive contrary motion (Var. I), sharp and unexpected dynamic contrasts (Var. II), trills (Var. IV), tempo contrasts which anticipate the first movement of the Piano Sonata, Op. 109 (Var. XIV), hymn-like writing (Var. XVII), and the long coda (final variation); Variation XXIII closely resembles the opening of his Piano Sonata, Op. 2, No. 2. The frequent inversions of chords, especially of the dominant seventh, provide both an interesting bass line and a harmonic drive. Mozart's piano variations are an obvious model, as are those by Beethoven's teacher in Bonn, Christoph Gottlob Neefe (1748–1798).

Influences on Beethoven's first period

Beethoven studied with Haydn for two years after arriving in Vienna in 1792 and subsequently took lessons from the contrapuntist J. G. Albrechtsberger (1736–1809) and Gluck's disciple Antonio Salieri (1750–1825). Their influence, as well as that of Mozart and the French Revolutionary composers, has been extensively discussed in the Beethoven literature, but three other composers also substantially affected his first-period works: Muzio Clementi (1752–1832), Leopold Koželuch (1752–1818), and Emanuel Aloys Förster (1748–1823).

A Roman by birth, Clementi was taken to England at the age of fourteen and spent most his life there, apart from concert tours and business trips. In the early 1780's he concertized on the continent, competed against Mozart (arousing his enmity) before the Emperor Joseph II, and entered into a tragic love affair which drove him from France in 1784 after he wrote some of his finest sonatas. After his return to London he wrote symphonies (now forgotten and mostly lost) in competition with Haydn, and during his long lifetime served as composer, teacher, publisher, and piano manufacturer. His sonatas, his most important compositions, extend from 1765 to 1821.

Clementi was a direct musical descendant of Domenico Scarlatti (1685–1757) and one of the great innovators in writing for the piano. He was the first important composer who really thought in terms of the modern piano, and his conception of the instrument is evident as early as the sonatas of Op. 2, written around 1770. Such characteristic forward-looking devices as powerful octaves, fast repeated notes, rapid chains of parallel thirds and sixths, fast scales and arpeggios, and thick, full, quasi-orchestral chords are often blended with legacies of the past like murky (broken octave) basses, two-voiced textures, or Scarlattian turns and ornaments. The sonatas of 1782 and 1783 (Opp. 7, 9, and 10) had a particularly strong impact on Beethoven. The singing, ornamental melodies over a slow harmonic rhythm or the sonority and spacing of the slow movement of Op. 9, No. 3 could easily be mistaken for a first-period Beethoven work, as can the Trio of the second movement of Op. 10, No. 1

EXAMPLE 2-2. Clementi, Sonata, Op. 10, No. 1, trio of second movement.

(Ex. 2-2) which so admirably exploits the singing low register of the piano.

After the Op. 14 sonatas, Clementi's compositions show less freshness of inspiration despite such magnificent exceptions as the sonatas in F-sharp minor and G minor of Op. 34 (1788). Most of his sonatas between 1784 and 1804 were written for concert tours or other commercial purposes and thus lack the personal feeling of his finest sonatas. His best late works, five sonatas and the *Gradus ad Parnassum*, were written between 1819 and 1826 and had a considerable influence on the second generation of Romantic piano composers.

Beethoven knew and esteemed Clementi's sonatas even though he did not meet him personally until 1807. Among Clementi's more discernible influences on the younger composer are the design of the first movement of the G minor Sonata (Op. 34, No. 2), in which the slow introduction is used in the development which probably was a model for Beethoven's "Pathétique" sonata; his use of rhythmic motives from his expositions in his development sections;

and his explosive developments and finales whose influence culminated in Beethoven's Sonata ("Appassionata"), Op. 57.

Many reasons have been advanced for the gross neglect of Clementi's compositions, among them Mozart's sarcastic personal comments ("a charlatan like all Italians") and incompetent editions of his music designed for pedagogical use rather than for musical merit; perhaps the chief reason is that aspiring pianists learn Clementi's sonatinas as youngsters and later regard them as representative of his oeuvre, which is like considering the "Minuet in G" and the *Album for the Young* typical specimens of Beethoven's or Schumann's music. Clementi is at his best a major composer of more than historical significance.

Leopold Anton Koželuch was one of the first Czech composers to migrate to Vienna toward the close of the eighteenth century. A prolific composer, many of his works display Romantic traits, best seen in the slow introductions to his sonatas which he sometimes repeats or echoes at the end of the first movement (a further influence on the "Pathétique" sonata). There are also striking similarities between Koželuch's and Beethoven's rondo-type sonata finales, sequences, and thematic contrasts in sonata expositions. The sonata from which Ex. 2-3 is taken was most probably written in 1785.

EXAMPLE 2-3. Koželuch, Sonata, Op. 15, No. 1, first movement: (a) introduction; (b) opening of first theme-group; (c) portion of second theme-group.

EXAMPLE 2-3 continued.

The chamber music of Emanuel Aloys Förster, whom Beethoven regarded highly and to whom he sent pupils who wanted to study composition, bears the same relationship to Beethoven's early string quartets as Clementi's and Koželuch's piano works do to his first-period sonatas. Mozart's "Haydn" quartets and late quintets are obviously Förster's points of departure. His style is quite contrapuntal (as could be expected of a composer who as a student arranged all the fugues from J. S. Bach's *Well-Tempered Clavier* for string quartet), and every member of the chamber ensemble has an important part to play. As Förster's String Quintet, Op. 19 (1802), shows, C minor meant to him what it did to Mozart and Beethoven. Such Beethovenian devices as a finale in minor with a fading-out coda ending in major, contrary motion in thirds even at the risk of dissonance, and a "bonus" recapitulation with more music than in the exposition can be encountered in Förster's works. He is not merely a forerunner and early contemporary of Beethoven (he gave up composing in 1803), but a significant if underestimated member of the Viennese Classic school of instrumental composition (Ex. 2-4).

EXAMPLE 2-4. Förster, String Quartet, Op. 16, No. 5, first movement (published 1798).

Beethoven's first period

This period of composition extends from approximately 1794 to 1800, with the "Spring" Sonata for violin and piano, Op. 24, the First Symphony, and the D major Piano Sonata, Op. 28 as the major terminal works. The piano, either in a solo capacity or in a chamber ensemble, is the dominant instrument.

Formal experimentation, deriving from Haydn's examples, is typical of Beethoven's early piano sonatas, with their structures ranging from the quite free forms of Op. 2, No. 2 and Op. 10, No. 2 to the clarity of form of Op. 22. The moods of the sonatas range from the tempestuousness of the two C minor sonatas to the placid contemplativeness of Op. 28 (called "Pastoral") and the playfulness of Op. 10, No. 2. Many of these sonatas are technically easy, but only an accomplished pianist can do justice to Op. 10, No. 3, the finest sonata of this period. Many of these sonatas have four movements, with the third generally termed "minuetto" but occasionally "scherzo." Perhaps because of Clementi's influence, Beethoven's piano sonatas are the most original of his first-period compositions.

Beethoven's chamber music for or with winds need not detain us long save to mention that his classicism is strongest in these works and that he abandoned this medium after his Septet, Op. 20 (which he came to detest) and the Serenade, Op. 25. His chamber music for strings consists of several duet sonatas of which the Op. 24 violin sonata is the most popular, a group of trios of which Op. 3 is really a divertimento, and the six string quartets, Op. 18, of which the first, fourth, and sixth are the most interesting. Orchestral music includes two rather conventional piano concertos (Opp. 15 and 17, the latter composed first) and the First Symphony. Its introduction was thought radical, for Beethoven omitted stating the unison tonic at the opening and began by going to the subdominant, establishing his tonic by circumscribing it. The second movement (as in the Op. 18, No. 4 quartet) contains contrapuntal *tours de force*, a legacy of his study with Albrechtsberger; the third movement is a full-blown scherzo though entitled "minuetto," and the finale has the playfulness of Haydn's last movements.

The transitional works leading to Beethoven's second period were written during his progressive loss of hearing; in his own words he described the history of this catastrophe:

June 29, 1801

I have been feeling, I may say, stronger and better, but my ears continue to hum and buzz day and night. I must confess that I lead a miserable life. For almost two years I have ceased to attend any social functions, just because I find it impossible to say to people: I am deaf. If I had any other profession I might be able to cope with my infirmity. . . . In order to give you some idea of this strange deafness, let me tell you that in the theatre I have to place myself quite close to the orchestra in order to understand what the actor is saying, and that at a distance I cannot hear the high notes of instruments or voices. . . . Already I have often cursed my Creator and my existence. Plutarch has shown me the path of *resignation*. If it is at all possible, I will bid defiance to my fate, though I feel that as long as I live there will be moments when I shall be God's most unhappy creature. . . . Resignation, what a wretched resource! Yet it is all that is left to me. . . .[2]

Of the principal works of this transitional period, the piano sonatas between Op. 26 and Op. 31 show most clearly the dissolution of the composer's earliest style and his groping for new means of expression. An irregular order of movements, with a slow movement first and the "sonata-allegro" movement at the end, characterize the Op. 26 and Op. 27 sonatas, the second of which is the popular "Moonlight;" novel, too, are the storminess of the "Tempest" sonata, whose slow movement was apparently influenced by the French funeral marches of the 1790's (but less so than the third movement of Op. 26), and the fine Op. 31, No. 3 sonata with its non-tonic opening, rich harmonies, and scherzo-like slow movement with sforzandi in unexpected places. Of the violin sonatas of Op. 30, the best is the second, a typical C minor work; also in this key is the powerful Op. 37 piano concerto, with a deeply expressive slow movement in the remote key of E major and an unusual finale. The most novel elements of the Second Symphony are the lengthy slow introduction to the first movement and the finale, whose capriciousness and playfulness exceed Haydn's. The "Kreutzer" Sonata for violin and piano (Op. 47) is the terminal work of the first transitional period.

Beethoven's second period

Most of Beethoven's popular works come from this period, which begins with the Third ("Eroica") Symphony and ends with such works as the "Emperor" Concerto and the incidental music to Goethe's drama *Egmont*. To this group of works belong the Fourth, Fifth, and Sixth symphonies; his most and least popular concertos; his only opera; some overtures; most of his songs; and the three string quartets of Op. 59; but only three piano sonatas.

The "Eroica" Symphony is the grandest and most grandiose specimen of the instrumental music of this time. Though the sonata had been gaining in length, the symphony had not, and Mozart's

---

[2] Emily Anderson (ed. and trans.), *The Letters of Beethoven* (London, 1961, 3 vols.), I, 59–60.

"Jupiter" Symphony (K. 551) was the most monumental of the preceding works in this medium. Attempts have been made to trace the influence of the French Revolution in the "Eroica" Symphony, chiefly its prominent triadic themes; further investigation may show that the overtures to the "rescue operas" may have contributed to Beethoven's symphonic "breakthrough."

Those who have studied this symphony have frequently commented on Beethoven's introducing a new "theme" in the development section of the first movement; this was not a startling innovation, for Mozart had done this, but what is novel is the new theme's reappearance in the immense coda. The second movement is a funeral march on an unprecedented scale, though Beethoven had made preliminary essays in his Op. 26 and Op. 31, No. 2 sonatas. The scherzo begins the vein of "cosmic humor" that culminates in the scherzo of the Ninth Symphony, and its prevalent stepwise motion is balanced by the difficult horn fanfares in the trio. The finale is a set of variations on a bass line with an accompanying melody which Beethoven had used as a contradanse and as a ballet movement in *The Creatures of Prometheus*, Op. 43; the Op. 35, or "Eroica" Variations, a piano work based on the bass line more than the theme, is complementary to, rather than a study for, the Third Symphony's finale. Beethoven is said to have preferred this symphony above all his others.

The Fourth Symphony is a contrasting and delightful (if unjustly neglected, like virtually all his works in B-flat major) interlude before the Fifth Symphony, in which Beethoven was trying to achieve a certain cyclic relationship, rhythmic as well as thematic, between some of the movements and within the first movement. The first movement is noteworthy for its intense concentration and the rhythmic motive which unites all its sections, but such interesting elements are absent from the repetitious second movement, a "double variation" in the style of Haydn. The third movement—anyone knowing the Beethovenian scherzo of the period will know why I hesitate to call it a scherzo—was considered the most "Romantic" of all the movements by contemporaneous critics and is bound to the noisy finale by a mysterious transition over a steady drumbeat. The triumphant finale in C major is an excellent specimen of the "optimistic" solution of the conflict inherent in the symphony in a minor mode (in the recapitulation of the first movement the second and closing theme-groups are stated in tonic major but are overwhelmed by the coda in minor); the return of a portion of the scherzo at the end of the development section is an inspired idea; but the coda is unequaled in sheer noise until the patriotic finales of the Russian nationalist composers later in the century. The exquisite Sixth, or "Pastoral," Symphony achieves its contemplative effects through light orchestration and slow harmonic rhythm.

These symphonies show Beethoven's increasing impatience with the limitations of the instrumental technique of his time. A virtuoso performer himself who had heard and composed music for the best living instrumentalists, he demanded a comparable facility from his orchestral musicians. One need but cite the demands on the horn players in the "Eroica" Symphony or *Fidelio*, or on the technique of the string bass players in the trio of the third movement of the Fifth Symphony; Beethoven had previously heard a string bass virtuoso playing his cello sonatas on this instrument. Beethoven even emancipated the trumpets and timpani from their previous noise-making and rhythm-emphasizing functions, yet he was no "orchestrator," and several conductors, notably Felix Weingartner (1863–1942), have tried to revise his scoring.

Among the concertos, the G major Piano Concerto (No. 4) is one of Beethoven's most serene and contemplative works, whereas the Fifth ("Emperor") is one of his most triumphant compositions. The Violin Concerto (Beethoven also wrote an alternative version as a piano concerto) shows the influence of the "military" concertos of G. B. Viotti (1755–1824) and Pierre Rode (1774–1830), the most renowned violinists of the period, but the "triple concerto," Op. 56, for piano, violin, and cello, is a minor work.

Before discussing the sonatas of the period, a digression is necessary to examine briefly the form that Beethoven had inherited. From Mozart he obtained clean craftsmanship and the idea that the violin in the duet sonata was an equal partner rather than an accompanying instrument; from Haydn the piquant surprises that could arise through experimenting with the formal structure; and from Clementi the conception of the rhetorical drama and conflict inherent in the form.

In the first movement, the center of gravity of the sonata of the time, the highly organized structure consisted of an exposition of thematic material heightened by the conflict of tonal centers as well as themes; a development, generally of previously presented material, whose conflicts came through thematic fragmentation and motivic development, often contrapuntally treated, underlaid by fluctuating and unstable tonalities; and a recapitulation restating the exposition with certain changes to insure that the second and closing theme-groups would appear in the tonic, thus resolving the conflicts in the exposition. Haydn, more than Mozart, contributed a slow introduction to the first movement, which Beethoven either spun out at great length (second and seventh symphonies) or reduced to a mere gesture (Op. 31, No. 2, Op. 78 sonatas). Of greater importance are Beethoven's codas, a device seldom used extensively by his predecessors save in several of Mozart's works in C major, but which Beethoven raised to the status of a second development section.

The formal structure and time-scale of the first movement of Beethoven's Piano Sonata, Op. 53, called "Waldstein" after one of the composer's first patrons, lies midway between the highly concentrated sonata-form movements of the Fifth Symphony or Op. 95 string quartet and the immensely expanded first movements of the "Eroica" and the Ninth symphonies. The first theme-group is based on motives rather than themes, and the transition is long in order to prepare the rather remote tonality of E major for the hymn-like second theme. A second transition leads to A minor for the closing group, which returns smoothly to the tonic for the repeat of the exposition but then, during the second playing of this section, modulates to F major, the tonality of the opening of the development. The latter is based on motives from the first theme-group and a figuration pattern from the second theme-group (measure 49 of the exposition), treated in sequence. The retransition to the tonic begins imperceptibly, sinks to a low point (measure 142) and then rises to a peak of climactic fury, all on the dominant of C major, then subsides through scales in contrary motion to the recapitulation, in which a "bonus" of eight measures (167–173) intensifies the feeling of the home tonic through deviations from it in delaying the inevitable.

Beethoven effectively reconciles the demands that the second and closing theme-groups be recapitulated in the tonic by beginning the former group in A major but (through A minor) closing in C major and, through a slightly compressed transition, beginning his closing group in subdominant minor. His emphasis on the subdominant leads to the coda, which starts in the remote key of D-flat major and, on motives from the first theme-group that had previously been worked over in the first development, rises to a climax; but the intensity decreases with a final statement of the second theme, a slowing down in the speed, and fermatas on the leading tone. A final rush, based on the first theme in the tonic, concludes the movement. One should note throughout the movement the transitional open spaces, the "lungs" which permit the music to breathe. Many similarities in principles of formal structure, emotional intensities, and scope are found between the "Waldstein" Sonata and the comparable work in minor, the popular "Appassionata" Sonata, Op. 57, in F minor like the storm movement of the "Pastoral" Symphony.

Fidelio, Beethoven's only opera, is a middle-period work although it underwent several revisions. The libretto was based on *Léonore, or Conjugal Love* by the French playwright Jean-Nicolas Bouilly (1763–1842), which had previously been set to music by two minor composers, Pierre Gaveaux (1761–1825) and Ferdinando Paër (1771–1839). Fidelio is virtually the last of the rescue operas and the only one which has survived in the repertoire. Though the lesser conventions of opera, especially those deriving from the *Singspiel*, were beneath Beethoven, as the opening and Rocco's "Gold" aria in Act I will testify, the composer's freedom-loving spirit and moral integrity rises to its height in Act II during the scene of Florestan in his dungeon cell, the climactic quartet of Act II when Leonore saves Florestan from his mortal enemy Pizarro, and the finale, in C major like the finale of the Fifth Symphony, with its triumphant echoes of the spirit of French revolutionary music. Of the four overtures which Beethoven wrote for the opera (contrast this with Rossini's using the same overture for at least three different operas!), the "Fidelio" overture written in 1814 generally is used to open the opera whereas "Leonore No. 3," a virtual symphonic poem recapitulating the high points of the drama, is performed during the change of scene for the finale of the second act.

The most experimental works of this period are the three string quartets of Op. 59 which Beethoven wrote for Count Rasumovsky, the Russian ambassador to Vienna who maintained a private string quartet. In homage to his patron, Beethoven incorporated Russian themes in each quartet; the theme of the trio of the third movement of the E minor quartet was also used by Musorgsky in the Coronation Scene in *Boris Godunov* (see Ex. 8-5). The F major quartet has a first movement on a grandly expansive scale, and its second movement is one of Beethoven's most unusual compositions because of the irregular resolutions of what seem to be dominant harmonies and its virtually unclassifiable form. The E minor quartet has a moving slow movement and a Hungarian-type finale which oscillates between C major and E minor, whereas the C major quartet closes with a fugue which too many performers play at breakneck speed.

Beethoven's overtures, written chiefly for dramas but transcending their original function as curtain-raisers, are among the principal ancestors of the symphonic poem. Among the best are the previously-cited "Leonore No. 3;" the overture to *Coriolan* (by Collin, not Shakespeare), a characteristic C minor work; and the overture to Goethe's drama *Egmont*, for which Beethoven also wrote the incidental music frequently called for in the drama. Beethoven's songs, a good many of which date from his middle period, are the most neglected of his compositions. Their air of nobility is most successful in the settings of devotional texts (Op. 48) by the German poet C. F. Gellert (1715–1769). The songs stem from and are the culmination of the heritage of J. F. Reichardt and other north German composers, rather than being precursors of the Lieder of Schubert.

Beethoven's second transitional period, which William S. Newman has called the "period of invasion" because of the French conquest of Austria and entry into Vienna during these years, is an experimental period and also the time when the composer's popularity was at its zenith. Among the major works of this period are the Seventh and Eighth Symphonies, the "Archduke" piano trio, the piano sonatas between Op. 78 and Op. 90, and the string quartets Op. 74 and Op. 95, as well as some lesser-known works like the Choral Fantasia, the Mass in C, and *Wellington's Victory*, or "Battle Symphony," Op. 91.

During this period Beethoven wrote genuinely neo-Classic works, the F-sharp and G major piano sonatas, Opp. 78 and 79, and the Eighth Symphony—homages to the past with an eye to the future. His other major works of this time are more experimental: the Seventh Symphony with its monothematic first movement and its preoccupation with rhythm; the virtually athematic first movement of the Op. 74, or "Harp," quartet; and the Op. 95 quartet with its astronomically high specific gravity unequaled until Sibelius's Fourth Symphony, unusual excursions into remote keys through enharmonic modulations, intensely concentrated first movement, and almost Rossinian conclusion. Whereas the first movement of the Op. 90 piano sonata is nearly as terse as that of the Op. 95 quartet, the second and final movement, almost Schubertian in its lyricism, is as spacious and expansive as the "Archduke" Trio, Op. 97.

Beethoven's sketches for the finale of his Eighth Symphony give insight into his creative process. Composition was not easy for Beethoven; thematic ideas, of which only the germ of the final form is evident in their initial stages, had to be laboriously revised and polished. His jottings and revisions were set down in sketchbooks, many of which have been preserved though scattered among many libraries. As a reviser of his sketches, he may be compared with the mother bear of mediaeval legend whose cubs were born formless and then literally licked into shape. Example 2–5 shows this process.

In the initial sketch for the finale (a), the basic ideas of the opening are evident: the major third in triplet rhythm at the opening, the consequent idea with a descending melodic contour (measure 5), and the flat submediant as a harmonic interval (measure 9). Sketch (b) seems to be a regression, although the descending melodic line is improved and continued, the meter receives its final designation as ¢ , and the contrast of triplets with duplets is not entirely abandoned. Sketch (c) Beethoven designated as "better": he restored the contrast of triplets and duplets at the opening but stopped the propulsive effect of the consequent idea. In the final form, the second measure of the earlier sketches is expanded through clever repetition, the chromatic alteration in measure 7 gives more harmonic

EXAMPLE 2-5. Beethoven's sketches for finale of Symphony No. 8, Op. 93:
(a) first sketch; (b) second sketch; (c) third sketch; (d) final version.[3]

[3] After Gustav Nottebohm, *Zweite Beethoveniana* (Leipzig, 1887), pp. 116–117.

(b)

(c) Meilleur

Final form
Allegro vivace

EXAMPLE 2-5 continued.

interest, the change of pitch location in measure 6 continues the effect of a descending melodic line, and the phrase is extended. The D-flat of the first sketch is saved until measure 17 and changed to a C-sharp, the reason for which is apparent only in the coda where it becomes the dominant of F-sharp minor.

Beethoven's final period

During this period, which began around 1815, Beethoven became almost totally deaf, led an eremitic and eccentric existence, and tried to gain custody of his nephew Karl, resulting in battles with the boy's mother and constant struggles between uncle and ward that culminated with Karl's running away and subsequently attempting suicide. Beethoven had increasing difficulty in conceiving, organizing, and shaping his musical ideas, which effected a lessened output of work, but among the compositions of this period are some of the most abstract and sublime ever written. Yet these works estranged Beethoven from his audience and alienated most of his colleagues, who could or would not follow him into the empyrean. From this period come his last five piano sonatas, his best bagatelles, his last five string quartets, the "Diabelli" Variations, the *Missa Solemnis*, and the Ninth Symphony.

This period can be called Beethoven's "contrapuntal" period. Fugues occur in the finales of the Op. 101, Op. 106 ("Hammer-klavier"), and Op. 110 sonatas, and contrapuntal devices characterize the variations of Op. 109 and the first movements of Op. 106 and Op. 111. The first movement of the C-sharp minor quartet (Op. 131) is a fugue, and portions of this fugue and the third of the variations from the slow movement of this quartet resemble the "paired imitation" of Josquin des Prez and his successors. The *Grosse Fuge*, Op. 133, orig-inally intended to be the finale of the Op. 130 quartet, is the apogee of Beethoven's abstract counterpoint. That Handel was his principal mentor is especially apparent in the "Consecration of the House" overture, Op. 124, and the fugal portions of the *Missa Solemnis*.

Beethoven overwhelmed the limits of Classical form in his sonata movements by blurring the demarcations between sections and theme-groups and in creating such gigantic structures as the first movements of the "Hammerklavier" Sonata and Ninth Symphony. Frequent changes of key and tempo characterize many of these movements; in the first movement of the Op. 130 quartet, of average length for this period, there are sixteen tempo changes and six changes of key signature, ranging from six flats to two sharps. These two signatures, representing the flat submediant and major mediant relationships of the tonic key of B-flat major, give further evidence of the composer's predilection, already apparent in his second period, for modulations by thirds in his sonata-form expositions.

The slow movements of Beethoven's instrumental cycles often become the musical centers of gravity, and sometimes (Opp. 109, 111) are final movements. Occasionally these slow movements have programmatic titles, like "Cavatina" in the Op. 130 quartet or "Song of a Convalescent's Thanksgiving to God, in the Lydian mode" from the Op. 132 quartet. Theme and variation form, often with a final variation containing chains of trills which add to the mood of sublimity, is common in these movements. As early as 1806 Beethoven became interested in variations on a ground bass (the C minor varia-tions, WoO 80), and the variations of his last period emphasize as constants the structure and basic harmonic scheme of the theme, with melody, meter, rhythm, pitch-locations, and other musical ele-ments as variables.

The composer-publisher Anton Diabelli (1781–1858) circulated one of his waltzes among a large number of composers with the request that each write a variation on it. Beethoven complied, and in fact wrote 33 variations on the theme; these not only explore all its harmonic, motivic, and musical possibilities but also, as Geiringer has shown [*Musical Quarterly*, L (1964), 496–503], fit into an architectonic scheme in which the number of variations conforms to the structure of the theme: eight groups of four variations each following the theme's eight four-measure phrases, with Variation 33 as an epilogue. In contrast to the grand scope of the "Diabelli" Variations are the *Bagatelles* of Op. 126 and the last four of the *Bagatelles*, Op. 119 (the others of this set having been composed earlier); they are enigmatically terse works which had a strong influence on Schumann and Brahms.

Just as the giant "Hammerklavier" Sonata stretches the capacities of performer and listener to the utmost, so does the Ninth Symphony. All its movements are immense specimens of their type—the first of sonata form, the second of the scherzo, and the third of the "double variation." The finale is a setting of Schiller's "Ode to Joy" for soloists, chorus, and orchestra, a project which had been in the back of the composer's mind for over 30 years. Its structure is essentially that of theme and variations, a form unusual in choral music, and a few of its notable moments may be cited: the recapitulation of snatches of themes from earlier movements, each rejected by an instrumental recitative in the cellos and basses; the simplicity of the theme, which led Spohr to reject it as a "Gassenhauer" (alley) tune; the sudden modulation at the end of the fifth variation from A major (dominant of the tonic) to F major (dominant of the new key of B-flat), one of the best illustrations of Beethoven's sudden shifting of tonal planes; the military march variation for tenor soloist and male chorus, with the ensuing triple fugue followed by the statement of the theme in its entirety for the last time; the introduction of new material (G major, 3/2) after which this new material is combined with the theme in a simultaneous double fugue; the sublime and almost impossible vocal cadenzas for the soloists; and the breathtaking coda.

On the other hand, the *Missa Solemnis* can be regarded as one of the greatest failures in the history of music. Despite its sublime moments, especially in the outer movements (Kyrie and Agnus Dei), the work is uneven, even patchy, and the overlong conclusions of the Gloria and Credo stupefy rather than edify. Though Handel's choral counterpoint influenced these sections, Cherubini inspired many of the quieter passages, and Haydn furnished not only the general structure but also, in his *Mass in Time of War in 1796* ("Pauken-messe"), the idea for the drumbeats and fanfares in the Agnus Dei. The personal prayers of the Kyrie and Agnus Dei and the setting in bold relief of the words "et homo factus est" in the Credo are Bee-thoven's own ideas.

What perplexed Beethoven's contemporaries most and led them to believe that he had either taken leave of his senses or, because of his deafness, had no idea of the sounds he was writing was actually a typical device of the period, "Romantic irony." Though this effect has been studied in the literary works of the time, its musical import has not been investigated. Romantic irony has been equated variously with parody, overstatement, exaggeration, misplaced em-phasis, or destruction and recreation of the object or mood to indi-cate mastery of the material. Often in his late works Beethoven creates a sublime mood only to destroy it, as in the fourth variation of the slow movement in the C-sharp minor quartet (Ex. 2-6a), or in this same quartet to contrive a musical practical joke (Ex. 2-6b); note the portrayal of musicians who seem to have lost their place in the music, their attempts to restore order, and their finally fiddling away *sul ponticello* (on the strings near the bridge) like an orchestra of infuriated dwarfs. Beethoven's supreme example of Romantic irony is the enigmatic pizzicato conclusion of his F major Quartet (Op. 135).

EXAMPLE 2-6. Romantic irony in Beethoven's Quartet in C-sharp major, Op. 131: (a) variation 4 in "fourth" movement; (b) coda of scherzo, "fifth" movement.

EXAMPLE 2-6 continued.

Beethoven's legacy

No composer of the nineteenth century could wholly escape Beethoven's influence, for his musical activity was so universal that he must be regarded as the trunk of the tree of nineteenth-century music from which so many branches sprang.

Beethoven gave the strongest impetus, at least for music, to the idea that art was a substitute for, or at least as noble as, religion. A

cluster of attitudes arose from this idea. The world, meaning publishers, music lovers, the middle-class audience, and the nobility (later
the state) owed the composer a living. He, in his turn, deliberately
aimed at creating the musical masterpiece, chiefly an instrumental
cycle with at least one movement in sonata form, since such a work
was the noblest, most serious, and most intellectually respectable
sort of musical composition. The gestation period for such works
was longer, as befits such higher-grade organisms; such works were
individual entities to be published as separate opus numbers rather
than in sets; and the greatest of these compositions were intended for
posterity rather than for the demands of the musical market. Performers, instrumental or vocal, should raise their technical skill or
vocal ranges to the composer's demands and the producer should
meet the composer's stipulation for an increased number of performers; this widened the resources on which the future composer could
call, but began to open a gulf between the composer, who became
a specialist rather than a performer who wrote his own repertoire,
and the journeyman musician or singer. The sociological features of
nineteenth-century music, to be further discussed in Chapter 10, became apparent in Beethoven's time, and he gave these trends a
powerful push partly through his own forceful personality, which
encouraged later composers along the same lines.

In his large instrumental cycles Beethoven displayed two contradictory attitudes: the first, implying tight condensation, fairly
strict construction, and even some degree of connection between
movements or their constituent sections, best shown in his Fifth
Symphony, Op. 95 Quartet, and Op. 101 Piano Sonata, continued
through Schumann and Brahms, and culminated in the later symphonies of Sibelius; whereas the second, characterized by an expanded
and loose construction, a flexible order and number of movements,
some programmatic elements, and even the implication that the symphony or sonata was what one chose to make it (most evident in the
Sixth and Ninth symphonies, "Hammerklavier" Sonata, and Op. 131
Quartet), can be found in Schubert, Berlioz, Chopin, Bruckner, and
Mahler. Beethoven widened the resources of tonality (macro-
harmony), though micro-harmonic innovations (coloristic chords)
were the property of his lesser contemporaries, and strove to elevate
counterpoint to the peak of nobility reached by J. S. Bach and
Handel.

Beethoven's influence on instrumental music or the large choral work was stifling, stultifying, or at least terrifying to subsequent generations of composers. Many of his younger contemporaries and successors focused their attention on forms which Beethoven had somewhat neglected, such as the song, song cycle, or small character piece, yet Beethoven had anticipated even these efforts in such works as his song cycle *An die ferne Geliebte,* Op. 98, and the *Bagatelles* of Op. 119 and Op. 126.

Bibliography

The literature on Beethoven is so copious that only a brief selection of the best studies can be suggested here. Alexander Wheelock Thayer's *Life of Beethoven* (1866–79), the standard biography (but one which does not discuss the music), has been re-issued in a fine annotated edition by Elliott Forbes (Princeton, 1964, 2 vols.). Emily Anderson's translation of the *Letters of Beethoven* (3 vols., New York, 1964) and O. G. Sonneck's *Beethoven: Impressions of Contemporaries* (New York, 1926) give an excellent portrait of Beethoven the man, whereas Donald Tovey's incomplete *Beethoven* (London, 1944) contains valuable insights into his works. A good one-volume critical biography of Beethoven is needed; the best is Marion Scott's *Beethoven* (London, 1934). *Das Werk Beethovens* by Georg Kinsky and Hans Helm (Munich, 1955) is for Beethoven's oeuvre what Köchel's catalogue is for Mozart's. Among the studies of Beethoven's works in individual genres are George Grove, *Beethoven and his Nine Symphonies* (reprint, New York, 1962); Donald Tovey, *A Companion to Beethoven's Pianoforte Sonatas* (London, 1951); William S. Newman, *The Sonata in the Classic Era* (Chapel Hill, 1963), pp. 501–542; with Clementi discussed pp. 738–759; and the studies of Beethoven's quartets by Joseph de Marliave (London, 1928), Daniel Gregory Mason (New York, 1947), Philip Radcliffe (London, 1965), and Joseph Kerman (New York, 1967). Gustav Nottebohm's *Beethoveniana* (reprint, 2 vols., Leipzig, 1927) is the best study of the sketches, and Allen Forte's *The Compositional Matrix* (Baldwin, 1961) studies the genesis of the Op. 109 piano sonata through its sketches.

3
Beethoven's Contemporaries

The first three decades of the nineteenth century have frequently been called the "Age of Beethoven." This term is somewhat erroneous, for although Beethoven was the greatest composer of this period and virtually all his contemporaries came at some time into his orbit, it must be recalled that a large number of significant composers were active between 1800 and 1830. All of them had their roots deeply sunk into the eighteenth century, and some considered themselves Mozart's legitimate heirs; most of them accepted Beethoven's earlier compositions while rejecting the works of his final period. Yet in a sense the composers to be discussed in this chapter were more progressive than Beethoven and, perhaps because they refused to compete with him and sought different means of musical expression, had a more immediate influence on most of the younger composers who reached musical maturity between 1830 and 1850.

Louis (Ludwig) Spohr (1784–1859)

Haydn was still composing when Spohr published his first work, and Wagner finished *Tristan und Isolde* in the year of Spohr's death. Though Spohr rejected most of Beethoven's music from the Fifth Symphony onward, he welcomed the early operas of Wagner. Though as a violin virtuoso he wrote most of his compositions for this instrument, wind players are his staunchest champions today, and he is best known now not through his music but for his autobiography, which gives a vivid picture of European musical life during the first three decades of the nineteenth century. Spohr was a universal composer, for he wrote even harp music (for his first wife) and works for piano as well as much chamber music, ten symphonies, choral music (including a Mass), operas, and concertos.

Spohr's chamber music ranges from duos for two violins to elaborately-scored works like the Nonet, Op. 31, for strings and winds. Quite typical are the solo quartets, which the composer described as being "for violin, with second violin, viola, and cello"; the first violin parts have twice as many pages as any other part and are really violin concertos with string trio accompaniments. His most interesting chamber works are his double string quartets (Opp. 65, 77, 87, 136), not for string octet but two opposed string quartets, or his chamber music with wind instruments like the Nonet (its slow movement is probably Spohr's finest composition), the Octet, Op. 32, and the Quintet for piano and winds, Op. 52.

Spohr's brilliant violin concertos have passed into virtual oblivion except for the Eighth Concerto in A minor, called "Gesangscene" because it was modeled after the Italian *scena ed aria*. His clarinet concertos, though not particularly grateful for the instrument, are sometimes played.

Spohr's ten symphonies range from 1811 to 1857; some have programmatic titles. The best is the Fourth, *Die Weihe der Töne* (Op. 86, 1832), which includes a romanza-type slow movement in which a lullaby, dance, and serenade are stated by themselves and then combined (with conflicting 3/8, 2/8, and 9/16 meters) in the manner of the three dance orchestras in the finale to Act I of Mozart's *Don Giovanni;* a dotted march in the style of Spontini; an "Ambrosian Song of Praise" in counterpoint to a fugato; and an extended chorale prelude in Bach's style. The curious "Historical Symphony" (No. 6, Op. 120) is "in the style and taste of four different periods": that of Bach and Handel (1720), Haydn and Mozart (1780), Beethoven (1810), and the "modern" period of 1840. The first movement is like a Baroque-era French overture; the second utilizes the chromaticism of Mozart's slow movements; the third is more like a fast minuet by Schubert than a "cosmic" Beethoven scherzo; and the finale, opening with a crashing diminished-seventh chord, is less "modern" than the later works of Beethoven or Schubert. The Seventh Symphony, titled "Earthly and Divine in Human Life" (Op. 121, 1841) and scored for two orchestras, anticipates the Liszt of *Les Préludes* in the second movement and the pseudo-religious Wagner of *Lohengrin* in the "Divine" finale. The program of the symphony would have appealed to both Liszt and Wagner, and Spohr's symphonies must be considered important antecedents of the symphonic poem.

Spohr's most important operas are *Faust* (1816), the first major opera based on Goethe's drama, and his masterpiece, *Jessonda* (1823). Spohr was intentionally trying to create the great German opera and selected as his models not only his idol Mozart but also the French rescue opera. The grand arias and finales are the most interesting portions, but his operas are not as attractive as Weber's because Spohr lacked dramatic instinct and musical economy; he envied Weber's ability to write popular operas.

Among Spohr's once-popular oratorios, the most representative are *The Last Judgment* (1826), *Calvary* (1835), and (his best work in this genre) *The Fall of Babylon* (1840). He also wrote a Mass for Ten Voices (1820) in which he tried to combine sixteenth-century contrapuntal techniques with the harmonies of Mozart's *Requiem.* Spohr's oratorios are out of fashion because they contain almost unbearably cloying movements characterized by such effects as over-use of 9/8 meter and slow tempos, a lavish use of chords of the diminished seventh and augmented sixth, and a melodic chromaticism often intensified by doubling the dissonant tones at the third or sixth below. Spohr's chromaticism stems from Mozart's, especially from such of his slow movements as those of the E-flat Quartet, K. 428, and the "Prague" Symphony, K. 504. Such passages

Andante

Fear   thou   not,   O   man   for thy   Re -

deem - er   liv - eth   He   that   died   is

ri - sen,   and   He   shall   live   to   all   e - ter - ni - ty,   and

He   shall   reign,   and shall   con - quer   all His   e - ne -

EXAMPLE 3-1. Louis Spohr, *The Fall of Babylon.*

EXAMPLE 3-1 continued.

as that shown in Example 3-1, with its wandering tonality finally settling into a cadence, influenced Spohr's successors.

Spohr's concertos had a strong influence on those of Mendelssohn and Chopin, and his chromaticism not only affected Wagner (Ex. 6-5b) but in its more sentimental vein the course of English Protestant church music. Though his music is of great historical importance, it lacks the sincerity and effusiveness of Weber's, the elegance of Field's, or the singing style and harmonic inventiveness of Schubert's.

Carl Maria von Weber (1786–1826)

Weber has been hailed as the first genuinely "Romantic" composer, the first "modern" composer, and the first orchestrator. Although he was chiefly a composer of piano music and operas, he also wrote two symphonies, a few Masses and other choral works, songs, chamber music, display pieces for clarinet and other wind instruments; he even began an autobiographical novel.

Weber's piano music is written in an extremely personal and individual style. With his large hands and long thumbs he could easily play the full chords spanning a tenth and the wide leaps in a rapid tempo which make his music so difficult for most pianists. A striking characteristic of his style is his transfer of orchestral idioms to the keyboard; not just a virtually orchestral range of sonority, as in Clementi and Beethoven, but an actual imitation of orchestral sounds, like the timpani strokes in the second movement of the Op. 24 piano sonata, the timpani rolls and horn-like arpeggios opening the Op. 39 sonata, or the string tremolos in the solo piano part of the Op. 32 concerto. Weber is the first composer whose piano works have been successfully transcribed for orchestra, as witness Berlioz's and Weingartner's transcriptions of *Invitation to the Dance* or Hindemith's *Symphonic Metamorphoses*, three movements of which are based on Weber's four-hand piano pieces. Other Weberian traits are a facile homophonic writing and a brilliance deriving from Mozart's sonata-rondo finales.

Weber's sonatas clearly show the weaknesses of early Romantic extended instrumental forms. The first movements have magnificent openings, but the lyrical themes are not suitable for development, the transitions sag, the second themes are not as strong as the first themes, and the developments are filled with sequences and passage work, often over diminished-seventh chords. The slow movements and scherzos are fine, but the finales, although containing breathtaking virtuoso passages, lack a quality of "summing up" the instrumental cycle. As a composer of four-hand duets for one piano, Weber deserves to rank with Mozart and Schubert, especially in the pieces of Op. 60. His variations are chiefly ornamental; the most interesting individual ones are those in "national" styles—mazurkas, Spanish dances, and especially polaccas, which are among his favorite vehicles for virtuosity.

The concertos, chiefly for piano or clarinet, have strong links with the eighteenth century through their quasi-martial openings. Noteworthy are the abbreviated concertos, especially the Konzertstück in F minor for piano, with its exuberantly joyous finale, and the Concertino for clarinet and orchestra. The two symphonies, both in C major and both dating from 1807, are remarkably surprising and fresh works, apparently modeled on Mozart's "Paris" Symphony (K. 297) and Beethoven's First Symphony; Weber's First, with its cyclic use of the raised fourth degree of the major scale, anticipates the "Turkish" elements of *Abu Hassan* and *Oberon*.

Weber's four best operas are his masterpieces. *Abu Hassan* (1812), with only three characters and one act, is a delightful Turkish Singspiel, a worthy successor to works on similar topics by Gluck, Grétry, and Mozart. The other three operas share certain characteristics: the supernatural "marvelous" element is important, and all incorporate "grand arias" for the protagonists with contrasting romances for the lesser characters, a legacy of the rescue opera. *Der Freischütz* (1821) and *Oberon* (1826) contain much nature-painting, with the real hero of the former the German forest in its benign (the huntsmen's chorus in Act III) or malignant aspects (the "Wolf's Glen" in the finale of Act II) *Euryanthe* (1823), a chivalric drama with an impossibly absurd libretto, is less successful than Weber's other operas, probably because in it he was striving to write the "great German opera." *Euryanthe* is considered "connected" and "through-composed" because the numbers are linked by accompanied recitatives and ariosos rather than by secco recitative or spoken dialogue, but set-numbers are easily distinguishable. Weber made some use of recurrent "reminiscence motives" associated with characters (especially the villainess Eglantine) or states of mind, a technique to be developed more fully by Wagner in his leitmotives.

Weber's operatic overtures are sonata-form movements skillfully constructed from the operas' main themes. The overture to *Oberon* is a good illustration: the introduction contains Oberon's horn call, the ritornello from the fairies' chorus in Act I, and the march for Charlemagne's court in Act III; the first theme-group is the conclusion of the Act II quartet; the second theme-group contains the middle section of Hüon's aria in Act I; and the closing theme, also developed in the coda, is the conclusion of Rezia's grand aria "Ocean, Thou Mighty Monster." Weber's technique of creating operatic overtures later degenerated into the thematic potpourris that were to become commonplace as preludes to operettas and musical comedies.

Weber's musical style contains elements common to both his vocal and instrumental music. His melody is highly individual, with much of its sweetness coming from an assimilation, rather than direct quotation, of the style of German folk and popular music. His themes are conceived in terms of regular phrases, but the bravura vocal themes seem pianistic. His use of non-harmonic tones on the beat produces a Romantically yearning quality and in rapid tempos gives an effect of brilliance, yet the harmonic background is diatonic in contrast to Spohr's modulatory-chromatic atmosphere. Weber's rhythm is very elastic, with much reliance on the ambiguity of hemiola, as when in 6/8 meter he produces the effect of 3/4. His love for dotted rhythms gives a martial tone to the first movements of his concertos and to his cantata *Kampf und Sieg*, written to celebrate Napoleon's overthrow, and provides a chivalric tone to his characterization of his knightly heroes (Ex. 3-2). Weber tends to over-use diminished-seventh chords in creating a daemonic atmosphere, as in *Der Freischütz* or the storm in *Oberon*. The chord of

EXAMPLE 3-2. Weber, Adolar's aria, Act I of *Euryanthe*.

the major ninth as a dominant harmony is a hallmark of his style.

It was as an orchestrator that Weber's influence was most pronounced. His orchestra is that of Beethoven, with the trombones as permanent members rather than occasional visitors, but he differs from his contemporaries by making imaginative and atmospheric use of the winds as solo instruments or choirs, especially the clarinet and French horn. The celebrated finale of Act II of *Der Freischütz* has been called an "arsenal of Romanticism" with its string tremolos, mysterious and spectral harmonies in the trombones or low woodwind instruments, and the special effects that accompany the casting of the magic bullets. Weber's unique keyboard style had some influence on Chopin and Mendelssohn, and his last three operas, especially their orchestral colors, had a strong effect on Berlioz and Wagner; the popularity of his music in France influenced the *opéra lyrique* of Gounod and Thomas. Weber's best works are his finest operas, the inner movements of his sonatas, and the four-hand pieces of Op. 60, and the clarinetist is grateful to Weber for having written some of the finest staples of his repertoire.

Franz Schubert (1797–1828)

Schubert was the youngest, most prolific, and musically most important of the composers discussed in this chapter, although he was initially the least appreciated, chiefly because most of his works published during his lifetime were songs or four-hand piano pieces and he was unable to appear in public as a performer. His musical fecundity can be shown by one striking illustration: during the year 1816 he wrote 179 compositions, ranging from dances for piano and songs to two symphonies, an opera, and the Mass in C major. Within each of the genres of his works, e.g., song, sonata, etc., one finds compositions ranging from triviality to inspired genius. Though he wrote for every available medium, he was least successful in composing operas or duos for solo instrument with piano.

Schubert's oeuvre may be divided into three chronological periods. The first extends from 1811 to 1819, the year of the "Trout" Quintet for piano and strings and the A major Piano Sonata, D. 664.[1] The second period ranges from 1820 to 1827 and includes such tantalizingly incomplete works as the Quartetsatz in C minor (D. 703), the "Unfinished" Symphony, and the C major Piano Sonata (D. 840), as well as his three great string quartets. The two piano trios and the song-cycle *Die Winterreise* are transitions to his third and final

[1] Schubert's works are known by their chronological numbering in O. E. Deutsch's *Schubert: Thematic Catalogue* (New York, 1951) rather than by their opus numbers, which are chronologically inaccurate owing to the amount of music published with opus numbers after the composer's death.

period, which embraced scarcely more than a year but contained his greatest compositions. It is most convenient to consider Schubert's works by genres rather than by periods, since his songs developed along a path different from his instrumental music and his dance music resists attempts at chronological ordering.

Piano music. Schubert composed at least 23 piano sonatas, some incomplete. Isolated early piano pieces may be sonata movements. The Sonata, D. 617, for piano duet and the Grand Duo in C, D. 812, which has been orchestrated in the mistaken belief that it was the sketch of a "lost" symphony, complete the list.

The sonatas display a considerable variety. Those from the A minor (D. 845, Op. 42) onward generally have four movements. They vary in total length from the exquisitely concise A major (D. 664, Op. 120) to the expansive last Sonata in B-flat (D. 960). Though a few begin with attention-getting boldness, most open with the quiet statement of a lyrical theme, often in question-and-answer form. The titles of the third movements oscillate between "minuetto" and "scherzo"; their trios contain some of Schubert's loveliest music. The slow movements are songlike, sometimes a theme and variations; characteristic of those in three-part, rondo, or modified sonata-form is a more active and interesting accompaniment at the reprise of the opening theme. The finales, the weakest movements, tend to sprawl and are generally inferior to the closing movements of the composer's best symphonies or chamber music. The sonatas lack the technical difficulties of those by Beethoven, Weber, or Hummel yet are scorned by many pianists, probably because of their general lack of brilliance and some passages which sound even more orchestral than Weber's piano music, e.g., the second theme-group of the A minor Sonata, D. 784, especially in the recapitulation.

Schubert's short character pieces derive not from the epigrammatic *Bagatelles* of Beethoven, but from the eclogues, dithyrambs, rhapsodies, and impromptus by two Czech composers residing in Vienna, Jan Vaclav Tomašek (Tomaschek, 1774–1850) and Jan Hugo Voříšek (Worzischek, 1791–1825). The form of these pieces is generally rondo with coda. The best known of Schubert's essays in the smaller forms are the *Moments musicaux*, D. 780 (*ca.* 1823) and two groups of Impromptus; the finest are the *Drei Klavierstücke*, D. 946, of 1828.

Schubert also wrote copious quantities of dance music—waltzes, Ländler, ecossaises, and "German dances," chiefly in waltz tempo.

The waltzes are not individual compositions but chains of dances like those of his contemporary Josef Lanner (1801–1843) or the later waltzes of the Johann Strausses (Sr., 1804–1849; Jr., 1825–1899), with each individual waltz containing six or more separate dances. The most interesting of the dance pieces are the polonaises and marches for piano duet. The spirit of Viennese popular music permeates not only the marches and dances but many of Schubert's larger works, for example the zither effect of the scherzo of the D major Sonata (D. 850, Op. 53) or the trio of the scherzo of the A major Sonata (D. 959).

Among Schubert's miscellaneous piano works are several sets of variations, for which he preferred a theme opening with a dactylic rhythm; short pieces which may be sonata movements; a magnificent Allegro in A minor for piano duet (D. 968); some rondos for piano duet which are allegretto, lyrical, and contemplative as opposed to the fast, flashy, and brilliant virtuoso rondos of his contemporaries; and a few divertimentos, all of considerable length, of which the most enjoyable is the *Divertissement à l'hongroise*, D. 818, one of the many souvenirs of Schubert's visits to Zselis as music master to the Esterházy family. The greatest of these miscellaneous compositions is the four-hand *Fantaisie* in F minor, D. 940, in which Schubert seemed to be aiming toward a one-movement instrumental cycle midway between Mozart's fantasies for mechanical organ (K. 594, 608) and a one-movement sonata. The work contains delightful and effective illustrations of the composer's love for contrasting minor and major forms of a theme (Example 3-3).

Orchestral music. Of Schubert's nine symphonies, the first six are early works, the Seventh is but a sketch (although attempts have been made to complete it), the Eighth is unfinished, and the Ninth (erroneously called the Seventh by some) was rejected by most orchestras during the nineteenth century. The early symphonies were written for the ensemble of the Imperial and Royal Stadt-Konvikt, where Schubert was a student; they call for an orchestra like that of late Haydn or early Beethoven but with solo flute and solo oboe assigned a more prominent role. It would seem that Schubert did not dare to compete with any of Beethoven's orchestral works written after *Prometheus*. Schubert's C minor Symphony (No. 4, D. 417) emulates the Beethoven of the C minor Quartet (Op. 18, No. 4) rather than the C minor sonatas or symphony; it has an unusually bumptious scherzo and some wonderful major-minor contrasts in the finale. The Second Symphony (B-flat, D. 125) is a

(a)   Allegro molto moderato

EXAMPLE 3-3. Schubert, *Fantaisie* in F minor, D. 940: minor and major forms of (a) opening theme; (b) second theme and coda.

(b)

(c)

EXAMPLE 3-3 continued.

EXAMPLE 3-3 continued.

Classic rather than a Romantic work, although like the other B-flat Symphony (No. 5, D. 485) its minuet is in minor. The Fifth Symphony has the instrumentation of early Haydn or Mozart—no heavy brass or timpani—and is the most popular of these early symphonies despite its weak slow movement.

The formal structure of the Eighth Symphony is Schubert at his most adventurous. In the first movement the introductory material dominates both the recapitulation and the coda (the recapitulation begins directly with the oboe-clarinet theme) and the idea of the second theme appears in the closing group. The unusual development section in the second movement has confused more than one analyst, and its second theme contains one of Schubert's most magical modulations and most beautiful contrasts between minor and major (C-sharp minor—D-flat major). Small wonder that the composer found it impossible to conceive a scherzo or finale which would be worthy of these two movements! In some respects the Ninth Symphony is a regression to earlier works, especially the Third Symphony and the Grand Duo for piano duet, yet on the other hand its "heavenly length" (Schumann's term), the imaginative writing for brass instruments, the insistent dotted rhythms and the drive of the finale influenced Schubert's logical successor, Anton Bruckner.

Most of the overtures, especially those "in the Italian style," show the influence of Rossini's domination of Viennese musical life during the 1820's. The so-called *Rosamunde* Overture was actually written for a drama called *Die Zauberharfe;* in this overture Schubert seems intoxicated by his first chance to write for an orchestra of professionals and in the tutti passages tends to overwhelm the listener with sheer volume of sound.

Chamber music. From his early youth Schubert was an avid violist in the family string quartet.[2] Thirty-six chamber works (excluding duet sonatas), some only fragmentary, can be counted; of these, the last three string quartets, the String Quintet with two cellos, the "Trout" Quintet, the piano trios, and the Octet are outstanding.

The chamber music with piano is represented chiefly by the two trios (D. 929 and 989) and the "Trout" Quintet, D. 667, so called because the fourth of its five movements is a set of variations on Schubert's song "Die Forelle." Noteworthy is Schubert's use of the singing tone of the piano, often in the high register, to the accompaniment of the strings. The Octet (D. 803), with its six movements a late example of the Classic-era divertimento, is among Schubert's most delightfully expansive works. Both the first and last movements have slow introductions, that of the finale quite ominous in contrast to the light-hearted main body of the movement. The slow movements include variations as well as one of Schubert's finest and most lyrical song-like forms. The effect of the winds is superb.

Of the string quartets, the ones in A minor (D. 804, Op. 29) and D minor (D. 810) are the most popular; the G major (D. 887) is seldom performed because of its length and its fatiguing effect on performers. The A minor Quartet is noteworthy because of its major-minor contrasts in the first movement and its somber third movement with a contrasting trio in major; the D minor for its daemonic energy, unusual for Schubert, in the outer movements and its slow movement, variations on his song "Death and the Maiden." The most sublime of his instrumental works is the Quintet in C major (D. 956) for string quartet with an additional cello, which provides a warmer sonority than the two violas of the customary string quintet. In the first movement, the opening theme contains some of Schubert's finest harmonic coloring, and the second theme-group is one of his loveliest ideas; the closing theme is a quietly mysterious Hungarian march, ending with a reminiscence of the second theme. Unusual features in this quintet include the somber trio of the light-hearted scherzo and the strange cadence, including the lowered second degree, in the Hungarian-style finale.

---

[2] The number of composers of magnificent chamber music who were also violists is amazing; besides Schubert one need only mention Mozart, Beethoven, Dvořák, and Hindemith.

Vocal music. During his lifetime Schubert was principally known as a composer of vocal music. He was unsuccessful in opera but wrote much fine choral music and can be regarded as the establisher of one of the few new musical forms of the nineteenth century, the Lied or art song.

Most of Schubert's larger choral works stem from his attempts to secure a position as a church composer that would provide him with both support and time for composing. His first four Latin Masses are early works and strongly influenced by Michael Haydn (1737–1806), but his A-flat (D. 678, 1822) and E-flat (D. 950, 1828) Masses are the last significant examples of the Viennese Classic Mass. The garbled texts of Schubert's Credo movements have been erroneously explained as stemming from either his carelessness or unorthodox beliefs, but he would not have been likely to jeopardize his chances for a secure position, and it is most likely that these Credos (along with his church works in the vernacular, like the "German Mass," D. 872) indicate the lingering effects of Joseph II's ill-considered attempts at "reforming" Austrian Catholicism some of which had yet to be purged from the Viennese liturgy. Schubert also wrote two major oratorios (*Miriam's Song of Triumph* and the incomplete *Lazarus*) and some delightful secular part-songs, many for male voices; their warm sonority encouraged some of Schubert's boldest harmonic experiments.

Schubert's Lieder must be understood in terms of the limitations of their predecessors. During the eighteenth century the atmosphere for solo song was restrictive: despite the efflorescence of German lyric poetry in the eighteenth century, the poets desired their works to be independent artistic productions, not merely librettos for song, and the composer was subject to the attitude "Sing your songs while composing them without using an instrument or adding a bass," which deprived the composer of the two areas in which l could operate most freely and independently: interesting accompan ment and refined harmonic expression. Poets preferred a sim strophic song that would support their verses; Schiller announced "constant strumming on the piano" as song accompanime many songs were printed on only two staves, with the r doubling the voice part, an indication that the pianist v the melody while playing.

Music assumed a more important role in the songs of the eighteenth century. Reichardt's songs are generally strophic.

hymnlike, with sometimes elaborate melodies with wide ranges and accompaniments generally limited to doubling the voice part or to broken arpeggiated chords in the right hand. Zelter's songs were more esteemed by poets than musicians and their influence on Schubert's songs was minimal. More important influences were the songs and ballads of Johann Rudolf Zumsteeg (1760–1802), Schiller's classmate; several of the ballads resemble the operatic scena with its ritornelli, accompanied recitatives, independent piano preludes and postludes, arias in differing tempos, and even passages in the style of melodrama with the text declaimed over the music. Reichardt used a similar technique in setting the grand monologues from the dramas of Goethe and Schiller, and this eventually developed into the secular cantata, exemplified by Mendelssohn's *Die erste Walpurgisnacht*. Less well known influences on Schubert's songs are the works of the Viennese song composers, especially Nikolaus Freiherr von Krufft (1779–1818), whose songs contain quasi-folksong melodies, independent piano accompaniments, and ventures toward the through-composed song.

Schubert's songs span his entire creative career, from 1811 to his death in 1828, and number more than 600, some of them different settings of the same poem. His choice of poets was quite catholic, including not only Goethe and Schiller but also lesser eighteenth-century figures like Klopstock, Hölty, and Matthisson; Romantic poets like the Schegel brothers and the early poems by Heine and Rückert; his versifying friends Schober and Mayrhofer; and German translations of songs by Shakespeare and Sir Walter Scott. Hölderlin and Eichendorff are the only significant German poets of the time whose works Schubert did not set to music.

Schubert's songs display a great variety but can be fitted into ‌tain broad classifications. The strophic songs, with the same ‌ody for each verse, include many of the fine songs in the cycle ‌ schöne Müllerin; they often have delightful piano preludes or ‌ludes. More common are modified strophic songs, in which ‌bert works changes in melody, accompaniment, or harmony ‌ shifting from major to minor or the reverse). Songs in ‌ er of the operatic scena are usually early works and in‌ Zumsteeg; they tend to be lengthy, sectional, with ex‌material (like the 60-measure piano interlude in "Der ‌," D. 111) and, as in Zumsteeg's comparable works, some‌ "interlocking" tonality with an ending in a key other than the original tonic. Condensations of the scena type led to Schubert's through-composed songs, sometimes in ballad style like "Der Erlkönig" (D. 328), and generally unified through recurring themes, tonal schemas, or accompaniment patterns.

In many of the strophic songs a frequent device is the placing of the melody exclusively in the vocal part with the accompaniment merely sustaining the harmony and creating rhythmic motion, as in Reichardt's or Krufft's songs; but Schubert's melody demands an accompaniment that will bring out its latent harmony. More frequent are the songs where the accompaniment holds the song together; who can forget the repeated triplets of "Der Erlkönig" or the varied patterns of "Ganymed" (D. 544)? The piano preludes and postludes, as well as many accompaniments, contain much descriptive tone-painting. The declamatory songs, often an alternation of declamation and arioso with recurring themes or tonalities unifying the work, are less frequent but include some of his greatest songs, ranging from "Gruppe aus dem Tartarus" (D. 583, 1817) to the Heine songs in the mis-named *Schwanengesang* (D. 957).[3] In "Memnon" (D. 541) the melodic line contains wide leaps, and in "Der Doppelgänger" (D. 957, No. 13) the declamation, reinforced by a dramatic accompaniment, borders on expressionism; such songs are the ancestors of the vocal styles of Wagner, Hugo Wolf, and even Schoenberg and Webern.

Among Schubert's favorite poetic categories are the hymn-like song, often on a topic dealing with Greek antiquity ("Lied eines Schiffers an die Dioskuren," D. 360) or the elegiac (the settings from Goethe's *Wilhelm Meister*). Some of the most popular are those dealing with nature, especially water or night, and those which approach (and have virtually become) folksongs, like "Der Lindenbaum" from *Die Winterreise*, D. 911. Space does not permit even a list of the great Schubert songs, for over a hundred can be considered such.

Schubert did not add expression marks to the voice parts of his songs, since he felt that the text was direction enough. Leopold von Sonnleithner, one of his contemporaries, described how Schubert wanted his songs performed:

---

[3] After Schubert's death the publisher Haslinger arbitrarily grouped these last songs together and affixed the title "Swan Song" to create a sentimental interest; *Schwanengesang* is not in fact a song-cycle.

[More than a hundred times] I heard him accompany and rehearse his songs. Above all, he always kept the most strict and even time, except in the few cases where he had expressly indicated in writing a ritardando, morendo, accelerando, etc. Furthermore he never allowed violent expression in performance. The Lieder singer, as a rule, only relates experiences and feelings of others; he does not himself impersonate the characters whose feelings he describes. . . . With Schubert especially, the true expression, the deepest feeling is already inherent in the melody as such, and is admirably enhanced by the accompaniment. Everything that hinders the flow of the melody and disturbs the evenly flowing accompaniment is, therefore, exactly contrary to the composer's intention and destroys the musical effect.[4]

Musical style. Schubert's most beloved melodies are generally in such salient places as the strophic or folk-like songs, the second themes of his sonata-form movements, his slow movements, and the trios of his scherzos. His rhythmic innovations are few but interesting; noteworthy among them are the displaced accents in the scherzo of his C minor Symphony; the hemiolas in the scherzo of his D major Sonata (Op. 53, D. 850) in which the macrorhythm consists of four measures of 3/2 followed by six measures of 3/4; or the cross-rhythms in the Allegro in A minor (D. 947). Two striking aspects of Schubert's harmony may be considered: color harmony and modulation. By the former is implied the non-functional use of such sonorities as diminished-seventh and augmented-sixth chords, for atmospheric and coloristic reasons rather than for modulation. Such color harmony may be a rhetorically amplifying device, as in the opening of the C-major String Quintet, or one for establishing a mood in the piano prelude of a song, as in "Am Meer" (D. 957, No. 12). Schubert's most notable modulations are generally abrupt, often sudden shifts to a mediant or submediant. Example 3-4 is one of his most magical modulations; although it seems like an extreme shift (C-sharp minor to C major), it can be best explained enharmonically as a shift from the dominant to its mediant (G-sharp major to B-sharp major). Another surprising effect is an abrupt change in the course of a leisurely transition to what one would expect to be the dominant, as in the *Grand Rôndeau* in A major, D. 951. In the

---

[4] Cited in O. E. Deutsch (ed.), *Schubert: Memoirs by his Friends* (London, 1958), p. 116.

EXAMPLE 3-4. Schubert, Sonata in B-flat major, D. 960, second movement.

course of a minor theme Schubert often ventures into the flat supertonic (Neapolitan), as in Example 3-3a.

The oft-told story of Schubert's starting to take lessons in counterpoint from Simon Sechter (1788–1867), the theorist later to be Bruckner's teacher, has created the legend that Schubert was not skilled in counterpoint, but his fugal writing is not easy to find fault with, and few composers could find more appropriate countermelodies for songlike themes. Schubert's formal weaknesses can be traced chiefly to his luxuriant melodic inventiveness and his leisurely attitude toward unfolding his musical ideas, but even his lengthiest transitions are far above the level of padding, and when he wanted to be concise, as in "Gruppe aus dem Tartarus" or the A major Sonata, D. 664, he was admirably successful. The legend that Schubert was a spontaneous composer who neither sketched nor revised is false, for his drafts for the B minor Symphony and *Fantaisie* in F minor show that he was as rigorous a self-critic as Beethoven or Brahms. Like all prolific composers, Schubert's work was uneven, but his best works are great and his weakest compositions possess touches of charm.

Lesser composers, mostly pianists

Space permits discussion of only a few of the numerous other composers active during the first three decades of the nineteenth century. Though during their time they were esteemed above Schubert and some of the other important composers discussed in this chapter, they are virtually forgotten today.

Unlike his fellow Czechs who migrated to Vienna, Jan Ladislas Dussek (Dušek, 1760–1812) went to northern Germany where he studied with C. P. E. Bach and helped transmit the ideas of this highly original composer to future generations. Though Dussek's early sonatas are *galant* works, from Opus 44 onward his compositions are frequently quite expressive, utilizing a "singing" style for the piano and some fine craftsmanship marred by excessive length, especially in the finales. His most significant work is the Sonata in F-sharp minor, Op. 61, the "Elégie harmonique" to commemorate the death of his pupil Prince Louis Ferdinand of Prussia at the battle of Saalfeld in 1806. The advanced chromatic writing and the restless syncopations (in the finale, only five measures are not syncopated) are a culmination of the "*Sturm und Drang*" style and also presage the works of Chopin and Liszt, the latter in the "heroic" portion of the opening of the development. Other noteworthy features of this sonata are the frequent key-changes within movements and the disintegration of the second theme-groups amid harmonic complexities, thus showing a free attitude toward tonality which was to increase in the music of Spohr, Liszt, and Wagner. Dussek's pupil Prince Louis Ferdinand (1772–1806), a nephew of Frederick the Great, was himself a highly original if undisciplined composer and highly esteemed by Beethoven and Spohr.

Johann Nepomuk Hummel (1778–1837), possibly of Czech ancestry, studied with Mozart and considered himself his principal disciple. A brilliant piano virtuoso and a prolific composer of piano, church, and chamber music, he succeeded Haydn as Prince Esterházy's music director and later held important posts in Stuttgart and Weimar.

Hummel's early works show harmonic crudities and even direct quotations from Mozart, particularly in the outer movements of his Op. 20 sonata, but his style later became more individual. Most noteworthy are the slow movements of his piano sonatas, with luxuriant fioritura figuration (even with 128th and 256th notes) well suited to the light action of the Viennese piano, as well as explorations of atmospheric devices and interesting sonorities and harmonic colors. Hummel's two piano concertos, along with Spohr's violin concertos, were the chief models for the soloist-dominated nineteenth-century concerto; his Septet, Op. 74, for piano, low strings, and winds, is quite interesting; and his Notturno for winds, Op. 99, shows in its variations that Schubert did not have an exclusive monopoly on Viennese charm and grace. Hummel's Masses, along with Schubert's, are the last major essays in the Viennese Classical style of church music; the E-flat and D major Masses are his best despite their stiff counterpoint, whereas the Mass in B-flat major is waltzlike in the Osanna and forward-looking in its tunefully sentimental effects, which were to characterize much subsequent church music.

His most significant work, the F-sharp minor Sonata, Op. 81 (1819), shows the new problems of the Romantic piano sonata. The opening theme contains the germ cells of the entire first movement; the slow movement is replete with the figuration which so strongly influenced Chopin; and the finale is dualistic, with much transitional material needed to reconcile the "Hungarian" gypsy opening with the "severe" fugal second theme—which shows that J. S. Bach's *Well-Tempered Clavier* was more widely disseminated than well-digested at this time.

John Field (1782–1837), Irish by birth and a pupil of Clementi, lived in Russia during most of his career. Though he also wrote sonatas, concertos, and chamber music for piano and strings, he is best known for his nocturnes and was the first to use the term for

EXAMPLE 3-5. Field, Nocturne in C minor.

piano music, since the notturnos of Hummel and Spohr are divertimentos for winds. Typical of Field's nocturnes are arpeggiated left-
hand accompaniments given sonority through the sustaining pedal,
over which the right hand plays, often in the high register, a
dreamily singing melody elaborated with fioritura and occasional
harmonic clashes with the left hand (Ex. 3-5); these devices had a
strong influence on Chopin. A less frequently encountered type of
nocturne consists of a suavely elegant melody with a simple accompaniment. Field influenced not only Chopin but the entire
course of Russian piano music from Glinka to Kabalevsky.

Paris was the locale of a number of transplanted German piano
virtuosos who developed techniques of performance and composition to astound the new middle-class audience whose musical background and taste were limited. The most noteworthy were Friedrich
Kalkbrenner (1785–1849), Henri Herz (1803–1888), Franz Hünten
(1793–1878), and the best of this group, Sigismond Thalberg (1812–
1871). The salon pieces of the American Louis Moreau Gottschalk
(1829–1869) stem from this tradition. The most respected of these
virtuosos was the violinist Niccolò Paganini (1782–1840), whose
satanic appearance and brilliant concertos and caprices captured the
imaginations of Berlioz, Schumann, and Liszt, although Spohr de-
tested his rival. Virtuosity, display, and showmanship are the primary constituents of this music, and the typical compositions are sets
of variations on popular operatic airs which decorate the melody
with arabesques. The musical value of most of these works is nil,
although Thalberg's larger works are respectable and Paganini's
caprices often show piquant and imaginative touches, especially the
A minor caprice which inspired variations by such later composers
as Brahms and Rakhmaninov. At least a cursory examination of the
virtuoso literature of this time is necessary to understand the reaction against it by Schumann, Mendelssohn, and Chopin, or the desire
of Alkan and Liszt to surpass it.

Bibliography

A good biography of Spohr is lacking. His autobiography (*Selbstbiographie*, Kassel and Göttingen, 1860–61, 2 vols.) exists in one English
translation (London, 1865) and a recent abridgement, *The Travels of*

Louis Spohr (ed. Henry Pleasants, Norman, 1962). Richard Hove's "Glemte noder II: Spohrs Kammermusik," *Dansk Musiktidskrift* XXXI (1946) is a good study of Spohr's chamber music. Good biographies of Weber are by Erwin Kroll (Potsdam, 1934), William Saunders (London, 1940), L. P. and R. P. Stebbins (*Enchanted Wanderer,* London and New York, 1940), and John Warrack (London, 1968).

Maurice J. E. Brown's excellent studies of Schubert's music include *Schubert: A Critical Biography* (London, 1958), *Schubert's Variations* (London, 1954), and *Essays on Schubert* (London and New York, 1966). Alfred Einstein's *Schubert: A Musical Portrait* (New York, 1951) is a fine appreciation, and Richard Capell's *Schubert's Songs* (2nd. ed., London, 1957) is an admirable study, as are O. E. Deutsch's *Schubert: Documentary Biography* (London, 1946) and his thematic catalogue of Schubert's works (New York, 1951). Arthur Loesser's *Men, Women, and Pianos* (New York, 1954) brilliantly captures the milieu of the Paris-domiciled piano virtuosos. The most recent study of Paganini is G. I. C. de Courcy's *Paganini the Genoese.* Studies of Field's and Dussek's music are needed, and the only important work on Hummel is Karl Benyovsky's *J. N. Hummel* (Bratislava, 1934; in German).

4

The German
Romantic Efflorescence

A large group of composers born between 1803 and 1813 dominated the music of most of the nineteenth century. The vacuum created by the deaths of Weber, Beethoven, and Schubert between 1826 and 1828 permitted the rise to prominence of younger composers, some of whom either died at an early age or changed their musical styles around 1850; it is with these men that this and the following chapter are principally concerned. Liszt and Wagner, on the other hand, took longer to mature as composers but compensated through long lives and continuing musical influence; their impact on the music of the century will be discussed in Chapter 6.

The years between 1830 and 1850 were particularly yeasty for music. The young composers, fictionally represented by Schumann's "League of David," were leagued against the "Philistines," with Paris and the German cities the principal arenas of the combat and with their battles fought in the press as well as in the concert hall or opera house. The young composers revered Beethoven, though his influence tended to paralyze their imaginations in writing in the larger forms; they highly esteemed Weber; and a few of them came to appreciate Schubert. They were more closely associated with the other arts, especially literature, than any preceding group of composers.

Felix Mendelssohn–Bartholdy (1809–1847)

Of all these composers, Mendelssohn was closest in spirit to the eighteenth century, chiefly through his impeccable craftsmanship and sense of proportion. A highly facile and prolific composer, he left a large amount of music that still remains unpublished, and his oeuvre still awaits the critical scholarship and cataloguing that, for example, Maurice J. E. Brown and Otto Erich Deutsch have done for Schubert's music.

Mendelssohn was second only to Mozart as a prodigy in composition. When we reflect that Mozart's first genuinely individual and independently meritorious works, like the G minor Symphony, K. 183, and the motet *Exsultate, Jubilate*, are the products of his sixteenth year, Mendelssohn's comparable precocity is apparent in such works from his sixteenth and seventeenth years as the Op. 20 Octet, the Concerto for two pianos, and the Overture to *A Midsummer Night's Dream*. Though it is fashionable to regard Mendelssohn's later works as representing a decline in his creative powers, such a verdict is as unjust as that which has been passed on Schumann's later compositions.

Mendelssohn's music must be evaluated by genres, not chronologically, and also in terms of the various facets of his creative personality: elfin and fey, soulfully expressive and sentimental, fussy-tempered, or elegiac. In various compositions Mendelssohn is the landscape painter, the Bach enthusiast, or the representative of Victorian and Biedermeier Protestantism. Many of these personalities exist isolated in individual pieces, single movements of an instrumental cycle, or even in theme-groups of a sonata-form movement constructed with impeccable craftsmanship.

Instrumental works. Mendelssohn revived the organ as a medium of composition. Although Beethoven, Ignaz Moscheles (1794–1870), and other pianists played the organ, they regarded it as a medium for improvisation rather than composition, and the near-century between J. S. Bach's last works and Mendelssohn's organ compositions are virtually a desert for the organist. Mendelssohn's organ sonatas are more like Baroque than nineteenth-century sonatas, for sonata-form movements are few, with the first movements preludes or even variations in the style of a chorale-partita. The Sixth Sonata (D minor) with its chorale variations, fugue, and concluding andante is considered the best of these works.

Mendelssohn's piano music is underrated, partly owing to the popularity of the *Songs Without Words* as teaching pieces or the tendency to regard his two concertos for piano as "student" concertos. An occasional performance of the *Variations sérieuses*, Op. 54, brings to light the finest set of piano variations between Beethoven and Brahms; it is Mendelssohn's greatest piano work. Such smaller works as the three fantasies of Op. 16 (especially the exquisitely elfin second one), the *Album Leaf*, Op. 117, and the *Capriccio*, Op. 18, are equal in musical value to the Schubert impromptus. The Beethoven of the sonatas between Op. 78 and Op. 90, Weber, and to a lesser extent Field were the chief influences on Mendelssohn's keyboard style.

Mendelssohn's chamber music is little known. One must admire the freshness of the Octet, Op. 20, especially the exuberant first movement and fey scherzo, and the craftsmanship of its sixteen-year-old composer. As in some of his other early work, Mendelssohn experimented with cyclic recapitulation in its finale. His once popular string quartets have virtually vanished from the repertoire, although Mendelssohnians plead specially for the F minor Quartet, Op. 80, one of his last compositions. Perhaps the best of his chamber works is the D minor Trio, Op. 49, with its elegiac first movement and fine scherzo; highly appreciated also are his two cello sonatas, especially the D major, Op. 58, with its exuberant first movement in typically Mendelssohnian 6/8 meter, flowing but not driving (Ex. 4-1); its second movement is wryly wistful.

Allegro assai vivace

EXAMPLE 4-1. Mendelssohn, Sonata in D major, Op. 58, first movement.

Mendelssohn's orchestral music is the best known part of his oeuvre. Nevertheless, twelve of his symphonies, mostly for strings, remain unpublished. An early Symphony in C minor is commonly but erroneously called his First, and the so-called Second Symphony, a choral cantata titled *Hymn of Praise*, is a relatively late work. The "Reformation" Symphony, given this title because of the "Dresden Amen" in its introduction and the elaborate treatment of Luther's hymn "A Mighty Fortress" in the finale, has a deft scherzo but a fussy first movement which shows the decline of the *"Sturm und Drang"* style, and a finale with skillful contrapuntal touches but several bombastic moments; it is interesting to compare it with the prelude to Meyerbeer's *Les Huguenots*, which also utilizes Luther's hymn. The "Italian" Symphony, in A major, is beloved because of the deftness and exuberance of the outer movements and the tenderness of its inner movements. (Mendelssohn did not publish the symphony, hoping eventually to revise its finale.) His finest symphony is his last, the "Scotch" (A minor), with its magnificently elegiac first movement, exquisite scherzo, wistful slow movement, and uneven finale. Of all his large instrumental works the best is the Violin Concerto in E minor, one of the few works in the history of music which appeals equally to performer, listener, critic, and audience.

Mendelssohn's programmatic overtures contain the best illustrations of his deft and skillful orchestral writing. The overture to *A Midsummer Night's Dream* was followed seventeen years later by additional incidental music to the drama, but the tendency to perform this music apart from the play has resulted in the unfortunate elimination of many fine individual pieces. The best overtures are seascapes, like *Hebrides* and *Melusine;* the dramatic portrayals (*Ruy Blas*) are weaker. Excellent examples of sonata form, these overtures stand midway between those of Beethoven and the symphonic poems of Liszt and had an important influence on succeeding generations.

Vocal works. During the nineteenth century Mendelssohn's choral works were ranked above his instrumental compositions. Among his large oratorios, *St. Paul* (1836) derives from Handelian dramatic oratorio, with some movements drawing on Bach's four-part chorale style; *Elijah* (1846) is a more felicitous fusion of these elements with the oratorio style of Spohr and the English anthem, its influence evident in the motet-like choruses like "Be not Afraid" and "He Watching Over Israel." The contemplative choruses and arias are the best moments in *Elijah*, and the confrontation of Elijah with the priests of Baal is a fine dramatic moment with effective touches of satire, but the dramatic choruses, e.g., "The Fire Descends," are inferior to their Handelian models, and in the conclusion of the first part too much reliance is placed on a jog-trot rhythm. Despite its shortcomings, *Elijah* is one of the finest large choral works of the nineteenth century, and was for a long time considered inferior only to Handel's *Messiah*. Among the other large choral works, the Anglican *Te Deum* (1832) is fine and the setting of Psalm 114 (1839) has a grandeur and nobility unsurpassed in Mendelssohn's works. The secular cantata *The First Walpurgis Night* (1833, revised 1843), a setting of Goethe, is a masterpiece containing Mendelssohn's best dramatic writing and loveliest land-scape painting. The models for this work are the dramatic cantatas by Andreas Romberg (1767–1821) and, despite attempts at imita-tion by Schumann, Gade, Brahms, and Dvořák, Mendelssohn's com-position never had a true successor and remains unique in the musical literature.

Mendelssohn's songs are the most neglected of all his works, perhaps because they follow the tradition of the strophic songs of the Berlin school, especially those of his teacher C. F. Zelter, rather than the ideas of Schubert. "Neue Liebe" is in Mendelssohn's best elfin vein and "Die Liebende schreibt" has the intimacy one asso-ciates with Schumann. A plea should also be made for the com-poser's charming duets for solo women's voices.

A capsule description of Mendelssohn's style is difficult to make in a limited space because of the many facets of his creative person-ality. The elfin and landscape-painting Mendelssohn is most familiar and popular today; such indications as "presto agitato" over a com-position in the minor mode will show the fussy-tempered Men-delssohn; and Example 4-1 shows the opening of one of his best exuberant works in 6/8 meter, a prevailing diatonic style, impec-cable craftsmanship, and singing melodies. Example 4-2 shows Men-delssohn in a soulfully elegiac mood: note the regularity of the phrases, the expressive but restrained harmony, the frequent internal cadences within a measure (the so-called "feminine endings"), and the wistful touches imparted by minor triads, mostly well prepared with secondary dominants, in an essentially major key. The four-part writing is in an almost vocal style, and one could imagine

Andante tranquillo

EXAMPLE 4-2. Mendelssohn, Variations, Op. 83, theme.

words, especially with religious import, set to the melody. Mendelssohn is least successful in writing music with a message or in portraying emotions of conflict or stress.

Though he seldom sketched works, Mendelssohn frequently returned to completed compositions (*Hebrides* Overture, D minor Trio, *First Walpurgis Night*) to make thorough revisions which are superior to the original models. He was not only a composer but a leading pianist, organist, and conductor of his day, and the administrative chores resulting from his efforts to make Germany the musical center of Europe hastened his early death. The Leipzig Conservatory which he founded set the model for professional music education in Germany as well as the Anglo-Saxon countries, and his endeavors to reform church music, though the most visible results were the anthems of the English Victorians, markedly contributed to the revived interest in the Protestant musical heritage of J. S. Bach and his predecessors, and also encouraged the infant discipline of musicology.

Robert Schumann (1810–1856)

German Romanticism, literary as well as musical, culminates in the works of Robert Schumann. His highly individual style, which derived from many sources, chiefly Beethoven, Schubert, and Dussek, had a strong influence on the absolute music of the later nineteenth century; he was a musical journalist who battled for new music; and his life and works are a neglected field for competent psychological study, since no other composer's music is so autobiographical.

Schumann's music may be divided into four chronological periods, each demarcated by a major crisis in his life. The first period, ending in 1833 with his attempted suicide, was the epoch of the Abegg Variations, Op. 1, and the Papillons, Op. 2, and terminated with the Intermezzi, Op. 5, on a theme by his future bride, Clara Wieck. The second period began in 1834 with his recovery of mental equilibrium and ended with his marriage to Clara in 1840 despite the continued opposition of her father. During these six years Schumann assumed the editorship of the *Neue Zeitschrift für Musik* and wrote his greatest piano compositions, beginning with *Carnaval*, Op. 9, and ending with *Faschingsschwank aus Wien*, Op. 26.

Schumann's marriage to his beloved Clara in 1840 inspired a "year of song" when most of his finest works in this genre were written; 1841 was the year of orchestral music, 1842 was the year of chamber music. Opinions vary as to the termination of this creative period; in his book *Greatness in Music* Alfred Einstein (seeking more for a round number than an accurate date) cites Op. 50 (his secular oratorio *Paradise and the Peri*, 1843); Georg

Knepler the year 1844; E. A. Lippman (article "Schumann" in *MGG*) 1847, the year of the D minor Piano Trio. The middle years of the 1840's were fallow for Schumann and saw his abandonment of musical journalism in 1844 and a breakdown in 1845, followed by a "cure by counterpoint" which resulted in the canonic studies and sketches for pedal-clavier (a piano with a pedal keyboard like that of the organ) and the fugues on B–A–C–H (B-flat–A–C–B-natural), replete with intricate contrapuntal devices.

It is fashionable today to deprecate the music of Schumann's last period, but the years between 1849 and 1851 were among his most productive and include his best neglected music. Yet his increasing mental deterioration resulted in his forced resignation as conductor in Düsseldorf in 1853, his attempted suicide in 1854, and his subsequent confinement in a mental institution until his death.

Piano music. Not only did the piano dominate Schumann's creative activity between 1828 and 1839, but most of his successful later works, particularly songs and chamber music, relied heavily on this instrument, and most of his essential musical characteristics are revealed in his piano music.

His split personality was incorporated in his earlier years in the imaginary characters Florestan and Eusebius, whom Schumann depicted in *Carnaval* and had "sign" individual articles in his journal and in the Davidsbündler Dances; a few of these dances and the F-sharp minor Piano Sonata, Op. 11, were written under joint authorship. Florestan is the capricious, tempestuous, impulsive figure who, in the dance beginning as in Example 4-3, "stopped, and his lips trembled sorrowfully"; Eusebius, on the other hand, is the contemplative, introspective dreamer (Ex. 4-4). In many of the compositions with epilogues (Davidsbündler Dances, *Arabeske, Dichterliebe*) Eusebius has the last word. Schumann's third personality, the judicious and arbitrating Master Raro, is first evident in Schumann's articles and becomes prominent in his music after 1844, especially in sonata-form movements and contrapuntal studies.[1]

In Schumann's earlier piano works the dominant idea is that of the masked ball, wherein various characters, portrayed in short epigrammatic character pieces, flit back and forth; the earliest example

[1] Schumann's mental illness was not schizophrenia but a manic–depressive psychosis; Florestan, Eusebius, and Raro can be viewed, therefore, not as split personalities but as the manic and depressive facets of his psyche, with Raro as a superego attempting to control the deviant personalities through contrapuntal and formal structures.

EXAMPLE 4-3. Schumann, Davidsbündler Dances, Op. 6, No. 9, "Florestan."

is *Papillons,* based on the masked ball toward the end of Jean Paul Richter's novel *Flegeljahre* which also contains the characters Walt and Vult, models for Florestan and Eusebius. *Carnaval* is another masked ball in which Clara Wieck (Chiarina), Schumann's temporary fiancée Ernestine von Fricken (Estrella), Chopin, Paganini, and the figures of the Italian commedia dell'arte appear in waltzes (influenced by Schubert's) and promenades; at the end Schumann's "League of David," his musical colleagues and their ancestors like J. S. Bach, Beethoven, and Weber, sally forth against the "Philistines," the purveyors of empty virtuoso piano music and the Classic epigonoi who, in Schumann's words, "wrote music by the yard." The Davidsbündler Dances, later works despite an earlier opus number than *Carnaval's,* are the culmination of the masked ball idea.

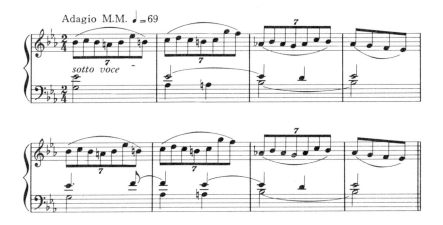

EXAMPLE 4-4. Schumann, *Carnaval*, Op. 9, "Eusebius."

This gave way to series of character pieces, either indefinite atmospheric portraits (*Fantasiestücke*, Op. 12) or the delightful pictures in the *Scenes from Childhood*, Op. 15; in later years Schumann returned to works of this type in the *Waldscenen*, Op. 82, *Bunte Blätter*, Op. 99 (incorporating movements withdrawn from *Carnaval*), and his tragic farewell to music, the *Songs of the Dawn*, Op. 133. His greatest piano works are the sets of large pieces, especially the *Symphonic Etudes, Kreisleriana*, the *Novelletten*, the *Faschingsschwank aus Wien*, and the *Fantasie* in C major.

Except for the later piano collections, the sets of piano pieces are not helter-skelter assemblages of individual pieces gathered into an arbitrary collection; they are often, if not always, unified by subtle means. Schumann's delight in musical acrostics is evident as early as his Abegg Variations (in German notation, the name is spelled out as A–Bb–E–G–G); *Carnaval* is based on permutations of the letters in the name of the Sudeten town of Asch near which Ernestine von Fricken lived; "Asch" (Ab–C–B-natural) is even permutated to S C H – u – m – A – n – n by using the notes Eb–C–B–A. Other unifying devices include the bass line of the theme of the Impromptus, a technique derived from Beethoven's "Eroica" Variations; harmonic structures in most of the *Symphonic Etudes;* and motivic connections between movements in his larger instrumental cycles, most evident in the G minor Piano Sonata, the

Piano Quintet, and the Fourth Symphony. Schumann was not consistent in his use of cyclic forms, however, and the analyst must not expect to find cyclic relationships in all of this composer's works.[2]

Schumann's middle-sized piano works, including single compositions like the *Arabeske* or *Blumenstück* as well as individual *Novelletten* or *Nachtstücke*, are modified rondo forms, often with codas. In the *Fantasie*, Op. 17, Schumann was aiming for a new kind of form, a modified sonata in three main sections with the first a very free sonata movement. In his sonatas his treatment of form is less skillful, for Schumann was empirically trying to revitalize this structure, but in his best symphonies and chamber music the force of his imagination triumphs over the weaknesses of his larger formal concepts.

Rhythm is Schumann's chief driving force. Following Beethoven's example in the first movements of the Fifth and Seventh Symphonies or the last movement of the C-sharp minor Quartet, he wrote many pieces dominated by insistent rhythms, either monorhythmic like the eighth of the *Kreisleriana* pieces or in sections with each dominated by a pronounced rhythm, as in the first number of the *Faschingsschwank*. Unfortunately, Schumann overworked the idea of insistent rhythm to the point of obsession; one can count the same pattern repeated 32 times in the finale of the Fourth Symphony, for example. Yet Schumann's masterly use of syncopation, hemiola, rhythmic displacement, polyrhythms, and syncopated harmonic rhythm makes him a master of rhythm comparable only to Beethoven, Berlioz, Brahms, and Stravinsky.

Schumann's harmony is seldom deliberately dissonant. More characteristic of his style is a lingering on non-harmonic tones in the melody with a gentle accompaniment aided by the sustaining pedal, typical of the "Eusebius"-like numbers such as the coda of the *Arabeske*. Another typical device consists of powerful march-like passages with full chords in both hands and a fast harmonic rhythm. Schumann's bass lines are superb and his harmonic imagination is best shown through his lavish use of inversions and secondary dominants. Schumann, as well as Chopin, was an innovator in writing around the tonic, as in Example 4-4, and thus directly contributed to the "psychological tonality" of Liszt and Wagner.

<hr/>

[2] A recent writer has gone so far as to conjecture that Schumann's themes were based on a numerological code. See Eric Sams, "Did Schumann Use Ciphers?" *Musical Times*, August 1965 (and the editorial comments); "The Schumann Ciphers," May 1966.

That Schumann was a magnificent melodist is shown not only in his songs but also in his piano music; one can imagine words to the seventeenth of the Davidsbündler Dances or the sixth of the *Kreisleriana*. Often Schumann will pluck, as it were, a melody from the notes of his accompaniment. Less frequent, as in the fifth of the *Kreisleriana*, are compositions based on motives rather than melodies, in which the interplay of motives, rhythms, and harmonies provides the musical interest. In some of the later works, like the fourth of the Marches, Op. 76, written under the stimulus of the revolutionary events of 1848, or the third of the *Bilder aus Osten*, Op. 66, Schumann concentrates on insistent reiteration of square-cut melodies.

Songs. Schumann wrote approximately 124 songs in 1840, the "year of song" during which he married Clara Wieck. These songs, furthermore, are the ones most frequently performed, whether individual songs like "Mit Myrthen und Rosen" and "The Two Grenadiers" or the song cycles *Myrthen*, *Liederkreis*, and *Frauenliebe und Leben*.

The most striking characteristic of Schumann's best songs is the close relationship between voice and piano. What Schumann had previously confided to the singing tone of the piano was now given to the voice but without placing the piano in the background as a mere accompanying instrument. Preludes, postludes, and interludes play a major role; the preludes are generally short, even to the point of merely getting the singer started, whereas the interludes often unify the song (as in "Der Nussbaum"), and the postludes continue and intensify the mood of the song after the singer finishes. The finest postlude is the conclusion of *Dichterliebe*, for it leads from the ironic mood of the last song back to the contemplative "Eusebius" mood of the first song of the cycle. Another trait of Schumann's songs is a close relationship between poetry and music; not since the troubadours, trouveres, and Minnesänger had words and notes been so beautifully united. Heinrich Heine's gently ironic verses inspired Schumann's best songs, as did the full-blown romanticism of Rückert and the nature poetry of Eichendorff; Robert Burns's poems inspired the best folklike settings. In Schumann's later years, when his creative imagination sometimes flagged, such good poems as those by Lenau set as Op. 90 or by Mary Queen of Scots, used in his last fine songs (Op. 135, 1852), roused his latent talents.

Schumann's strophic songs are generally simple and folklike;

those of Op. 79 are vocal companions to his *Album for the Young*. The declamatory songs, like "Ich grolle nicht" from *Dichterliebe*, are more melodious than Schubert's, and the chordal, hymnlike songs are generally late works. The song-cycles are unified in various ways: cyclic interrelationships in *Dichterliebe*, similarities between the outer songs in *Frauenliebe und Leben*, or tonal relationships between songs in *Myrthen, Liederkreis*, or the Mary Stuart songs.

Orchestral music. Schumann's orchestral works include four symphonies and a quasi-symphony without a slow movement (the *Overture, Scherzo, and Finale*, Op. 52); concertos for piano (Op. 54) and cello (Op. 129) as well as some miscellaneous concert pieces, the best of which is the *Konzertstück* for four horns, Op. 86; and four overtures, the earliest written in 1851. In recent years the symphonies have seldom been performed, and the Cello Concerto is neglected because its contrasts are too subtle, its poetic atmosphere too unrelieved, and its virtuosity too unevident, though cellists know how difficult it is.

The First Symphony is partially cyclic; more so are the Second and Fourth. In the Second Symphony, the main theme of the slow movement (in minor) becomes the second theme (in major) in the finale. All the movements are related in the Fourth Symphony, a highly concise work based on germ-motives like Beethoven's Fifth Symphony which set a pattern for symphonic writing that continued well into the twentieth century with Sibelius' Seventh Symphony. In some of these orchestral works Schumann attempted to dissolve the boundaries between movements, most successfully in the Cello Concerto.

In his book *Style and Idea* Arnold Schoenberg effectively contradicted the frequently-encountered nonsense about Schumann's "poor" orchestration by stating that if the orchestration were changed much of the typically Schumannesque quality of these works would be lost. Schumann wanted certain tone-colors and especially wanted blends of tone, subject to the natural limitations of the brass instruments (it is interesting to note the virtual liberation of his horn parts in the later orchestral works) and we should not blame the composer for not wanting his orchestral works to sound like those of Mendelssohn or Berlioz.

Chamber Music. Most of Schumann's best chamber music was written in 1842, the year of the three string quartets, the Piano Quintet, and the Piano Quartet. After his breakdown of the mid-

1840's Schumann renewed his interest in this medium with three piano trios, two violin sonatas, miscellaneous chamber music including winds, and even piano accompaniments for Bach's solo violin and solo cello works and for Paganini's caprices.

That Beethoven's later works were Schumann's models is most evident in the Piano Quartet; it is not mere coincidence that E-flat is the common key of this work and Beethoven's Op. 127 string quartet. Schumann's string quartets are the finest between Schubert's and Brahms's, but the most exciting of his chamber works is the Piano Quintet. Cyclic relationships abound in this work, one of the most striking being the combination of the opening themes of the outer movements as a double fugue in the coda of the finale. All of the chamber works show some kind of formal experimentation in attempting to create new paths for the sonata form and scherzo (A major Quartet) or finale, especially the Piano Quintet. The D minor Trio, Op. 63 (1847) is a complex work which demands many hearings to reveal its message; late Schumann can be almost as difficult for the listener as late Beethoven. In this work the lyricism is hectic, and several portions, especially in the second movement and finale, give the impression that Schumann is merely going through the motions; yet few passages in chamber music are as striking as the *sul ponticello* section of the first movement, and some of the Trio's harmonies are quite adventurous.

Choral music. Schumann came late to this genre. His first published choral work, *Paradise and the Peri*, a secular oratorio, contains fine movements but is hindered by Thomas Moore's saccharine text. His *Mass*, Op. 147, and *Requiem*, Op. 148, both written in 1852 for Düsseldorf, are not difficult works but are quite effective. *Manfred*, Op. 115 (1848–1849), based on Byron's poem and scored for narrator, chorus, and orchestra, is a splendid work; its overture is the most frequently performed of Schumann's later compositions, and though the choral parts are subsidiary there is much fine music to accompany the narration, especially in nature-painting scenes like the invocation of the witch of the Alps; the appearances of the shade of Astarte contain some of Schumann's most expressive music. His one opera, *Genoveva* (1850), was beset with numerous problems, not the least of these the libretto; a continuation of the mediaeval-chivalric legend with virtually continuous set-numbers like *Euryanthe*, *Genoveva's* greatest misfortune was its having been composed after *Tannhäuser* and *Lohengrin*.

Schumann's greatest late work, which may well be the finest neglected composition of the entire nineteenth century, is his *Scenes from Faust*, composed between 1844 and 1853. Rather than select numbers which would make a continuous narrative, he selected individual scenes, mostly from the second part of the drama. Considerable cyclic unity joins the scenes; the solos are among the few instances where Schumann could transfer his mastery of song composition to the brief aria with orchestra; the declamation, especially that of Faust, must have been studied by Wagner; and the third part contains the most sublime music between Beethoven's death and Brahms's full maturity. A comparison of Schumann's original conclusion with his later version of the ending provides an excellent illustration of how his first thoughts were superior to his revisions.[3]

The German Romantic legacy

Mendelssohn's music became the model for the "academic" composer of Protestant antecedents, especially in Germany, Scandinavia, and the Anglo-Saxon countries. At the opening of the twentieth century a violent reaction against his music took place which has only slightly abated. Schumann's legacy, on the other hand, was more widely disseminated. His aesthetic of song writing found many imitators, chiefly his disciple Robert Franz (1815–1892), who published about 350 songs between 1843 and the onset of deafness in 1868. Unfortunately Schumann's enthusiastic emotional expression and fine harmonic coloring was later debased into the "Hearts and Flowers" sentimentality so well exemplified by the *Hochzeitmusik* of Adolf Jensen (1837–1879) or the drawing room and wedding songs of the American, Oley Speaks (1874–1948).

Schumann's ideas of instrumental music and especially the instrumental cycle were a happy mean between those of Mendelssohn and Berlioz, and thus strongly influenced the revival of instrumental music after 1860, and not in Germany alone. Brahms was most affected by Schumann's music, but Saint-Saëns, Fauré, Chaikovsky, Grieg, and even Sibelius and Rakhmaninov must be counted among his disciples. Undoubtedly, Schumann's example liberated Liszt from

[3] See Donald Mintz' fine study of this work in *Journal of the American Musicological Society*, XIV (1961), 235–256.

being merely a purveyor of virtuosic galops and opera transcriptions, and his harmony led to the "psychological tonality" of Liszt and especially Wagner.

Bibliography

The standard biography of Mendelssohn in English is Eric Werner's *Felix Mendelssohn, A New Image of the Composer and His Age* (New York, 1963); unfortunately, the author overstates Mendelssohn's "modernism," and the book suffers from an awkward translation. Many of the letters have been translated into English (*Mendelssohn's Letters*, transl. Gisella Selden-Goth, New York, 1945). Percy M. *Young's Introduction to the Music of Mendelssohn* (London, 1949) is quite serviceable.

No biography of Schumann has the immediacy of J. W. von Wasiliewski's (Dresden, 1858; English translation, *Life and Letters of Robert Schumann*, Boston, 1871); this study by one of the composer's closest associates deserves a new and annotated translation. Joan Chissell's *Schumann* (London, 1948) is the most adequate biography in English, for André Boucourechliev's *Schumann* (New York, 1959) is filled with Romantic overstatements (if also beautiful illustrations).

5
Italian and
French Romanticism

Musical Romanticism developed later in Italy and France than in Germany and Austria. The reasons are easy to explain: in Italy, opera was the dominant medium and its audiences were conservative until the 1840's, the period of the drive for the unification of Italy (the *Risorgimento*), whereas in France the rescue and revolutionary operas of the 1780's and 1790's gradually disappeared with the advent of the Directory and the subsequent rise to power of Napoleon.

Italian opera, 1813–1853

The Italian operas of Gioacchino Rossini (1792–1868) are the culmination of the Neapolitan opera of the eighteenth century and thus represent the close of an old era rather than the beginning of a new one. Though only a few of his comic operas and some of his overtures are performed today, he was the most popular composer in Europe during the 1820's.

Rossini's first success was *Tancredi* (1813), and so many serious and comic operas streamed from his prolific pen that he enjoyed an international reputation by the time he was 30. In 1824 he settled in Paris, where he produced French versions of his Italian works and wrote two of his masterpieces, the opéra comique *Le Comte Ory* (1828) and *William Tell* (1829). With the latter, his career as a composer of operas ended, though he continued to compose short piano pieces, songs, and church music. Among the reasons advanced for his refusal to continue operatic composition, the most probable are his difficulties with the régime of Louis Philippe, which assumed power after the July Revolution of 1830, and his distaste for competing against Meyerbeer.

Rossini's opera overtures are among the most exciting and thrilling works in this genre. They generally consist of a slow introduction, a main section in abridged sonata form with the development section replaced by a transition back to the tonic, and a coda in a faster tempo. Characteristic of them are piquant woodwind solos, driving rhythms, and crescendos consisting of a repeated motive to which additional instruments are added in succession.

Rossini's arias often follow a stereotyped form which includes a slow introduction featuring florid and highly ornamented vocal writing, an allegro with virtuoso fireworks for the singer and sometimes solo instrumentalists as well, and a *cabaletta* in an even faster tempo, designed to elicit a shower of applause. Rossini was assailed for writing out his vocal ornaments, but it is necessary to remember (as Spohr testifies about his travels in Italy during this time) that both singers and instrumentalists inserted ornaments into anything they were performing, and Rossini merely codified an established tradition. The assertion has been made that Isabella Colbran, his principal singer, mistress, and later wife, was losing her voice and that Rossini ornamented her parts to conceal her vocal deficiencies, yet similar "coloratura" writing occurs in the principal male roles.

Rossini's ensembles are pseudo-canonic, with each singer entering in turn, but they bear only a surface relationship to the contrapuntal writing in Cherubini's operas or Beethoven's *Fidelio* and are really strophic with only very rudimentary counterpoint. His choral writing, like that of his successors, is extremely simple since most chorus singers of the time could not even read music.

Touches of Romanticism are most evident in Rossini's serious operas, with their plots derived from literature or history (in contrast to the involved plots, which derived from the popular theatre, of the comic operas), and in the faint tinctures of chromaticism in his slower melodies (see Ex. 5-1) in contrast to the diatonic rapid vocal melodies which often sound as if designed for the clarinets in a military band.

EXAMPLE 5-1. Rossini, Cavatina, "Bel raggio lusinghier," *Semiramide*, Act I.

Rossini was the true composer of the counterrevolution which spread over Europe after 1815. In his novel *Le Rouge et le Noir*, Stendhal describes an ultra-Royalist salon where the only fit topics of conversation were Rossini and the weather. The Paris of the Bourbon restoration, the London of George IV, and the Vienna of Metternich were most hospitable to Rossini's music; this hampered the careers of Beethoven and Schubert during the 1820's, and in France younger composers like Auber and Herold were driven to strong efforts to emancipate themselves from his influence. Though the anti-Rossini strictures of Boieldieu, Spohr, Wagner, and others were partially motivated by chauvinism and professional jealousy, it is nevertheless true that his influence in most European countries was stifling and perhaps explains why Italy and France lagged behind Germany in developing a Romantic musical idiom.

Italian Romanticism during the 1830's is best seen in the music of the Sicilian born Vincenzo Bellini (1801–1835), who wrote almost exclusively for the operatic stage during his short career. Bellini is most praised for his long, arched vocal melodies, which require a superb singer, almost always a soprano, for their proper performance (Ex. 5-2); he may have absorbed this style through his teacher Nicola Zingarelli (1752–1837), whose generally undistinguished operas contain progressive moments like the aria "Ombra adorata aspetta" from *Giuletta e Romeo* (1796). A large number of Bellini's melodies consist of passages with a prevailing dotted rhythm

EXAMPLE 5-2. Bellini, *La Sonnambula*, Act I.

that occasionally imparts a martial cast (see Ex. 5-3a). A trait typical of Bellini's ritornelli, later adopted by Verdi, is an interruption of the melody just before the final cadence, after which the prevailing accompaniment pattern is re-established and the singer begins.

Bellini's harmonic resources and orchestral palette are limited, often producing an effect of monotony, yet he was often able to create an effective psychological scene setting, as in the opening of Act II of *Norma*. Bellini excels as a melodist and as a musical psychologist.

Gaetano Donizetti (1797–1848) represents the lusty, vigorous side of post-Rossinian Italian opera. A very prolific composer, few of his many operas have survived in the repertoire, and these usually as vehicles for a star singer: *Lucia di Lammermoor* for a soprano, *L'Elisir d'amore* for a tenor, *Don Pasquale* for a comic baritone. Less artistically gifted than Bellini, much of his music contains a vitality that often skirts the vulgar. He also had a gift for the "big scene," like the sextet and "Mad Scene" from *Lucia*. His sentimental melodies are replete with parallel thirds and sixths (see Ex. 3c). The principal fact about Bellini's and Donizetti's operas is that they were written for particular singers during a period of vocal virtuosity.

Giuseppe Verdi (1813–1901) was the greatest Italian composer of the nineteenth century. Though his musical development was slow and his first major work, *Nabucco* (based on the Biblical story of King Nebuchadnezzar) was not performed until 1842, his career as a composer spanned more than fifty years. His work can be divided into four major periods; for the sake of chronological organization and to account for the changes in his musical style after 1853, this chapter will include only the works of his first two periods, with the operas and other compositions after *La Traviata* to be discussed in Chapter 9.

Verdi's operas before 1851 have been scorned and disdained by aesthetes because of their vulgarity, earthiness, and unashamed portrayal of raw emotions, the techniques for which came largely from the operas of Saverio Mercadante (1795–1870); these works nevertheless display a powerful dramatic sense, deep psychological insights (especially in *Luisa Miller*, his masterpiece of this period), and a skillful treatment of the devices which he inherited from Bellini and Donizetti (Ex. 5-3).

EXAMPLE 5-3. (a) Bellini, *Norma*, Act I; (b) Verdi, *Luisa Miller*, Act I; (c) Donizetti, *Lucrezia Borgia*, Act I duet; (d) Verdi, *La Traviata*, Act III.

fe - sa a te sa - rò.

(b) Allegro moderato

Ah! fu giu-sto il mio so - spet - to I - ra e duol m'in-va-de il

pet-to D'og-ni be-ne il ben più san-to sen-za mac-chia io vò l'o-nor,

(c)

Di pes-ca-to - re ig- no-bi - le esser figliuol cre - de - i,

Moderato

A - ma tua-ma-dre, e te - ne - ro Sem-pre per lei ti ser - ba,

pre - ga che l'i - ra pla-chi - si del - la sua sor - te a cer - ba

EXAMPLE 5-3 continued.

EXAMPLE 5-3 continued.

An understanding of Verdi's early work is incomplete without a knowledge of the political drive for the unification of Italy known as the *Risorgimento*. Many of Verdi's early operas (*Nabucco, I Lombardi, La Battaglia di Legnano*) are thinly-disguised political tracts into which the audiences could read appeals for liberation from foreign, especially Austrian, domination. Passages that seem like vulgar, bouncy brass band music are really intonations of the mass songs of the revolutionary Carbonari or "Young Italy" movements, and Verdi's early period really closed with the suppression of and temporary setbacks to the unification movement after the Austrian victories over the Italian insurgents in 1849.

Verdi's operas of the early 1850's—*Rigoletto, Il Trovatore,* and *La Traviata*—can with equal correctness be considered the culmination of the works of his early period, as products of a self-contained period, or as harbingers of the future. The first two operas are concerned with the portrayal of such violent emotions as murder, torture, kidnapping, seduction, dishonor, and hatred, with little concern for the subtleties of musical or dramatic character portrayal, whereas *La Traviata* is a psychological drama, a bourgeois tragedy in contemporaneous dress.

EXAMPLE 5-4. Verdi, *Rigoletto*, Act I.

Ma in al - tr'uo - mo qui mi can-gio!

EXAMPLE 5-4 continued.

Many of the traits of Verdi's earlier operas survive in *Rigoletto* and *Il Trovatore* and can best be seen in the soldiers' chorus from the latter opera, the bouncy chorus of courtiers in Act II of *Rigoletto*, or stereotyped set-numbers like "Di quella pira" in *Il Trovatore* or the duet at the end of Act III in *Rigoletto*. On the other hand, musical tendencies which were to flower in Verdi's later operas become apparent at this time; foremost is an impassioned musical declamation, neither recitative nor aria nor Wagnerian sung speech, which is most comparable to the vocal parts in Monteverdi's Venetian operas of the 1640's. As a general rule, such declamation is given to the baritone (Ex. 5-4). The combination of subtle harmonic refinements, effective ritornels which set the scene rather than merely announce a favorite aria for the audience, and restraint in the use of vocal fireworks or other musical stereotypes gives greater depth to the soprano arias, evident in the "Miserere" from *Il Trovatore*, Gilda's aria in Act II of *Rigoletto*, or the whole third act of *La Traviata*.

French operatic genres

French opera throughout its history presents a Hegelian picture of thesis, antithesis, and synthesis. The thesis is the serious, stately, and sometimes pretentious *grande musique* of Lully, Rameau, Gluck, Meyerbeer, or d'Indy, whereas the antithesis is the *petite musique agréable* of *opéra comique*, operetta, or parodies of serious works. The synthesis occurs when the *petite musique* approaches its serious counterpart in style and topic, as in the rescue opera or *opéra lyrique*.

Gluck's legacy persisted in France longer than in any other nation. The nobility of his style, combined with the powerful expressive devices of the "*Sturm und Drang*" which were brought to Paris by German instrumental composers, the melodious tunes of the eighteenth-century *comédie mêlée d'ariettes*, and the ideals of the French Revolution contributed to the rescue opera which arose in the mid-1780's but lost its vitality after 1800. Gluck's ideas were also continued by Antonio Salieri (1750–1825), who spent most of his life in Vienna; Luigi Cherubini (1760–1842); and especially Gasparo Spontini (1774–1851), whose grand historical operas, like *La Vestale* and *Fernand Cortez*, display a heroically monumental simplicity, contain rich orchestration, and were to influence both Berlioz and Wagner. At the same time, *opéra comique* was reverting to its earlier form of a sentimental play interspersed with musical interludes, chiefly syllabic and strophic ariettes, romances, and couplets, with simple ensembles and finales. In 1800 the leading composer in this genre was Nicolas Dalayrac (1753–1809), who also wrote rescue operas and string quartets.

During the first two decades of the nineteenth century the rivalry of François-Adrien Boieldieu (1775–1834) with Niccolò Isouard (1775–1818) stimulated the growth of *opéra comique*. Boieldieu was the better composer, but Isouard could write more popular tunes and had the better librettos, many of which poke fun at the pretensions of bourgeois society. The rivalry exhausted both men: Isouard died in 1818 and Boieldieu's muse was fallow between that year and 1825.

The advent of Rossini in Paris threatened to extinguish a viable French school of composition. After the failure of his *Olympie* in 1819 Spontini left for Berlin, and the younger French composers shamelessly aped Rossini's musical mannerisms. Yet *opéra comique* as a native French genre was revived in 1825 with Boieldieu's *La Dame blanche* and *Le Macon* by the prolific D. F. E. Auber (1782–1871). *Opéra comique* was to enjoy two decades of success with such works as Auber's *Fra Diavolo*, *La Part du diable*, and *La Sirène*, and *Zampa* and *Le Pré aux clercs* by L. J. F. Herold (1791–1833). Though Rossini's influence remained audible in the overtures and the vocal fireworks of the *première chanteuse de roulades*, the French style was most prominent in the delightful ariettes, deft ensembles, and the prevailing dance-like rhythms (Ex. 5-5). Around 1845, with the later works of Auber and the early works of Ambroise

EXAMPLE 5-5. Herold, *Le Pré aux clercs*, Act III.

Thomas (1811–1896), *opéra comique* assumed a depth of seriousness and expression which was to become the *opéra lyrique* of the 1860's.

Auber's *La Muette de Portici* (or *Masaniello*, 1828) was the first example of French Grand Opera, characterized by a historical plot with elements of realism, influenced by the historical dramas of Friedrich Schiller and the historical novels of Sir Walter Scott (1771–1832), and a mixture of various musical styles, from the quasi-symphonic and the grand aria to the trivial dance tunes of the ballet. It was designed to appeal to all the tastes of the middle-class audience which patronized the *Opéra* after the July Revolution brought the high bourgeois class to power. The influences of Spontini were strong on Auber's work and its immediate successor, Rossini's operatic swan song *William Tell*. Of the composers of Grand Opera, Giacomo Meyerbeer (1791–1864, *recte* Jakob Beer) was the most important.

Meyerbeer, a virtuoso pianist in his boyhood, studied operatic composition in Italy before becoming a permanent resident of Paris in 1826. In 1831 he composed *Robert le diable*, which established his reputation as a composer of Grand Opera. *Les Huguenots* followed in 1836, *Le Prophète* in 1843, but his masterpiece, *L'Africaine*, though begun in 1838, was not performed until after his death. The supreme musical eclectic of all times, Meyerbeer combined virtually every known device in his operas for the sake of creating telling effects. His style ranges from the crassest vulgarity, as in the "Shadow Song" from *Le Pardon de Ploërmel* (1859) or the quickstep in *Les Huguenots* derived from the Lutheran chorale "Ein' feste Burg," through devices which had a telling effect on the listeners of the time but today seem bombastic, as in Example 5–6, to the expressive moments of the love duets in *Les Hugenots* and *L'Africaine* and Vasco da Gama's grand air "Ô Paradis" in Act III of the latter opera. Meyerbeer rivaled Berlioz in introducing new orchestral effects. Much

Andantino

Pour cet - te cau - se sain - te   o - bé - is - sez sans crain - te   o -

bé - is - sez sans crain - te   à mon Dieu   à mon Dieu à mon

très doox

Roi !   Comp - tez sur mon cou - ra - ge en -

tre vos mains j'en - ga - ge,   en - tre vos mains j'en -

ga - ge   mes ser - mens, mes ser - mens   et ma foi mes sermens et ma foi !

EXAMPLE 5-6. Meyerbeer, *Les Huguenots*, Act IV.

of his music has a veiled effect, because of his predilection for extreme flat or sharp keys and the resulting absence of open-string sonority; his harmonic effects, chiefly enharmonic modulations, were widely plagiarized. Meyerbeer had an extremely important influence on the opera of the second half of the century, especially on Wagner's earlier operas, the nationalist historical operas of eastern Europe, and Verdi's operas between *La Traviata* and *Otello*. The exoticism of *L'Africaine* and the orientalia of Félicien David (1810–1876) were models for such operas as Verdi's *Aïda* and Saint-Saëns' *Samson and Dalila*.

Opéra lyrique, which began around 1850, was a more intimate counterpoise to the grandiose operas of Meyerbeer, and the best works in this genre have a charm and delightfulness not present in any of the contemporaneous schools of operatic composition; Charles Gounod (1818–1893), Ambroise Thomas, and Jules Massenet (1842–1912) are its best composers. The plots deal almost exclusively with love and are often distortions of literary masterpieces; the classic example is Thomas's version of *A Midsummer Night's Dream* in which Queen Elizabeth, Shakespeare, and Falstaff are among the *dramatis personae*. The expressiveness of *opéra lyrique* comes chiefly through piquant chromatic seasonings, compound meters (especially 9/8 and 12/8), and long, lyrical melodies, frequently with "feminine" endings in internal cadences. Although Thomas's *Mignon*, Gounod's *Faust* and *Romeo and Juliet*, and Massenet's *Manon* are regarded as the leading exemplars of this genre, Georges Bizet's (1838–1875) *Carmen* belongs to this tradition despite the Spanish local color and the realism of the libretto.

The Hegelian cycle was further continued by the rise of operetta as an antithesis to *opéra lyrique*, a genre scorned by Théophile Gautier as "Gluckism . . . broad, slow, slow . . . going back to plainchant." Adolphe Adam (1803–1856), a pupil of Boieldieu and a prolific composer of *opéras comiques*, began a lighter style of composition which culminated in the vivacious operettas of Jacques Offenbach (1819–1880), whose musical style is summed up in the title of one of his biographies, *Can–Can and Barcarolle*. Much of Offenbach's music faithfully depicts the vulgarity of Napoleon III's "Second Empire"; however, his posthumously-performed masterpiece, *The Tales of Hoffmann*, is free of the tawdry effects that characterize most of his operettas and should be considered one of the last *opéras lyriques*. The dramatic ballet rose to a peak in nineteenth-century France; one should mention especially the scintillating ballet music of Léo Délibes (1836–1891), who also wrote lyric operas. After 1870, opera became only one of many forms of musical expression open to French composers and lost its position of almost exclusive domination.

Fryderyk (Frédéric) Chopin (1810–1849)

Chopin permanently left his native Poland in November 1830 and settled in Paris in the following year. In *Lutetia* (1837), the poet Heine evaluated him as a composer and pianist of the first rank and the darling of the aristocratic public of Paris; assessing the national influences on Chopin's music, Heine remarked that Poland contributed chivalric sensitivity and historical sorrow; France, grace and easy charm; and Germany, Romantic melancholy. (One might add that Italy gave Chopin his melodic cantilena through Bellini's music and the traditions of operatic singing, including ornamentation.) Heine continued that Chopin "is therefore neither Pole, Frenchman, nor German; he betrays a much higher origin . . . from the land of Mozart, Raphael, Goethe; his true fatherland is the realm of poetry."

Chopin was essentially a composer for the piano; the songs and chamber music are peripheral in his oeuvre, though his Cello Sonata is the most significant duet sonata between those of Beethoven and Brahms. Chopin was furthermore basically a composer in the smaller forms, for only two piano concertos and three of his four sonatas are viable instrumental cycles, and his longer compositions in the free forms (polonaises, scherzos, ballades, fantasias, etc.) consist of a skillful linking together of ideas proper to the smaller forms. Yet only in the preludes is he a miniaturist like Schumann, Grieg, or MacDowell.

Although the influences of Hummel, Field, and Weber are pronounced in the early works, written before his departure from Poland, many of Chopin's individual stylistic traits are evident in these compositions. The best of them, like the Polonaise for cello and piano, the slow movements of the two concertos, several of the Etudes, Op. 10, and the Variations, Op. 2 (which elicited Schumann's remark, "Hats off, gentlemen, a genius!") could not be mistaken for works by any other composer. Most of Chopin's popular compositions were written between 1831 and 1840, a period of composition which can be demarcated by the Nocturnes, Op. 9, and the B-flat minor Piano Sonata. His last period begins with such major works as the F-sharp minor Polonaise and the A-flat major Ballade and, except for a few mazurkas and waltzes written during his last series of illnesses, concludes with the Cello Sonata, Op. 45 (1846). The best of these late works contain a spaciousness of conception (which was not always successful) and interesting refinements in the smaller works, like the cross-rhythms in the so-called "Minute" Waltz.

Most of Chopin's smaller compositions are dances and are exemplified by the Polish mazurka and the international waltz. The forms, basically ternary, are sometimes expanded into rondos. Though such dances as the E-flat (Op. 18) and G-flat (Op. 70, No. 1) waltzes and the D major Mazurka (Op. 33, No. 2) are suitable for dancing, as witness their orchestral transcriptions in the ballet *Les Sylphides*, most of the dances are as highly stylized as the movements of J. S. Bach's suites; representative specimens are the A minor Waltz (Op. 34, No. 2) or any of the mazurkas in C-sharp minor. The mazurkas, spanning Chopin's entire creative career, show the greatest variety in mood and contain some of the most interesting melodic and harmonic ideas of any of his compositions.

Chopin's middle-sized works include relatively minor genres like the variations and impromptus as well as such major works as the nocturnes, scherzos, polonaises, and ballades. The nocturnes, popular because of their relative technical ease, range in expression from salon pieces like the F-sharp major (Op. 15, No. 2) to such major works as the C-sharp minor (Op. 27, No. 1) and G major (Op. 37, No. 2); the C-sharp minor (Ex. 5-8a) is one of the composer's most pessimistic compositions, relieved by a stirring middle section and a consolatory coda, whereas the G major has some of the composer's most adventurous modulations; the later nocturnes are less interesting. Among his four scherzos, the one in B-flat minor is most frequently performed; the middle section of the one in B minor is the Polish Christmas carol "Lulajze Jezuniu."

Chopin's six mature polonaises are considered his most important group of compositions and display a wide variety of mood: delicacy in the C-sharp minor, funereal lament in the E-flat minor, a stirring processional quality in the A major (the so-called "Military" polonaise), lament in the C minor with its harmonically interesting trio, Sarmatian wildness in the F-sharp minor, and powerful virtuosity in the A-flat major.

Of the fantasias, the relatively early and posthumously published *Fantaisie Impromptu* is on a small scale and is one of Chopin's most popular works, especially in its simplified versions. The *Polonaise-Fantasia* (Op. 61), a late work, contains a magical introduction whose harmonic freedom may possibly have influenced Liszt and Wagner, yet despite its beautiful sections it does not give the impression of a genuinely unified work. The Fantaisie in F minor, Op. 49, is one of the composer's most significant works; apart from the opening march its structure resembles a free sonata form and is a magnificent counterpart to Schumann's Fantasia, Op. 17. The G minor, A-flat major, and F minor Ballades are among Chopin's most important compositions (though the C major Ballade is less successful) and excellently illustrate his technique of creating a large work through juxtaposing and effectively repeating short sections which by themselves would have been admirable preludes or nocturnes.

Chopin's few large instrumental cycles have been dismissed by critics from Schumann and Liszt to the present because of their supposed imperfections in form. The two piano concertos, both early works, stem from the tradition of Dussek and Field, and Spohr's influence is strong in the F minor Concerto. Apart from the juvenile C minor Sonata, Chopin's three essays in this genre consist of the B-flat minor (Op. 35) and B major (Op. 58) piano sonatas and the G minor Cello Sonata; common to these sonatas are recapitulations which begin directly with the second theme-group in the first movement, with the first theme either omitted because of its having been worked over so intensively in the development (B-flat minor Sonata) or presented in a kind of "mirror" recapitulation (Cello Sonata); Brahms was somewhat influenced by these. The finales range from the terse, enigmatic, toccata-like finale based on triplet figuration in the B-flat minor Sonata, a complete antithesis to the "optimistic" or "climactic" finales of the nineteenth-century instrumental cycle, to the well-developed and extensive finales of the other two sonatas.

Chopin's melody ranges from figuration and passage work whose main interest is harmonic and pianistic to a languid cantilena with its ornamentation often derived from vocal music, particularly the vocal portamento; Chopin would often exquisitely vary his melody with ornamental figuration, as in the F minor Ballade. Many of Chopin's singing melodies, whether major (the Op. 9, No. 2 Nocturne or the middle section of the *Fantaisie Impromptu*) or even minor (Op. 63, No. 3 Mazurka) were carried over into twentieth-century popular music.

Chopin's "modal" effects do not derive from deliberate and consistent use of the lowered second and seventh or sharpened fourth degree of the scale but from the ambiguity between the diatonic and altered forms of these scalar degrees. The early polonaises of Op. 71 best show the ambiguous leading tone, whereas the mazurkas contain the best illustrations of the conflict between the raised and natural fourth degrees of the scale (Ex. 5-7a, b) often found in Slavic folk music (Ex. 5-7c). The lowered second degree of the scale is the reverse of the leading tone's drive to the tonic; this gives the melody in Example 5-8a its despairing character and in another composition results in the kind of cadence typical of Bartók's music, where the leading tone and lowered second degree are sounded simultaneously (Ex. 5-8b).

Liszt perceptively remarked that Chopin's main harmonic contributions were the extension of chords, chromatic and enharmonic inner parts, and embellishing notes in melodic figuration which derived from Italian vocal ornamentation. Abraham has coined the term "tonal parenthesis" to describe the extension of chords; it con-

EXAMPLE 5-7. Ambiguous use of raised and natural fourth degree of scale in (a) Chopin, Mazurka, Op. 56, No. 2; (b) Chopin, Mazurka, Op. 50, No. 3; (c) Slavic folk music (from Jan Seidel, ed., *Národ v Písni*, Prague. 1941, p. 247).

EXAMPLE 5-8. Lowered second degree of scale in (a) Chopin, Nocturne, Op. 27, No. 1 and (b) Chopin, Mazurka, Op. 56, No. 3.

sists of a passage, in fast harmonic rhythm containing mostly dominant-tonic relationships, which starts in the home key and returns to it and thus cannot be considered a true modulation. One of the simplest illustrations of this device is shown in Example 5-9. In larger

EXAMPLE 5-9. Chopin, Nocturne, Op. 9, No. 2.

and later works like the sonatas, ballades, and fantasias the tonal parentheses are longer and more extensive and often involve lavish keyboard figuration. One of Chopin's favorite modulatory points of departure is an unresolved dominant-seventh chord in third inversion, fortissimo, followed by runs and scale passages. Non-tonic beginnings are among Chopin's favorite devices; among them are the opening of the G minor Ballade with a cadential formula beginning with the "Neapolitan" chord (its root the flatted supertonic) which continues into the opening theme of the Ballade, and the magnificent dominant preparation of the A-flat major Polonaise. The mazurkas Op. 17, No. 4, Op. 24, No. 2, and Op. 59, No. 1 are wonderful specimens of tonal ambiguity equalled only by the A minor Prelude. Chopin sometimes relied on an "interlocking" tonality in which a composition begins in one key and ends in another; for example, the C major Ballade ends in A minor (Chopin's deliberate intention, according to Schumann).

Ignaz Moscheles's comment about Chopin's "harsh modulations which strike me disagreeably when I am playing his compositions" has been quoted out of context so often that the remainder of his statement needs to be supplied; he further said that such modulations no longer shocked him, since when Chopin played them "he glides over them in a fairy like way with his delicate fingers." Moscheles evidently could not play Chopin's music with understanding, for almost all of Chopin's dissonances are passing, not to be intensified or emphasized, and are an integral part of his (as well as Schumann's) piano coloring. Chopin's harmony had some influence on that of Liszt and Wagner (compare the ending of the Op. 48, No. 2 Nocturne with the finale of the *Faust Symphony* and the "Magic Sleep" motive of Act III of *Die Walküre*), but had its strongest impact on early twentieth-century composers like Ciurlionis and Skryabin, who extended Chopin's ideas to perhaps the ultimate reaches of tonal harmony.

Chopin's rhythm, though dominated by the dance, is highly flexible; one need but think of the cross-rhythms between 3/4 in one hand and 6/8 in the other in the A-flat Waltz, Op. 42, and the E major Scherzo. He has two kinds of rubato: one kind where, in his words, "the singing hand may deviate . . . but the accompanying hand must keep time," appropriate music in which the steady left-hand accompaniment supports the right hand's silvery washes of color, often in irregular groupings of notes, characteristic of the *Berceuse* and *Barcarolle;* another kind is an alteration of tempo, either slowing or quickening, necessary for his nocturnes or stylized dances.

Chopin carefully marked the proper preparation of his trills, and the performance of his compound appoggiaturas should be generally on the beat as in the eighteenth-century style. Since the pedals of Chopin's time gave the piano less sustaining power than today's, the composer's indications for pedaling should be approached with caution.

Hector Berlioz (1803–1869)

Occasionally a composer will appear whose music is so original and so apart from the musical mainstream of his time that he is misunderstood not only by his contemporaries but also by succeeding generations. Gesualdo, Wilhelm Friedemann Bach, Janáček, and Varèse are such composers, and Berlioz is the only nineteenth-century composer to be compared to them.

In comparison with his contemporaries, Berlioz's oeuvre is relatively scanty, consisting of a dozen major works plus songs, concert overtures, occasional pieces for ceremonial occasions, and early works written for the Prix de Rome competition during his student days. Frequently several years elapsed between completion and performance of a major work; one of the most tragic passages in Berlioz's memoirs is his account of the deliberate suppression of a symphony lest its composition, completion, and performance beggar him and his family. Berlioz earned his living not through composition but through musical journalism, arrangements of Weber's and Gluck's operas for performance in Paris, and poorly paying sinecure positions. Few composers have had to persist in their creative work in the face of so much official discouragement, misunderstanding, and lack of support; comparable examples are more apparent in the annals of science or medicine.

Berlioz's works may be divided into three chronological periods. The first was one of apprenticeship and chiefly devoted to writing works in competition for the Prix de Rome, which would provide a government stipend for study in Italy and Germany; these compositions served as sources of themes and ideas for later works, and Berlioz has been critized for such borrowings—by critics who forget similar re-uses of ideas by a host of composers, including J. S. Bach and Handel. The second period began with the *Symphonie Fantastique* (1830) and ended with the *Damnation of Faust* (1846, although some numbers were written in 1829). The final period culminated in his greatest work, *Les Troyens* (1856–1859, performed 1863). It is difficult to speak of chronological changes of style in Berlioz's music, for no other composer's music shows so much difference between adjacent works, yet even in his earliest compositions his individuality is unmistakable.

Berlioz was the last heir of the grand, monumental, Classic tradition of Gluck, Lesueur, and Spontini, and took Beethoven's innovations, especially those of the Ninth Symphony, as points of departure. Weber's operas and the best ideas of the lyrical aspects of French *opéra comique* were lesser influences. One cannot state with certainty whether Berlioz or Chopin was the first to employ certain new structural and harmonic devices, or whether Berlioz or Meyerbeer initiated certain orchestral effects. Certain it is, however, that Berlioz's visits to England, Germany, and especially Russia had a most invigorating effect on the younger composers of these countries. His *Treatise on Instrumentation* founded the science of orchestration; he was among the first of the modern conductors, being driven to this profession by the indifference or incompetence of the conductors in Paris; and his writings on music are equalled only by those of Eduard Hanslick (1825–1904) and George Bernard Shaw.

Berlioz is one of the most misunderstood composers. His tempestuous life and love affairs were well publicized, but much of his apparent eccentricity was a kind of "role playing" on his part to help call attention to his music. The occasional massive effects which he required for what is essentially a very small fraction of his music were easy subjects for caricature: Berlioz's riding in a horse-drawn giant bass drum summed up his music in Parisian circles, and even today the general impression of Berlioz's music held by those not well acquainted with his works is that of noise, tempest, daemonic dissonance, and legions of brass and percussion players.

Berlioz's religious works show the contradictions of his style. The *Requiem* (1837) and what he called his "Babylonian" and "Ninevite" *Te Deum* (1855) are the two works which have been most responsible for the legend about the noise and immense numbers of players necessary to perform his music, yet *L'Enfance du Christ* (1855) is a delicate, gentle work which derives not only from the intimate oratorios of Lesueur but also from the socially conscious aspects of the French Catholic revival during the nineteenth century. In a class by itself is the song cycle *Nuits d'été* (1841), with its long melodic lines for the voice and subtle orchestration; this work wholly contradicts the typical misconceptions of Berlioz's music.

Berlioz's operas have been unsuccessful not on musical or dramatic grounds or even because of their vocal problems (though a few singers gave Berlioz the excuse that his music would ruin their voices) but because they are not adaptable to the limitations of the conventional operatic stage. *Benvenuto Cellini* (1838) is known today only through its overture and the "Roman Carnival" entr'acte. *Les Troyens* is in two parts: *La Prise de Troie* is too short for an evening's production, whereas *Les Troyens à Carthage* is too long. *Béatrice et Bénédict* (1862), the composer's last work, is a deft *opéra comique* in the best traditions of this genre and the one opera by Berlioz which can best be accommodated to the restrictions of the stage; as a musical farewell it ranks with Verdi's *Falstaff* or the last movement of Beethoven's Op. 135 quartet as a masterpiece of gentle, enigmatic humor.

Aside from the concert and operatic overtures, Berlioz's five remaining works are large orchestral compositions, with or without voices. Four of them have been called "symphonies" although only the first, the *Symphonie Fantastique*, really deserves this title. *Harold in Italy* (1834), with an obbligato solo viola, is neither symphony nor concerto but a bit of both. The "dramatic symphony" *Romeo and Juliet* (1839) contains extensive choral passages in its outer movements, but its central second movement is purely orchestral, for Berlioz felt that such scenes as Romeo's solo meditation, the ball, and the love scene between Romeo and Juliet would be best expressed without the hindrance of words. The *Funeral and Triumphal Symphony* (1840) is exclusively for winds, although strings and a chorus were subsequently added to the finale; it consists of a grand funeral march, an "oration" for solo trombone, then after a thrilling fanfare an "apotheosis" in quick-march style. The change of instrumentation in French army bands, wherein oboes and bassoons were supplanted by saxophones and saxhorns, has made this work a rarity in performance. The symphonic idea disappeared with *Lélio* (1832), an unsuccessful "sequel" to the *Symphonie Fantastique* that adds narrator and chorus to the orchestra. *The Damnation of Faust* is neither symphony, oratorio, opera, nor cantata; seldom performed in its entirety, it is generally known by such orchestral excerpts as the Racoczy March.

Berlioz's musical style is misunderstood because it differs so greatly from that of his contemporaries or even his immediate successors, and his antecedents like Spontini and Lesueur are unfamiliar even to musical scholars. Berlioz is the true founder of the "modern" orchestra, as his stipulation for numbers of instruments, especially in the string section, shows. Berlioz demanded his additional performers not for volume but for sonority, especially in his brass writing; he knew that it took many string players to achieve a true pianissimo, and he wanted additional winds in order to have unified tone colors on a chord. He requested additional timpani not only to have a triad or four-part chord playable on those instruments but also to provide additional sonority for orchestral chords on the mediant. Occasions where volume for volume's sake is demanded are few in his music; more characteristic are passages with extremely delicate scoring (third movement of the *Symphonie Fantastique* or the inner movements of *Harold in Italy*) or a festive brilliance of violins and winds in their high registers (the ball scene of *Romeo and Juliet*). Berlioz was the first composer to utilize fully the improvements in instruments, particularly the French woodwind and brass instruments, that had resulted from the technological and metallurgical innovations of the Industrial Revolution.

Largely because of the satirical "Amen" fugue in the *Damnation of Faust* and Ferdinand Hiller's remark that Berlioz believed "neither in God nor in Bach," Berlioz has been erroneously viewed as a hater of counterpoint. His contrapuntal point of departure was the last movement of Beethoven's Ninth Symphony, and the number of fugal passages in his works, of which the finale of the *Symphonie Fantastique* or the introductions to *Harold in Italy* and *Romeo and Juliet* are representative, should lay to rest any statements that Berlioz was anti-contrapuntal; in fact, the opening chorus of the *Te*

Deum is as good fugally as any of Mendelssohn's essays in this genre. Berlioz's most characteristic contrapuntal device is the combination of two themes, often for a programmatic purpose; this derived from the double-fugue variation in the last movement of Beethoven's Ninth Symphony.

Berlioz' harmony is strikingly original, chiefly because of his free use of diminished-seventh chords as modulatory pivots, his love for "weak" or so called "modal" progressions to the third or sixth degrees of the scale, his employment of orchestral timbres to reinforce harmonic change or to underline the part writing, and his use of seemingly arbitrary or even dissonant effects which on closer examination are surprisingly logical: the relationship between B natural and C natural in the second movement of *Harold in Italy* at first seems gratingly dissonant but highly reasonable after one hears the coda of this movement. Berlioz hated abuses of non-harmonic tones, especially appoggiaturas, and criticized even the tame use of them in Herold's *Zampa* (1831) as well as Wagner's more radical employment of these effects in *Tristan*. One of Berlioz's favorite dissonances consists of suspensions delayed well past the expected moment of resolution. He also delighted in the flat submediant, often in an inner part, as an expressive degree of the scale.

Berlioz's melodic gifts escape many listeners because his melodies are often long, asymmetrical, and even seemingly arbitrary: recently the melody in Example 5-10 has been claimed as a quasi-serial melody, but note how the sparse accompaniment and harmony give it a tonal direction. Berlioz often loved to reharmonize melodies on their recurrence, a technique best shown in the second movement of *Harold in Italy*. Berlioz's melody also has a wonderful rhythmic flexibility, seen not only in Example 5-10 but also in the opening allegro of the *Benvenuto Cellini* overture and the horn theme of the hunt and storm in *Les Troyens*.

Rhythm is the most exciting aspect of Berlioz's music. In his letters and memoirs he repeatedly complained about the inadequacies of many orchestral musicians in coping with his rhythmic writing. It is not so much the use of syncopation or rhythmic experiments like the 7/4 meter of the dance of the soothsayers in *L'Enfance du Christ* that makes his rhythm so original, but the subtle "sprung rhythms," the cross-rhythms, the entrances stipulated where the performers do not expect them, the differences between macro-

EXAMPLE 5-10. Berlioz, *Romeo and Juliet*, Part II (Romeo Alone).

rhythm (meter) and the microrhythm of individual lines or short groupings of notes, and even what Renaissance composers would have called "proportions" (the coda of the third movement of *Harold in Italy*).

Berlioz's form is loose but logical. His use of the recurrent *idée fixe* in the *Symphonie Fantastique* and the recapitulation of previously heard themes in *Harold in Italy* (deriving directly from the finale of Beethoven's Ninth Symphony) and the *Requiem* was supplanted by less obvious and systematic procedures in his later works. According to Barzun, rhythm and tempo have structural functions for Berlioz. Tonality does not play as important an organizing role in his music as it did in the works of his Germanic contemporaries, and Berlioz must share with Chopin the responsibility for weakening the obvious effect of tonality as a major structural device.

For the listener, the impact of the effects in Berlioz's music often obscures the unconventional and original treatment of other musical materials. So much is made from the idea of contrast: compare the sheer massiveness of the *Te Deum* with his meticulous attention to detail, especially in varying the accompanimental patterns of a repeated theme, or the variety and brilliance of his allegros with his deliberate use of monotony to create an expression either of humility (the offertory of the *Requiem*) or of inexorable, relentless power (the "Judex crederis" of the *Te Deum*). Berlioz paints a better picture of Hell than any other composer (*Symphonie Fantastique, Damnation of Faust*) but his contrasting heavens are rather bland. Berlioz's structural niceties are often obscured by the wealth of detail and effect in his transitional passages.

Berlioz changed many elements of his style from work to work. With the "apotheosis" of the *Funeral and Triumphal Symphony* or the *Reverie and Caprice* for violin and orchestra he showed that he could write in a popular vein, but his heart was in the monumental works, which were accepted by only a limited segment of his audience. Each of his major works differs in several essential respects from its companions, and Barzun has pointed out the disagreement among students of Berlioz's music concerning which of his works is the greatest or most representative. Few composers, moreover, are less amenable to pigeonholing, categorizing, or the tracing of influences; Berlioz exists in a kind of splendid isolation, though his influence is greater than generally supposed or was generally admitted.

Bibliography

The panorama of Italian opera is best seen in the biographies of Rossini by Stendhal (Henri Beyle, Paris, 1824, annotated English translation New York, 1957); Francis Toye (London, 1934); and (the most complete study) Giuseppe Radiciotti (Tivoli, 1927–1929, 3 vols.); of Donizetti by Herbert Weinstock (New York, 1964); of Verdi by Francis Toye (London, 1931), Frank Walker (New York, 1962), and, in German, Hugo Gerigk (Potsdam, 1932). A scholarly study of Bellini's music is needed.

W. L. Crosten's *French Grand Opera* (New York, 1948) is an unsurpassable study of the cultural milieu of this genre. Martin Cooper's *Opéra Comique* (New York, 1949) and my dissertation on D. F. E. Auber (University Microfilms, 1957) survey the lighter counterpart, but *opéra lyrique* has yet to receive a definitive examination. Offenbach's work is marvelously studied in its cultural milieu in Sacheverell Sitwell's *La Vie parisienne* (London, 1937) and Moss and Marvin's *Cancan and Barcarolle* (New York, 1954).

Chopin's life and works have produced chiefly rhapsodic, quasi-poetical appreciations, not only from critics (for example, J. G. Huneker, *Chopin: The Man and His Music*, New York, 1901) but even from scholars (Hugo Leichtentritt, *Chopin*, Berlin, 1905). Gerald Abraham's *Chopin's Musical Style* (London, 1939) is a splendid study of his music,

31668

and Arthur Hedley's *Chopin* (London, 1947) corrects many of the legends about this composer. Edward Waters's annotated translation of Liszt's *Life of Chopin* (New York, 1963) makes available a fine appreciation and memoir.

Jacques Barzun's *Berlioz and the Romantic Century* (Boston, 1950, 2 vols.) is a superb "life and times," strongly influenced in its musical commentary by Tom S. Wotton's *Berlioz* (London, 1935). Special studies of Berlioz's musical style are contained in the special number (1956) of *La Révue musicale*, and I am greatly indebted to Philip Friedheim's study of Berlioz's harmony in *Music Review* XXI (1960). A new edition of the composer's complete works is in progress, and it is hoped that his literary works (available as complete works only in German) will receive English translations comparable to Jacques Barzun's version of *Evenings with the Orchestra* (New York, 1956). Ernest Newman's annotated translation of Berlioz's *Memoirs* (London, 1932; reprint New York, 1966) is a literary classic.

6

The Music
of the Future

The year 1848 is the dividing point in the musical as well as the narrative, social, and cultural history of the nineteenth century. The revolutions of 1848 and 1849 which convulsed continental Europe all ended in failure. During this time Berlioz and Chopin sought safety in England; Schumann and Johann Strauss paid tribute with marches, the former to commemorate the revolutionaries and the latter to celebrate the victors; Liszt wrote his heroic elegy *Funérailles* as a memorial to his friends who fell in the Hungarian uprising; but Wagner was so actively involved in revolutionary activities that he was driven into exile.

Though literary historians consider 1848 the terminal date of

Romanticism, the changes in music that took place after that year gave nineteenth-century Romanticism in music a new lease on life which was to be valid for another 45 years. It is true that the deaths of Mendelssohn, Chopin, and subsequently Schumann created a vacuum which was filled by Liszt and Wagner, though these two composers had written important works before 1848; that Berlioz and Verdi substantially changed their musical styles; and that as Meyerbeer's reputation was waning, *opéra comique* and Grand Opera coalesced into *opéra lyrique*. Yet all the new developments had important roots in the immediate past, and though 1848, like 1870, is an important "watershed date" in the general history of the nineteenth century, it is not a year marking stylistic convulsions like 1600, 1740, or 1910; 1848 is a date dividing a musical epoch like 1550, 1690, 1770, or 1933.

Terms like "music of the future" and "new German school" are often used to describe some of the musical developments that took place after 1848, but neither Liszt nor Wagner consciously used them. The phrase "music of the future" has been attributed to a hanger-on in Liszt's circle and became a pejorative term among conservative critics in Germany and France; the term "new German school" appropriately describes only the compositions by Liszt and his circle during the 1850's and 1860's. This "new music" had several important antecedents: Beethoven's late works, Berlioz's and Chopin's compositions, and less "respectable" parents like Spohr, Spontini, and Meyerbeer.

Protagonists of the "new German school" felt that Beethoven had said all that was worth saying in the media of absolute music and that the symphonies, sonatas, and string quartets produced after his death were inferior to their models. Spohr and Berlioz had shown that the program symphony was a way to a new ideal of expression, and Berlioz had also revealed the new orchestral colors available to the composer. Paganini exhibited a new concept of virtuosity which Liszt transferred to the keyboard, and Weber, Spohr, and Berlioz had been the principal founders of the discipline of conducting. Beethoven's ideas for the enrichment of the large instrumental cycle had been continued in one-movement forms incorporating in themselves the ethos of the entire cycle—Schubert's F minor *Fantaisie*, Moscheles's Sonata in F-sharp minor, Schumann's C major *Fantasy*, and Chopin's last two ballades, for example. The declamatory songs of Schubert were just becoming known. Although the Italianate "number opera" provided opportunities for the singer, it was dramatically false and musically sterile; Meyerbeer's grand operas were more theatrically effective but made too many concessions to the public. Harmony and instrumental colors were to provide the main channels for musical expression in new forms, instrumental or vocal, and thus provide edification and emotional release for an audience that had to be specially trained through musical journalism.

Ferenc (Franz) Liszt (1811–1886)

Liszt was born only 30 miles from Vienna, his mother was Austrian, and from childhood he resided chiefly in central or western Europe; though bearing a Hungarian name he could not speak the language (he was most at home in French), and despite his Hungarian rhapsodies he was not a truly nationalist composer. He was, in fact, the most international musical figure between Gluck and Stravinsky.

Liszt's works fall into five chronological periods with the years 1839, 1848, 1861, and 1869 as the approximate points of demarcation. His work, however, has not been subjected to the searching examination or chronological-bibliographical study that the works of other major composers have received. He revised most of his early works during the 1850's, and his songs span his entire career without revealing the radical changes of, for instance, his piano music.

First period. Virtually all the works of Liszt's Parisian period (1826–1839) were either unpublished or were revised several years later. The changes were chiefly in the pianistic layout and structural cohesion, and Liszt may have delayed their publication until he felt that the public was ready for his new musical ideas. The important works of this period are the first two books of the *Années de pèlerinage* (Switzerland and Italy), the *Transcendental Etudes*, and the *Grand galop chromatique* (1838), the only major work of this period which Liszt did not later revise.

Most of the *Transcendental Etudes* are works of great virtuosity, although "Paysage" with its premonitions of Brahms's style, the delicate "Feux follets" with its use of a motive which Bartók later employed in his Fourth String Quartet, and "Harmonies du soir" provide poetic contrasts. The final version of 1852 was a simplification of the virtually insuperable pianistic difficulties of the

EXAMPLE 6-1. Liszt, excerpts from "Mazeppa," *Transcendental Etudes*.

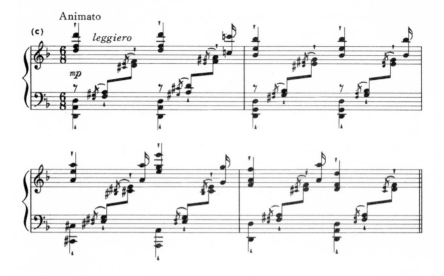

EXAMPLE 6-1 continued.

1826 and 1839 editions. The fourth of these etudes well illustrates the varied treatment of a melody which Liszt developed into the "transformation of themes," as Example 6-1 shows.

In contrast, the individual pieces of the *Années de Pèlerinage* range from the quietly lyrical ("Eclogue," "Sposalio") to full-fledged symphonic poems for the piano like "Vallée d'Obermann," the most remarkable work in the two sets, or the dissonances of "Il Penseroso," which anticipate the strange harmonies of his late works. Such harmonic devices as altered chords or unresolved dissonances are evident in these early compositions. The *Grand galop chromatique*, a fine specimen of bravura display, anticipates not only Offenbach's can-cans but also the circus-like music with piquant dissonances later effectively employed by Prokofiev and Shostakovich. Though these works seem advanced in style, one must remember that these works were contemporaneous with the most popular piano compositions of Schumann and Chopin; Liszt was later to write polonaises, ballades, and a berceuse with a pedal point on D-flat like Chopin's. Paganini's violin playing influenced not only Liszt's keyboard technique but also his sense of "showmanship," whereas Berlioz's influence was important chiefly in guiding Liszt's steps toward program music.

Second period. Liszt spent the years from 1839 to 1847 as a touring virtuoso and had little time for composition, though he began to write songs and sketched several of the works which were later to be completed in Weimar after he had retired from his hectic performing career. The most representative works of this period are his piano transcriptions, though some of these date from his Paris years and he continued to arrange works in other media for the piano throughout his life. The operatic transcriptions were meant to be appreciated by those who knew their operas well and were among the most popular works on Liszt's tours. He also transcribed songs, chiefly Schubert's or his own (the Petrarch sonnets and the *Liebesträume* were originally songs); orchestral works by Beethoven and Berlioz; and even J. S. Bach's Weimar organ works. In a day when permanent symphony orchestras were rare, Liszt's transcriptions brought many unfamiliar works before the general public and undoubtedly aroused in many the desire to hear the original versions. During these virtuoso years Liszt showed himself altruistically willing to devote his talents to playing the major works of Schumann and Chopin, since they were physically incapable of doing so.

Third period. From 1848 to 1861 Liszt was musical director and conductor in Weimar, producing concerts and conducting operas. During this period he wrote his most frequently performed large compositions, devoted his energies generously to helping Berlioz and Wagner, revised most of his compositions from his earlier periods into their final form, and assumed responsibility for the writings on music which appeared under his name.

The piano works of this period include the intimate Consolations and the *Harmonies poétiques et religieuses,* essentially a continuation of the *Années de pèlerinage,* which include reworkings of earlier compositions, transcriptions, and the grand heroic elegy *Funérailles* (its middle section, similar to the trio of Chopin's A-flat major Polonaise, has given rise to the legend that this piece is a "tombeau de Chopin"). The two polonaises, two ballades (the second fine if repetitious), and a few shorter works seem directly inspired by Chopin. The most significant of Liszt's piano compositions of this period, and the most influential piano composition for the second half of the nineteenth century, is the B minor Piano Sonata, completed in 1853 and dedicated to Schumann.

For this one-movement, cyclically-connected structure which combined the salient elements of contrast and unity of both the sonata-form first movement and the multi-movement instrumental cycle, Liszt had several precedents: the later fantasies of C. P. E. Bach, Mozart, and Schubert; the C major Fantasy of Schumann; a one-movement *Grande sonate mélancolique* (1814) by Moscheles which surprisingly anticipates Liszt's rhetorical devices; and the ballades, *Polonaise-Fantasie*, and F minor Fantasy of Chopin. Liszt pursued this one-movement form to its logical conclusion not only in the B minor Sonata but also in his symphonic poems and A major Piano Concerto.

Figure 6-1 shows in outline form the combination of structures in the Sonata in B minor, with its significant motives and some of their transformations. Note the overlapping between "development" and "slow movement," although the finale corresponds with the re-capitulation. The apparently capricious introduction, with its tonal center of G minor, is later seen as an ingeniously logical procedure: G is a pivot note for the diminished seventh that serves as the dominant of B minor. A tonic chord of B minor in root position (which earlier composers would have considered essential to establish the tonality) does not appear until the start of the transition to the second theme-group. Notice how the "closing group" is a lyrical transformation of the originally driving and hectic motive C.

Much of the "development" corresponds to the slow movement of an instrumental cycle. New material (X), which is a contrast through its tonal stability in F-sharp major and its homophonic texture, is introduced and later returns in the coda. The use of motive A in the return of the introduction, with a tonal center of F-sharp, leads one to expect a tonal as well as thematic recapitulation, but the enharmonic reading of F-sharp as G-flat and its use as a springboard for the diminished seventh as the dominant of B-flat minor, the key of the fugue, is a surprise; the proper "recapitulation" occurs only with the appearance of the "second theme" (motive D) in the tonic B major. Despite transient modulations, the coda is in B major throughout.

Unity in other respects is only apparently broken down: although there are 15 changes of key signature, 12 major tempo changes, and 17 changes of time signature, these have mostly structural functions; the "second theme" is in 3/2 meter, most of the key changes are in the development, and most of the tempo changes are in the coda. That Liszt intended this work to be one of high integrity rather than a virtuoso showpiece is shown by its ending, quiet and almost mystical rather than a shower of fireworks.

Among the other important works of the Weimar period are compositions for piano and orchestra, three of them major works. The earliest of these, the E-flat Piano Concerto, loosely adheres to a four-movement form with cyclic interrelations between movements, an omnipresent first theme, and interesting transformations, with the lyrical theme of the slow movement becoming the bumptious march of the finale. The A major Piano Concerto is a more successful work, in one movement with two contrasting themes, the first of these subject to the greatest variety of changes. The *Totentanz* is a set of free variations on the "Dies Irae" chant of the Requiem Mass and the finest example of Liszt's "satanic" compositions, which had so much influence on Stravinsky and Prokofiev.

As a result of the urgings of his friend the princess Carolyne de Sayn-Wittgenstein, Liszt directed his attention to purely orchestral compositions and while in Weimar wrote twelve of his thirteen symphonic poems and two programmatic symphonies. Though he needed help in orchestrating the *Mountain Symphony* (the weakest and most padded of his symphonic poems) and the first version of *Tasso*, with the final version of this work Liszt showed that he could handle the orchestra effectively if somewhat conventionally, his scoring more like Spohr's than that of Berlioz or Wagner.

The symphonic poems on one hand derived from the concert overtures of Beethoven and Mendelssohn and on the other from the programmatic symphonies of Spohr and Berlioz; in scope and extent they occupy a position midway between overture and symphony. Programmatic works, their general structure corresponds to that of the B minor Sonata. *Les Préludes* is the finest structural specimen, with *Tasso*, *Mazeppa* (based on the fourth transcendental étude, with elaborate introduction and coda), *Orpheus* (a restrained work which many regard as Liszt's masterpiece in this genre), and the *Battle of the Huns* the other major works. These and Liszt's other symphonic poems influenced virtually every subsequent composer except such devotees of absolute music as Bruckner and Brahms: one can clearly see the influence of *Orpheus* on Franck, *Héroide funèbre* and *Mazeppa* on Mahler, and *Tasso* and *Die Ideale* on Richard Strauss; and the achievements of the eastern European nationalists or the French composers after 1870 would have been unthinkable without Liszt's orchestral works.

Of Liszt's symphonies, the *Faust Symphony*, composed in 1854 and first performed in 1857, is regarded by many as Liszt's greatest composition. Its introduction is very "modern," with much use of

		MOTIVE
Introduction: Lento assai		A
"First movement"	Exposition: allegro energico	
	1st "theme-group" (B minor)	B, C
	Transition	B, C, then A
	2nd "theme-group" (D major)	D
	"Closing group" (D major)	C′
	Development	B, C′
"Slow movement"		
Recitativo		D, then C, B
Andante sostenuto		X
Quasi adagio		C′, D
	Retransition (F-sharp major)	X, C, A
"Finale"	Recapitulation: allegro energico	
Fugue	1st "theme-group"	
	(B-flat minor)	B, C
	Transition (B minor)	B, C; A; B, C
	2nd "theme-group" (B major)	D
	"Closing group" (B major)	C′
Coda (B major)	Stretto quasi presto	C′
	Presto	A
	Prestissimo	B
	Climax	D
(B major)	Peroration	
	Andante sostenuto	X
	Allegro moderato	C, B
	Lento assai	A

FIGURE 6-1. Liszt, *Sonata in B minor.*

FIGURE 6-1 continued.

FIGURE 6-1 continued

the augmented triad, and could easily be mistaken for a work by d'Indy or Skryabin. The first movement, "Faust," contains most of the themes of the symphony, whereas the second movement, "Gretchen," is chromatically lyrical and almost sensuous. The third movement, "Mephistopheles," is most interesting, for the Faust themes are diabolically parodied (Mephistopheles cannot create, only destroy, and Gretchen's theme escapes his distortions). The work concludes with a setting of the final chorus from Goethe's drama. The *Dante Symphony* is less successful; although the first movement, "Inferno," depicts the empty desolation of Hell and is more terrifying than Berlioz's lurid canvases, the second movement, "Purgatory," is wandering, vague, and goes nowhere. In the concluding "Magnificat" (Liszt made no setting of "Paradise") the composer uses many secondary triads with unexpected resolutions in a manner which almost anticipates that of Vaughan Williams.

Liszt's songs are the least known of all his works. The Petrarch sonnets and *Liebesträume* are more successful in their piano versions, but "Es muss ein Wunderbares sein" has the intimacy of Schumann; "Tristesse," a late song, anticipates the chromaticism of Hugo Wolf; and the best song, "Ihr Glocken von Marling," anticipates the lyric song of the twentieth century. Many of Liszt's songs have overwritten piano accompaniments, and "Die drei Zigeuner" even sounds like a Hungarian rhapsody with vocal accompaniment; the French

songs, of which "Oh! quand je dors" is the best, belong to the tradition of the romance rather than the German Lied.

Fourth period. After several disappointments in his efforts to
make Weimar a major musical center, Liszt resigned his post as
musical director in Weimar in 1858 and in 1861 followed Princess
Carolyne to Rome. After deciding not to marry her, Liszt went
into a period of semi-retirement and focused most of his attention
on religious works. Of the important piano compositions of the
time, the Legends have religious topics, but in style they and the
Mephisto Waltz (better in its piano than its orchestral version)
hearken back to the Weimar period, during which years Liszt had
become interested in choral music.

Liszt's first major Mass, the festive Mass for the dedication of
the basilica in Esztergom (Gran), dates from 1855 and is orchestrally and stylistically related to the best symphonic poems, the
Consolations, and the *Harmonies poétiques et religieuses;* along with
the very subjective setting of Psalm 13, it exemplifies Liszt's ideas
for a "humanitarian" church music which would be "devotional,
strong, and drastic—uniting on a colossal scale the theatre and the
Church, dramatic and sacred, superb and simple, fiery and free,
stormy and calm, translucent and emotional." In this statement—
and in these works—one is reminded not only of the social Catholicism of the Abbé Lamennais and his followers who remained in the
Church but also of the "triumphalism" of Pius IX, Pope from 1846
to 1878 and a friend of Liszt. In contrast, the *Missa Choralis* (1865)
is a very austere work for chorus with light organ accompaniment,
without any of the fanfares, cymbal crashes, and rich harmonies of
the Esztergom Mass or the Hungarian Coronation Mass of 1867.

Liszt's two oratorios, *St. Elizabeth* (1857–1862) and *Christus*
(1862–1867), are similarly contrasting, for the former is virtually
an opera, akin to the historical works of Meyerbeer and early Wagner, whereas the restrained *Christus* resembles in spirit the *Missa
Choralis.* Most of Liszt's organ works date from this period and
range from short offertory-like numbers to such extended works as
the fantasia on the chorus "Weinen, klagen" from J. S. Bach's Cantata No. 12 (known better, in a modified form, as the "Crucifixus"
of the B-minor Mass).

Fifth period. Liszt's "twilight," as Szabolcsi has called it, began
in 1869 and was marked by a sharp change in style, as astonishing
as that in the music of the late Beethoven or Stravinsky. Though in

public life Liszt was constantly shuttling between Rome, Budapest, and Weimar, the recipient of many honors and the teacher of an international coterie of piano students, in his creative life he was essentially cut off from the main currents of music, his late works refused by publishers or rejected by his former disciples.

These late works, almost entirely works for the piano or for the church, show harmonic experimentation and a breaking down of tonality. *Via Crucis* (Stations of the Cross), his major work of this period, contains contrasts between austere modal harmonies and adventurously altered chords, a free use of the augmented triad (found also in his late piano piece "Unstern"), and even the whole-tone scale. Many of the piano works contain clashing harmonies employed with the economy and even brutality of Musorgsky. In contrast, the last book of *Années de pèlerinage* is a major source for a new kind of effect: to quote Szabolcsi, "anybody desirous of becoming thoroughly familiar with French impressionism has to begin with Liszt's 'Eclogue' and 'The Fountains of the Villa d'Este' so as to be able to continue with Debussy's gardens and Ravel's fireworks."

Liszt, rather than Berlioz or Wagner, is the true seminal figure for twentieth-century music, occupying the same position in the history of music as Dunstable for Renaissance music or C. P. E. Bach for Romantic composers. The variegated facets of his musical personality found many echoes—the heroic in Mahler, the satanic diabolism in late Mahler, Stravinsky, and Prokofiev, the landscape painting (how different from Mendelssohn's) in Debussy and Ravel, the economy of means and use of striking dissonances in Schoenberg's Op. 11 piano pieces and in the works of Bartók (who considered Liszt more important than either Wagner or Richard Strauss in the development of music). Example 6-2 shows Liszt's effect on two turn-of-the-century composers who are not generally considered among his disciples, Grieg and MacDowell.

Liszt's other activities, such as his altruistic efforts on behalf of composers from Chopin to Rimski-Korsakov, or his training of a whole school of pianists, influenced music in other ways. He is truly the dominant figure of the "progressive" trends in music, even though many today reject his aesthetic, his melodrama, his rhetoric, his optimism—which shows most clearly in the apotheoses of his symphonic poems—as well as his lapses of taste into bombast, roar-

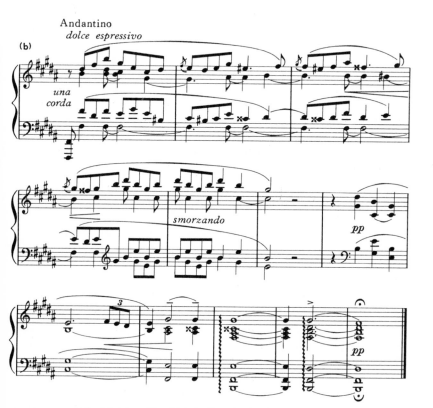

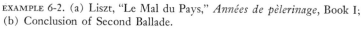

EXAMPLE 6-2. (a) Liszt, "Le Mal du Pays," *Années de pèlerinage*, Book I;
(b) Conclusion of Second Ballade.

ing chromatic octaves, delicate chromatic filigrees at cadences, or
overly rich harmony; those who dislike Liszt's music on these grounds
should examine his more astringent late works.

Richard Wagner (1813–1883)

Wagner is still the most controversial composer of the nineteenth century. Though his influence on the subsequent history of music was not as overwhelming as was once believed, no one can deny his important position in the second half of the century, the magnitude of his achievement, or the problems he posed for virtually every operatic composer who came after him. We should therefore look at the musical milieu from which his operatic ideas came (his other works are relatively unimportant in comparison), his chronological development as seen in his operas, and the salient aspects of his musical style.

After Weber's death in 1826 German opera became provincial again, for Germany, still a geographical abstraction, lacked the musical centralization and splendor of Paris or the many urban agglomerations of Italy which supported opera. Musical conditions outside Berlin and Vienna were rather primitive, and German opera had to compete with the French and Italian repertoire, which was better sung and easier to conduct or perform. The "great German opera," for these and other reasons, seemed an unattainable dream, though models existed in Beethoven's *Fidelio* and Weber's *Euryanthe;* Spohr labored in vain, Mendelssohn and Liszt evaded the challenge, and Schumann made the last unsuccessful attempt with *Genoveva* in 1850. Some of the younger German composers saw in *Der Freischütz,* Weber's most popular opera, a model: Albert Lortzing (1801–1851) found his inspiration in the folklike *Gemütlichkeit* of Max's aria in Act I or the Huntsmen's chorus in Act III, while the horror story elements like the Act II finale inspired Heinrich Marschner (1795–1861) in *Der Vampyr* (1828) and *Hans Heiling* (1833). French and Italian influences dominated the most successful German works like *Martha* (1847) by Friedrich von Flotow (1812–1883) and *The Merry Wives of Windsor* (1849, its third act a minor masterpiece) by Otto Nicolai (1810–1849).

Wagner's ideal was a German opera which would occupy an artistic position and status equal to that of the greatest symphonic music, with the theatre a locus for edification and ennoblement rather than entertainment (an idea that Schiller had pursued since the mid-1780's) and through his ambition, his will, and his egomania he succeeded, after numerous setbacks that would have broken ordinary spirits. The help he received from Spontini, Liszt, King Ludwig of Bavaria, and the cult that grew up around his music was valuable, but his single-minded and egocentric determination was the principal factor in his eventual triumph; even some of his obstacles were of his own making.

Wagner's early works extend to 1848; his juvenilia need not detain us here, and the student of his music should concentrate on his four major operas of this period: *Rienzi* (1840, performed 1842), *The Flying Dutchman* (1841, performed 1843), *Tannhauser* (1845), and *Lohengrin* (1848; performed 1850, though the composer, then in exile, was not to hear it until much later). *Rienzi* is a grand historical opera written, it was thought, to outdo Meyerbeer, but its real parents are the grand operas of Spontini; only its overture is generally known, but this work established Wagner as an operatic composer and obtained for him a post as conductor in Dresden. *The Flying Dutchman*, a work of greater significance, is the first of the "psychological dramas" in which Wagner was to excel, and his first practical demonstration of his theory of myth as the best source of plot for the music drama. *Tannhäuser* and *Lohengrin* are syntheses of Grand Opera devices, psychological music drama, and the mediaeval legends that excited many Romantics.

One who studies these works is struck by the various points at which Wagner either adheres to or departs from the operatic conventions established by Weber or Meyerbeer. Despite the continuous texture, arias and "set-numbers" are evident. *The Flying Dutchman*'s arias are overwritten, especially Senta's ballad in Act II; Elisabeth's "Dich, teure Halle" in *Tannhäuser* is a magnificent specimen of the traditional grand aria; and Wolfram's song to the evening star in this opera shows that Wagner could write a "hit tune" as well as any composer. Not until *Lohengrin* did Wagner display a thorough mastery of the duet. Wagner's large-scale ensembles are the most spectacular parts of these early operas and are most successful when they follow traditional conventions, like the march in Act II or the pilgrims' choruses in Acts I and III of *Tannhäuser*. Most of his finales follow the Spontini-Meyerbeer tradition, with the whole company on the stage; the weakest finale is that of Act II of *Tannhäuser* with its prolix tournament of song and its hero's praising the charms of Venus in the chivalric accents of Weber's knightly heroes like Adolar or Hüon. *Lohengrin* contains the most interesting departure from the conventional spectacles, for they become muted, restrained, and subdued, and what seems to be a massive buildup to a climax in Elsa's procession in Act II is thwarted by Ortrud's denunciation. In all these operas Wagner shows a great love of contrast: Act III of *The Flying Dutchman* is an excellent illustration, for Wagner contrasts effectively the merrymaking of the Norwegian sailors with the spectral atmosphere of the Dutchman's ship.

In retrospect, Wagner did not make as much of a break with traditional operatic and musical conventions as either his enemies or his admirers claimed. Wagner's treatment of the voice in his early operas is quite noteworthy: though the voice dominates the orchestral accompaniment, much of what is to be sung is in a measured, quasi-melodious recitative akin to arioso (Wagner insisted that his singers perform from the standpoint of dramatic realism rather than for vocal effect), with the orchestra interjecting comments or even serving as a giant continuo. At times this could result in dull music, as in the duet in Act I of *The Flying Dutchman* between Daland and the protagonist, but it could also rise to the heights of dramatic declamation, as in the hero's narrative in Act III of *Tannhäuser*. Wagner's orchestra in these operas is not unusually large, and the additional resources he demands are chiefly for on-stage fanfares, but in *Lohengrin* he discovered the expressive effects of the English horn and bass clarinet. Wagner's use of the brass ranges from the "heavy artillery" noise of *Rienzi* to the great restraint of *Lohengrin*. Harmonically, Wagner was no more adventurous than Spohr, Liszt, or Chopin at this time; it is Spohr's chromaticism that pervades the Pilgrims' chorus and Elisabeth's prayer in *Tannhäuser*. Beginning with *Lohengrin*, Wagner associates keys with certain characters or incidents: A major (also the key of the prelude) for Lohengrin, F-sharp minor for the conspiracy of Telramund and Ortrud, A-flat minor for accusations. In his recitatives Wagner is most tonally adventurous: in "Die Frist ist um" of Act I in *The Flying Dutchman* he uses one of his finest recitatives to get from B minor to C minor, but the ensuing aria has a conventional tonal scheme. The third act of *Tannhäuser* shows how Wagner was groping to achieve the dramatically and tonally unified structures characteristic of his later operas: the heightened declamation, accompanied by reminiscence motives, of the hero's pilgrimage (in A minor) is a harbinger of his later style, but set-pieces like the Pilgrims' chorus and Elisabeth's prayer are reminiscent of the grand opera tradition, and the tonality of E-flat major begins and closes the act.

With *Lohengrin*, Wagner stopped composing, not only because his time was occupied with disputes with his superiors in Dresden, participation in the abortive revolution of 1849, proscription and exile to Switzerland, but because he felt that this opera marked a terminal point in his musical style. He had found it necessary not only to write his operas but also to train his performers and educate his audience; now he would need to begin all over again, first by setting forth in several essays what opera should be. His numerous statements need not detain us, since he was too good a musician to be completely fettered by theories, even his own. In 1850 he began his sketches for his tetralogy *Das Ring der Nibelungen*. He was not to complete this cycle until 1874. *Das Rheingold* was finished in 1854 and *Die Walküre* in 1856, but he abandoned *Siegfried* in the middle of the second act in 1857, not to resume work on this opera until 1869. The twelve-year hiatus was filled by *Tristan und Isolde* (1859), originally intended as a "practical" opera which would not require elaborate staging or scenery, and *Die Meistersinger* (1861), Wagner's most beloved opera, hailed even by those who dislike his other works. *Die Götterdämmerung*, the last and greatest of the *Ring* cycle, was completed in 1874 and *Parsifal*, his last opera, in 1882.

Wagner's new kind of opera had many antecedents: the "symphonic style" of the operas by Mozart, Cherubini, and Beethoven; the continuous texture of Weber's *Euryanthe* and Meyerbeer's mature operas, in which the boundaries between the set-numbers were blurred; and the cyclic instrumental forms, with thematic linking, from Beethoven's Fifth Symphony onward. Wagner's concept of the *Gesamtkunstwerk*, where all operatic devices are united in a whole, stemmed not only from Gluck's operas but also from the dramas of Goethe, Schiller (whose *Die Braut von Messina* of 1803 would have been the first *Gesamtkunstwerk* had there been adequate musical and theatrical resources in Weimar), and Schubert's friend Franz Grillparzer (1791–1872). Even at his most innovative, Wagner preserved links with the musical past.

Only in *Das Rheingold* (effective because of its stage effects and fast action) and *Siegfried*, the least popular of Wagner's mature operas, did the composer's theories interfere with his instinctive musical and theatrical sense. Wagner's vocal melody, often just another strand in the orchestral texture and chiefly devoted to expressing the text, is sometimes perfunctory or is doubled by the orchestra, yet one sometimes finds full-fledged arias or dry but measured recitative, with the string section serving as the continuo. Wide leaps, generally fifths or minor sevenths, are one of Wagner's favorite expressive devices; the most extreme example may be found in Kundry's part in *Parsifal*, which established a precedent for the even wider leaps in the operas of Richard Strauss, Schoenberg, and Berg. Wagner's vocal melody is seldom "tuneful" and is designed to carry the short textual lines and quick exchange of dialogue in the dramatic poem. Wagner's declamation demanded a new type of singer,[1] but there were several precedents for those roles which demanded endurance: Meyerbeer's heroic tenors or the heroines of Cherubini's *Medea*, Beethoven's *Fidelio*, or Weber's *Euryanthe* and *Oberon*.

Except for the on-stage brass instruments, Wagner used in his early operas a more conventional and less adventurous orchestration than Berlioz. The orchestra in the *Ring* is the largest because Wagner was creating an entire dramatic world in which special effects were necessary. In Wagner's orchestra the increased number of wind instruments allows a homogeneous timbre on a chord; the English horn and bass clarinet (especially in *Tristan*) are as expressive for Wagner as the clarinet and horn were for Weber; the Wagner tubas for the *Ring* provide a solemn tone-color to contrast with that of the horns or the heavy brass (best seen in the "Annunciation of Death" in Act II of *Die Walküre*); the contrabass trombone and tuba extend the compass of the brass section downward. Correspondingly, an increased number of string players is required to balance the additional wind instruments. Wagner's fortissimos are not constant, and he could orchestrate as delicately as any of his successors. His design for the sunken orchestra pit at Bayreuth, with the brass and percussion farthest under the stage, proves conclusively that he was interested more in sonority than in volume. Several features are typical of Wagner's orchestral sound: extended vertical structures with many doublings of chord-tones; upward extension of the ranges of the string instruments; frequent division of the string sections into many parts; string unisons on short turning figures accompanying a sonorous wind melody, evident as early as the overture to *Rienzi;* a great use of the cellos and even violas as melodic instruments; and a lavish employment of both fingered and

---

[1] It is interesting to note that throughout the history of his operas their heroines have been better cast than their heroes (Heldentenors), most of whom were originally baritones.

bowed tremolos. Wagner gave his orchestra a substantial "inside" through writing for valved brass instruments, especially the horns,[2] and such dramatic brass unisons as the trombone entrance in the *Tannhäuser* overture or the "treaty" motive in the *Ring* are still vividly exciting.

The leitmotive is Wagner's most important external means of unifying his operas. In its simplest definition, the leitmotive is a musical identification of a character, an object, or a state of mind. In Wagner's early operas the leitmotive is melodic and should really be termed a "reminiscence" motive which reinforces the impression of a situation which occurred earlier (Verdi and Erkel were among the more conspicuous utilizers of this device). In his mature operas Wagner treats the leitmotives differently, owing much to the thematic transformations of Berlioz, Schumann, and especially Liszt; other precedents for such melodic, rhythmic, and harmonic alterations of still recognizable motives can be traced back to Beethoven's development sections and even the development of subjects and countersubjects in J. S. Bach's fugues. Most of Wagner's leitmotives are melodic, but a striking chord progression (Ex. 6-3a) or even a rhythmic pattern (Ex. 6-3b) may suffice to recall earlier incidents.

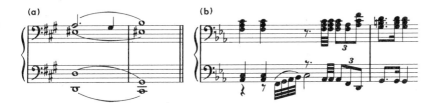

EXAMPLE 6-3. Leitmotives from Wagner's *Ring:* (a) Destiny; (b) Hunding.

The transformation of leitmotives occurs through distortions of intervals or rhythmic patterns and reharmonizations, less often through combinations of leitmotives. Significantly, the great majority of leitmotives in Wagner's mature operas are "open at both ends" in that they can be preceded or followed by a modulation, or the leitmotive itself can be modulatory, often enharmonically; Example 6-3a constantly fulfills this function in the last three operas of the *Ring*. Attempts have been made to reduce the basic number

[2] Adam Carse, *The History of Orchestration* (London, 1925), p. 274.

of leitmotives and to find relationships between apparently dissimilar ones; like all the sweeping theor¨˙ ˙hat have been applied to Wagner's unconscious creative process, there are grains of truth in such attempts, but also a tendency to read too much into the existing musical evidence. There is some association between leitmotives and keys, evident in the earliest sketches for the *Ring:* the Valkyries ride in B minor, the Norns spin in E-flat minor; and just as Brünnhilde awakens, in *Siegfried,* to a harmonic progression from E minor to C major, so Siegfried, in Act III of *Die Götterdämmerung,* regains consciousness after his assassination by Hagen to the same progression, but from E-flat minor to C-flat major. Often there is much repetition of leitmotives, since Wagner did not wish to leave too much to the audience's imagination; thus in Act I, Scene 3 of *Die Walküre,* where Siegmund discovers the sword in the ash tree, the "sword" motive is repeated some twenty-one times. One of the essential functions of the leitmotive is to substitute for the dramatic "aside," wherein the audience is informed of a situation not known to the actors on the stage; a good example occurs in *Siegfried,* when the orchestra tells the audience of Mime's plot against the hero.

The *Ring* contains the most extensive use of leitmotives because of the necessity for continuity in this long tetralogy which depicts a mythological universe divorced from mundane reality. Leitmotives are fewer in the other operas; because they depend so much on atmosphere (especially *Tristan* and *Parsifal*), there is less need for recapitulatory reminiscence, and the few leitmotives used are even more striking and have more of an individual character than those of the *Ring.* Leitmotives are essential ingredients of Wagner's musical fabric, which has been called "endless melody" and which is really a replacement of authentic cadences with deceptive cadences or other modulations. Though leitmotives sometimes occur in the voice part they are usually embedded in the orchestra.

As the leitmotive is Wagner's most important external unifying device, tonality is his most important internal architectonic means. Wagner's macrotonality[3] extends over long stretches of time-space

---

[3] Macrotonality may be defined as the general tonal plan of a composition, whereas microtonality deals with the tonal centers of short individual sections. One may therefore speak of the macrotonality of a sonata-form move-

through his use of a "psychological" tonality more evident to the ear than to the eye. This derived from the tonal plateaux in Beethoven's longer development sections; the "writing around the tonic," by emphasizing its dominant, so characteristic of Schumann, Chopin, and Liszt; and Chopin's "tonal parentheses" and lengthy dominant preparations. We should also remember that after 1850 it was no longer necessary to define the tonic of a key by stating it in root position on a strong beat; when this occurs it is usually a signal that a modulation is about to take place.

Wagner has been called a "chromatic composer," but even in *Tristan*—his most notoriously chromatic work—he writes lengthy diatonic passages, as in the parts associated with Kurvenal. In the more chromatic sections Wagner achieves tonal stability by using "tonal cells" which often consist of a major or minor triad (the tonic), usually inverted, and containing a leitmotive; a diminished or half-diminished seventh chord; a dominant seventh, also containing a leitmotive; then a deceptive cadence, after which another character often sings or there occurs an orchestral interlude. The "open-ended" leitmotives permit several possible resolutions—sometimes to the tonic, more often to the dominant or a new tonic through a deceptive cadence, or to a diminished-seventh chord, which even in traditional practice has four possible resolutions. The longer leitmotives, like those signifying Valhalla or Siegfried's destiny, can be treated sequentially to give the effect of rising tonal plateaux. When Wagner concludes a musical section within a scene, the cadence is often to the dominant of the tonic. When he interrupts the effect of tonal stability he uses deceptive cadences or coloristic harmony, chiefly the famous "Tristan chord" or another chord of the half-diminished seventh or the augmented triad, yet in the passage shown in Example 6-4 he uses a diatonic leitmotive to pull the music from a tonally ambiguous area (augmented triads in sequence) to a new tonal center through modulation.

Tonality is Wagner's chief architectonic device. A study of scenes in Wagner's opera shows a frequent, though not invariable, use of melodic, dramatic, and tonal inner patterns organized either in a three-part structure (A-B-A) or a so-called "Bar" form

---

ment and the microtonality of the second theme-group of the exposition. In Wagner's operas, macrotonality refers to an act or even a long scene whereas microtonality describes a smaller portion built around a certain tonal center.

sein Stamm ver - fiel mir, un - er -

löst soll der Hei - li - gen Hü - ter mir schmachten,

und bald, so wähn' ich, hüt ich mir selbst den

Gral. Ha - ha!

EXAMPLE 6-4. Wagner, *Parsifal*, Act II.

SCENE	DRAMATIC ACTION	TONAL CENTER

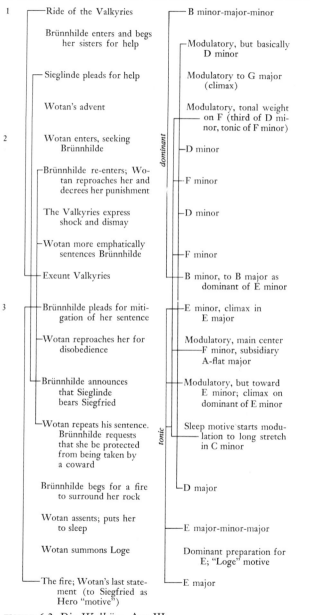

FIGURE 6-2. *Die Walküre*, Act III.

(A-A-B); this latter pattern is chiefly associated with *Die Meister-singer* but occurs elsewhere: the opening 67 measures of Act III, Scene 3 of *Die Walküre* is a bar-form with introduction. Sectional divisions within scenes are often marked by orchestral interludes. Massive dominant preparations occur in individual acts: the "Ride of the Valkyries" of Scene 1 of Act III is in B minor, and the scene and motive recur in the same key at the end of Scene 2; this is preparation for the E minor-major tonality of Scene 3, with E major the basic key of Wotan's farewell, the "coda" of the third act. Wagner had several significant models for his frequent use of "inter-locking" tonality in his operas, especially in the large-scale dramatic and choral works of composers from Monteverdi to Beethoven.[4]

In discussing Wagner's "micro-harmony" (individual chords and their immediate contexts) one must remember that many of the most typical "Wagnerian" progressions were very much in the air during the first half of the nineteenth century; Example 6-5 shows a few specimens of one chord. Wagner neither invented these har-monic ideas nor was he the last to use them, but by employing them in striking dramatic and musical configurations he made them seem exclusively his own. His followers misinterpreted his harmonic thought by trying to write harmony for its own sake and by seeking completely new and novel sonorities and effects.

Certain operas get their "tone" from individual chords. The "Tristan chord" in Example 6-5 and other uses of the half-dimin-ished-seventh chord in a non-functional role, especially in the love duet in Act II, are the basic atmospheric ingredients of *Tristan*. The major-minor sonority of *Die Meistersinger* is given variety by the use of the half-diminished seventh in its functional role as a chord of the dominant ninth with missing root. The augmented triad supports the chromatic portions of *Parsifal* in portraying pain and anguish (Wagner may have easily copied this idea from Liszt) but has no independent significance in Wagner's other operas: in *Die Meistersinger* it accompanies Walther's rejection by the Master-singers and especially Beckmesser, in *Die Walküre* it is the harmoni-zation of the "Ho-jo-to-ho" motive of the Valkyries, and in *Die Götterdämmerung* it distorts diatonic leitmotives.

---

4 Graham George's "The Structure of Dramatic Music 1607–1909," *Musi-cal Quarterly*, LII (1966), 465–82, contains many interesting ideas on "inter-locking" tonality which deserve more detailed and extensive treatment.

EXAMPLE 6-5. (a) Beethoven, Sonata, Op. 31, No. 3, first movement
(1801–1804); (b) Spohr, *Der Alchymist*, Act II (1830); (c) Wagner,
Tristan und Isolde, Prelude (1859).

Wagner's counterpoint is not traditional but is empirically derived from part-writing. Following Berlioz's example, he combined
leitmotives for programmatic purposes, but such passages as the
combination of three motives in the prelude to *Die Meistersinger*
are *tours de force* rather than normal practice. Wagner's bass lines,
especially in the *Tristan* prelude, repay study, and the active inner
parts in his chromatic passages inspired Richard Strauss and the
young Schoenberg.

Wagner's music, especially his mature operas, did not become
internationally known until the last quarter of the nineteenth century, after the construction in 1876 of the *Festspielhaus* in Bayreuth,
which became a place of pilgrimage for aspiring musicians. The
international Wagner cult was more literary than musical, and Debussy's remark that Wagner had been "a beautiful sunset mistaken
for a dawn" was lost not only on composers but also on musical
historians. Those who tried to follow directly in Wagner's footsteps
were generally unsuccessful: Engelbert Humperdinck (1854–1921)

had the best luck with his *Hansel and Gretel* (1893) in which German folksongs and children's songs were blended with a fairy-tale libretto in a musical fabric similar to that of *Die Meistersinger*. Though Wagner's chromaticism and empirical polyphony inspired Hugo Wolf, Richard Strauss, and Schoenberg, the reaction against his heavy sonorities and mythologizing led to the lightened textures and sonorities of much French music, culminating in Debussy and Fauré.

Wagner created more problems for the future of opera than he solved. Despite Nietzsche's claim that Georges Bizet's *Carmen* had "Mediterraneanized" music, the "number opera" was equally a dead end for the composer, and its future was that of entertainment music like Franco-Viennese operetta and American musical comedy or of deliberate archaism, as in Stravinsky's *The Rake's Progress* (1951). The composers who chose to follow Wagner's operatic path had to choose between two pitfalls: was the music to be subordinate to the text and accompany a vocally declaimed libretto, as in the *Ring*, or was opera to be a "symphonic poem with words" like *Tristan?* These questions still remain unanswered.

Other composers

A few other composers were allied with the trends of the "music of the future" and thus deserve at least brief mention. Charles-Valentin Alkan (*recte* Morhange, 1813–1888), an eccentric, eremitic composer of Jewish origin, wrote piano works of nearly impossible length and difficulty, of which his Symphony for Piano and his "Aesop's Banquet," the variations which conclude his *Etudes in all the Minor Keys,* are his best. Alkan paralleled rather than influenced Liszt, and Franck is the most important composer who came within his orbit. Many pianists concede the effectiveness of Alkan's music in performance but question whether they are worth the time that must be spent to master their intricate technical difficulties.

Of all the composers in Liszt's circle, Peter Cornelius (1824–1874) was the best. Because so much of his time was spent in being Liszt's secretary and translator, his output was limited. *The Barber of Bagdad* (1858) is a masterpiece which is excelled only by *Die Meistersinger* and *Falstaff* among nineteenth-century comic operas and contains exquisite Lisztian harmony without sentimental effusions, one of the finest love duets in the literature, and magnificent choral writing. Cornelius's expressive art-songs, of which the *Christmas Songs* of Op. 8 are good illustrations, undoubtedly influenced the sensitive religiosity of many of Wolf's songs. Those acquainted with Cornelius's works deplore the altruism which drove him to furthering the careers of Liszt and Wagner instead of writing more music.

Though associated with Liszt, the highly prolific Joachim Raff (1822–1882) was an eclectic whose early works were influenced by Mendelssohn and whose late works presage the revival of Baroque instrumental forms. He wrote in all genres, but chiefly instrumental music; the Third (*Im Walde*) and Fifth (*Lenore*) are regarded as the best of his eleven symphonies, and his "geographical suites"— musical travelogues—provided models for Richard Strauss's *Aus Italien* and the *Caucasian Sketches* of M. M. Ippolitov-Ivanov (1859–1935). The music of Felix Draeseke (1835–1913), who considered Liszt's late works too radical, is almost hilariously eclectic but is better constructed than Raff's.

Bibliography

Humphrey Searle's *The Music of Liszt* (London, 1954) is the best survey of this composer's works, and Bence Szabolcsi's *The Twilight of F. Liszt* (Budapest, 1959) is a good if slightly chauvinistic account of his late years; it contains a musical supplement. The writings appearing under the composer's name are the thoughts of Liszt and his feminine circle, drafted in French and organized and translated into German by Cornelius.

Chappell White's *An Introduction to the Life and Works of Richard Wagner* (Prentice-Hall, 1967) is an excellent starting-point, with a fine annotated bibliography. The standard biography in English is Ernest Newman's monumental *The Life of Richard Wagner* (New York, 1949, 4 vols.). Robert Donington's *Wagner's 'Ring' and Its Symbols* (London, 1963) is an interpretation according to Jungian psychology and searches for thematic interrelationships; it has a more extensively annotated bibliography than White's study. Elliott Zuckerman's *The First Hundred Years of Wagner's Tristan* (New York, 1964) exaggerates the posthumous influence of his opera.

7

The Rebirth of Absolute Music

An observer of the musical scene living in 1860 would have been forced to conclude that sonatas, symphonies, and string quartets would soon be as extinct as the canzona or the trio sonata, yet during the next four decades absolute music, the world of the instrumental cycle, won a new lease on life even though it did not dominate the minds of composers as it had during the Classic period. Nor was this revival a repudiation of the aesthetic of Berlioz, Liszt, and Wagner, for the harmonic, structural, and orchestral resources of the "music of the future" were at least partially retained, and in France and the Slavic nations many composers owed allegiance to both camps by writing both instrumental cycles and symphonic poems.

The principal composer to keep the ideals of absolute music alive during the heyday of Liszt and Wagner was Robert Volkmann (1815–1883), a German who spent most of his life in relative obscurity in Hungary. Volkmann is best known for his light, tuneful chamber music, of which the best examples are the B-flat minor Trio, Op. 5 (dedicated to Liszt) and the string quartets in G minor, Op. 14, and E-flat major, Op. 43. His two symphonies are interesting; the First, in D minor, furnished Borodin with the structural model for the first movement of his Second Symphony. Of greatest import for the future were Volkmann's serenades for strings, prototypes not only for Chaikovsky's but also for the Opp. 1 of two important twentieth-century composers, Leoš Janáček and Carl Nielsen. Two lesser German composers of absolute music deserve mention: Carl Reinecke (1824–1910), a solid and prolific composer whose concertos and duet sonatas are his best works, and Max Bruch (1838–1920), best known for his Violin Concerto and "Kol Nidre" (though he was not Jewish), but whose most representative compositions are his large choral works.

Anton Bruckner (1824–1896)

A cathedral organist in Linz and later a professor of counterpoint in Vienna, Bruckner is known today chiefly through his symphonies (eleven, two unnumbered) and his church music. Although many of the anecdotes about his naiveté and humility can be dismissed as *petite histoire*, his deep humility, piety, and personal integrity made him the most noble figure of nineteenth-century music. They also contributed to a lack of self-confidence in his musical ability, complicated by few opportunities to hear his music performed; he was thus led to consent to revisions, often disastrous, of many of his best works.

Bruckner is the direct descendant of the Beethoven of the Ninth Symphony and the Schubert of 1828. Though he esteemed Wagner highly, the Bayreuth master's chief influences were on aspects of his instrumentation and certain harmonic devices, chiefly techniques of enharmonic modulation; the Third Symphony (see Ex. 7-2) most clearly shows Wagner's influence. As far as Bruckner was concerned, Berlioz, Schumann, and Liszt might not even have existed.

From his Third Symphony onward, Bruckner utilized certain musical devices which are virtually fingerprints of his style, yet he gave them enough variety to avoid mannerism. One can almost reconstruct a "typical" Bruckner symphony—with the reservations that the Fourth and Sixth symphonies are "lighter" works and that the last three symphonies soar to a pinnacle of achievement. Bruckner begins his symphonies "out of nothingness," sometimes with a string tremolo (Fourth, Seventh, Ninth Symphonies), a rhythmic pattern (Sixth Symphony), or, rarest of all, a slow introduction (Fifth Symphony, the allegro opening with a soft tremolo). The first themes are usually based on either the open fifth or the triad. Bruckner called his second themes "song themes"; in slow movements and finales as well as in first movements, the theme will be closely interwoven with a counterpoint which is an essential part of the theme-complex, and the composer's love for exploring possible permutations of the themes in invertible counterpoint adds to the length of the second theme-groups. The closing themes can be forceful (Fifth Symphony, finale) or quietly stark (Seventh Sym-

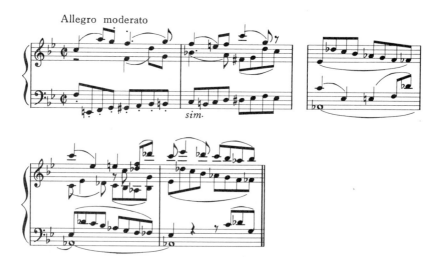

EXAMPLE 7-1. Bruckner, Symphony No. 5, finale, recapitulation of second theme-group. Note the use of pseudo-imitation in the first section and double counterpoint in the second.

phony, first movement). Bruckner's expositions are not cluttered with padded transitions; often, after a pause, he will begin a new theme-group without preparation, which adds to the granitic effect of his symphonies.

Bruckner's developments are like Schubert's in that both composers rely on repeating themes in sequence; the great double fugue of the development in the finale of the Fifth Symphony is an exception. Bruckner's recapitulations are shorter than his expositions and his codas are modeled on Beethoven's. In these codas one best sees a favorite Brucknerian device: a crescendo consisting of an immense buildup out of nothingness, over a pedal point, frequently culminating in the glowing sonorities of the full brass section.

Except for the slow march of the Fourth Symphony, the slow movements are Bruckner's centers of symphonic gravity; they generally consist of solemn hymnlike adagios in sonata form, with the contrasting "song theme" often a letdown in the mood of exaltation. The scherzos are often deliberate and ponderous, less often (as in the Sixth Symphony) fantastic; the trios range from the dance-like one in the Fourth Symphony to the mysteriously shadowy one of the Ninth.

Like the other composers of the century, Bruckner struggled with the problem of the finale; there is none for the Ninth Symphony, though Bruckner began this composition in 1887. Sometimes themes from previous movements will be recapitulated in the finale, and there are sometimes sharp contrasts between the themes, often with programmatic significance; in the last movement of the Third Symphony the juxtaposition of a dance-like melody with a trombone chorale symbolized for Bruckner a funeral ceremony inside a church with street life going on outside its portals. A climactic chorale is a frequent, but not essential, ingredient of his finales; that of the Fifth Symphony is treated in counterpoint with the fugue subject that figures in the first theme-group of this movement.

Bruckner's melodies tend to be long, based either on a triad or on wide leaps, and often treated as "double sequences" a third apart, which leads, in notation, to what seems to be a frightening enharmonic thicket, since part of the sequential treatment includes a Schubertian love for contrasts between major and minor. A sequence from A major, for example, can include F major, D-flat major, and C-sharp minor. In the passage shown in Example 7-2, Bruckner begins his melody in the tonic, modulates to distant areas, and returns securely to his home key; here one can see the roots of

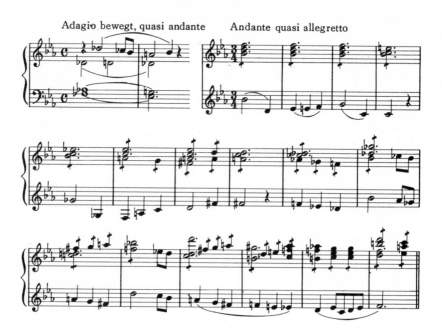

EXAMPLE 7-2. Bruckner, Symphony No. 3, second movement.

Hindemith's melodic-harmonic style. Bruckner's rhythmic finger-print is the contrast of triplets and duplets in a given melody; when they occur in cross-rhythms (Fifth Symphony, second movement; Sixth Symphony, first movement) they create an effect of intricacy.

When Bruckner used rich altered chords he employed them as functional harmonies to go from one tonal center to a transient internal center. Often, after a pause, Bruckner shifts his tonal planes abruptly, a device derived from Beethoven's late works. His orchestration has been criticized as "organist's scoring"; frequently one hears an effect comparable to changing organ manuals (from pure string color to woodwind color to another "manual" of glowing brass), in tutti passages he uses the tuba like an organ pedal playing an active bass line, and his tremendous octave passages, either against string figurations or powerful unisons with 32′, 16′, 4′, and 2′ "registrations," produce a massive organ-like effect; yet he eschewed the reedy, flutey, or "voix céleste" sonorities of his fellow organist-composer César Franck.

Bruckner's well-meaning but hopelessly misguided pupils per-suaded their mentor to agree to many disastrous cuts in his sym-phonies; after his death they changed his orchestration to achieve a more Wagnerian blend and committed mayhem on his music, for example, hacking out most of the recapitulation of the finale of his Fifth Symphony. In explanation, but not defense, one should mention that this was a period when musicians "improved" the works of their predecessors; thus Grieg's second piano parts for Mozart sonatas, MacDowell's reharmonization of Bach's Anna Magdalena book, and the differing revisions of Monteverdi's *Orfeo* by d'Indy and Respighi.

Much of Bruckner's church music, especially the motets, derives from the ethos of the Cecilian reformers who sought to restore Catholic church music to a pristine *a cappella* purity, but his Masses in D minor and F minor and his *Te Deum* are in the tradition of Viennese symphonic church music; despite many lovely passages, especially the Benedictus of the F minor Mass or the contrapuntal *tours de force*, these works sound overwritten. A magnificent synthesis of symphonic and Cecilian trends in church music is the E minor Mass (1866, revised 1882), which succeeds where Spohr failed in his attempts to unite sixteenth-century counterpoint and nineteenth-century harmony.

Bruckner failed to found a "school" of composition, and during his lifetime he seldom heard his symphonies in their entirety or without some kind of fiasco. Though his influence on Mahler was strong, it was not overwhelming, and linking the two composers together is as unjustified as bracketing Bach with Handel or Debussy with Ravel.

Johannes Brahms (1833–1897)

Though writers agree on the existence of a youthful period ending around 1855 and a final period beginning in 1891 with the works from Op. 114 onwards, Brahms's creative life is difficult to arrange chronologically. It is difficult to speak of internal "periods" in his music (although Geiringer's citation of the *German Requiem* as a dividing-point is quite convincing) since Brahms's first work for any medium has a certain tentative and experimental quality about it, even as late as the First Symphony or the Violin Sonata in G major, and since on the other hand even in his very early works one finds so many salient traits of his mature style. One can best speak of periodization in the forms and media for which Brahms wrote.

Piano music. Brahms's first published works include three piano sonatas, evidence that he was beginning his career as a "strict" composer; a marvelous Scherzo, Op. 4, the earliest work he deemed fit for publication; the Ballades, Op. 10; and some variations, crowned by the magnificent Variations and Fugue on a Theme by Handel, Op. 24, which Wagner praised, and the virtuoso Variations on a Theme by Paganini, Op. 35. Brahms thereafter limited himself to short piano pieces: those of Op. 76 are highly concentrated; the Rhapsodies, Op. 79, are magnificent specimens of his *"Sturm und Drang"* Romantic piano writing; and the short piano pieces from Op. 116 through Op. 119 are the culmination of his achievement as a piano composer.

These brief pieces bear such noncommittal titles as "capriccio," "rhapsody," and especially "intermezzo." Generally ternary in form, the individual sections show highly subtle internal links and are often inter-related. The few passionate pieces (e.g., Op. 116, Nos. 1 and 3, are restrained and concentrated in comparison with the Rhapsodies of Op. 79; others, like Op. 116, No. 5 and Op. 118, No. 4, are highly abstract plays on rhythmic motives. Such warm and contemplative pieces as Op. 118, No. 2 and Op. 116, No. 4 may be contrasted with the somber Op. 118, No. 6, the songful Op. 117, No. 1, and the reflective Op. 119, No. 1. These late pieces are the complete antithesis of the Romantic "salon piece"; comparing them with Liszt's Consolations shows a striking contrast between the aesthetic of two different composers working within the same self-imposed limitations.

Brahms often sketched his larger chamber or orchestral works for two pianos; the scanty original literature for this medium counts among its cornerstones the two-piano versions of the Piano Quintet and the Haydn Variations. Among the fine works for piano duet are the Waltzes, Op. 39; the intricate and difficult Variations on a theme by Schumann, Op. 23; the Liebeslieder Waltzes, to which vocal parts were later added; and the familiar Hungarian Dances, which helped start a virtual avalanche of "national" dances for piano duet of which those by Dvořák, Grieg, Moszkowski, and Gilbert are the most worthy successors.

Chamber music. This medium occupied Brahms during all his creative periods and contains perhaps his best work. In number of performers, the range is from duet sonatas to string sextets, and there are interesting contrasting timbres in the Trio for horn, violin, and piano (Op. 40) and the Trio for clarinet, cello, and piano (Op. 114).

In all the media except for quintets, the first work reveals not only a certain tentativeness, as if Brahms were exploringly feeling his way, but also a certain expansiveness, for each first work tends to be longer than its successors. The B minor Trio, Op. 8, the first of his chamber works, was originally so long that Brahms later condensed it drastically, but it is still his longest chamber work. These first works often have a serene contemplativeness, as in the B-flat String Sextet (Op. 18) and E minor Cello Sonata (Op. 38), but the extremely somber C minor String Quartet (Op. 51, No. 1) is a striking exception. As a rule, the second work in each medium is the best or most "Romantic" in its effusiveness, especially the A minor String Quartet (Op. 51, No. 2) or—Brahms's most "Romantic" chamber work—the A major Violin Sonata (Op. 100). The third work in each medium can either be the most "Classical," like the B-flat major String Quartet (Op. 67), or the most abstract, like the D minor Violin Sonata (Op. 108).

The growth of professional string quartets stimulated Brahms's muse; his chamber works, unlike Volkmann's, are not for amateurs playing *Hausmusik*. Generally his chamber music is highly restrained, disciplined, and even somber (C minor Quartet, B minor Clarinet Quintet), but few more exuberant chamber works exist than the gypsy rondo which closes the G minor Piano Quartet (Op. 25) or the light-hearted first movement of the B-flat String Quartet. A few of his chamber works have an almost "orchestral" sound, especially the two string quintets, and Schoenberg thought that the G minor Piano Quartet should be given orchestral garb. Many performers of the duet sonatas complain that the competition with the piano is an unequal one, and that the close relationship between solo instrument and piano is uncongenial to the type of virtuoso who considers his instrument the center of a duet sonata.

Orchestral music. Though Brahms's four symphonies are no longer considered the acme of his oeuvre, they are still among the major orchestral works of the nineteenth century. His four concertos—two for piano, one for violin, and the "Double Concerto" for violin and cello—revert to the Beethovenian tradition of a symphony with obbligato solo instrument. The two early Serenades (Opp. 11, 16) and the "Tragic" and "Academic Festival" overtures complete the short list.

Not only is the first work in each orchestral genre tentative, whether serenade (Op. 11), concerto (Op. 15), or even symphony (Op. 68), but when each is compared with a work written soon after it in another genre, as with the A major Serenade and the Second Symphony, the second work shares the expansiveness of the first. Brahms's orchestration, stemming from that of Beethoven and Schumann, is characterized by great restraint in using orchestral "heavy artillery" and by a rather dark brown, somber coloring thanks to the importance of the violas, the blended tone-colors, and the doubling of notes, particularly the thirds of chords, in the low registers (a characteristic also of his piano and chamber music). Only in the D minor Piano Concerto does he write poorly for his instruments. The serenades are works for chamber orchestra; in the second, in A major, he even (as in the first movement of the *German Requiem*) omits violins.

Songs. Brahms wrote over 200 songs in the tradition of the German Lied. Except for the Romances from *Magelone* (Op. 33), settings of a poetic cycle by Ludwig Tieck, and the *Four Serious Songs* (Op. 121), on Biblical texts, Brahms avoided the song cycle, preferring to write a group of songs to texts by a variety of poets.

From a strictly evolutionary standpoint Brahms's songs are regressive, for he limited the role of the accompaniment to short preludes and postludes, occasional interludes, and to doubling the vocal melody or playing arpeggiated chords, often in cross-rhythms, without however any semblance of hackneyed accompanimental patterns. The voice is the center of attention; the occasional wide leaps demanded are generally triadic, and irregular (three- or five-measure) but balanced phrases frequently occur. The most typical songs are either those in folksong style ("Sonntag" from Op. 47, or the German folksongs with piano accompaniment) or are slow and contemplative, like "Sapphic Ode," "Feldeinsamkeit," or "Wie bist du, meine Konigin." When he examined a song by another composer, Brahms would cover all the parts except the vocal melody and the bass, evidence that he considered these the most important elements of a song.

Choral music. Only Handel and Mendelssohn can be said to have written as grateful music for choral voices as Brahms, a choral conductor who thoroughly understood the medium. His choral music is the culmination of the German tradition, embracing not only the large festival chorus but also the small mixed, male, or women's chorus that fulfilled important social as well as musical functions. Brahms's largest accompanied choral work, the *German Requiem*, is based on Biblical rather than liturgical texts and contains not only dramatic fugal passages and a song-like soprano solo in the fifth movement but also, in the outer movements (in F major, one of the composer's favorite keys) and the fourth, the finest choral writing of the century. Among the shorter accompanied works the exquisite *Nänie* and *Song of Destiny* deserve particular mention. His *a cappella* choral works include not only motets based on the seventeenth-century choral tradition, which Brahms thoroughly understood by having conducted these works as well as several of J. S. Bach's cantatas, but also delightful arrangements of folksongs.

Musical style. As with any major composer, a capsule description of Brahms's musical style is difficult to make, but several stylistic traits are prominent in his music. His melodies emphasize the triad (characteristic also of German folksong, in which he was deeply interested), and triadic leaps give a virile strength and energy to even the most contemplative passages. When the melodies tend to be long, as in reflective works like the B major Trio, E minor Cello Sonata, and B-flat major String Quintet (like the opening melodies of Beethoven's "Archduke" Trio or Schubert's B-flat Piano Sonata, D. 960), they indicate that the work is to be on an extensive time-scale. Brahms's long melodic arches are evident even when interruptions must be taken for breath, as in the songs or the slower movements of the works for clarinet, or when the melody itself is seemingly broken up by rests, as in the third movement of the Op. 108 Violin Sonata. As Example 7-4 will show, his handling of simple phrases and extending them motivically is magnificent.

Rhythm is Brahms's driving force, and his treatment of this element, which he shared with Beethoven, Schumann, and Berlioz, raises his music far above that of his contemporaries like Raff and Reinecke, who were too easily satisfied with static or jog-trot rhythms inseparable from the meter. Though Brahms occasionally used irregular meters or (like Schumann) added another beat to a measure to extend a phrase or delay a cadence, he generally relied on syncopation, sometimes united with a syncopated harmonic rhythm (as in the first movement of the Third Symphony) that gives the impression to the casual observer that the conductor is a fraction of a beat behind or ahead of the orchestra. Cross-rhythms, with triplets in one hand and duplets in the other, are most obvious in his piano music and song accompaniments and are one of his favorite ways of giving added interest to a homophonic passage.

Brahms's most striking rhythmic device is his use of hemiola, which pervades most of his movements in 3/4 or 6/8 meter. Quite often this is a "sprung rhythm" wherein a prevailing pattern in 3/4 will give way to measures of 6/8 or vice versa, and there are also combinations of the two meters to provide another variety of cross-rhythm.

Though Brahms was the most contrapuntal composer of the century, he was the least ostentatious about it and in this respect is surpassed only by Mozart, for even in Beethoven's music one often senses that the composer is deliberately calling attention to his use of a "learned" device. Especially in the large choral works Brahms's fugues are "accompanied," perhaps to keep the rhythmic

EXAMPLE 7-3. Selected rhythmic devices in Brahms' music: (a) Color prolationis hemiola (Horn Trio, Op. 40, last movement); (b) Hemiolar cross-rhythms (Violin Sonata, Op. 78, first movement); (c) Duplets, triplets, and color prolationis (B-flat Quartet, Op. 67, first movement, coda); (d) Syncopated harmonic rhythm (Handel Variations, Op. 24; end of second variation leading into third variation).

Var. 3

EXAMPLE 7-3 continued.

propulsion from sagging (the fugues in the third and sixth movement of the *German Requiem* are excellent illustrations), but in the
motets he reverts to more archaic techniques. The best instrumental
fugal finales conclude the E minor Cello Sonata and F major String
Quintet; Beethoven's keyboard fugues in the late sonatas are the
most obvious models, but the ultimate ancestor is J. S. Bach's *Well-
Tempered Clavier* rather than the organ fugues of the Weimar
epoch which Liszt and his disciples were transcribing as virtuoso
piano solos. In his variations Brahms took great delight in canonic
problems, as Bach did in his "Goldberg" Variations, and in setting
compositional limitations for himself, especially in the use of invertible counterpoint, where soprano and bass melodies may exchange places, or of such difficult tasks as occur in the tenth of the
Schumann Variations, Op. 9, where the bass line is the mirror image
of the soprano melody. Occasionally Brahms utilized ground bass
techniques, as in the finales of the Haydn Variations and the Fourth
Symphony.

Though Brahms used many of the harmonies of the "new German school," particularly the half-diminished seventh chord as
dominant preparation in cadences, to him harmony was strictly
functional, neither coloristic or rhetorical. Along with his love for
folksong came a desire for authentic sounding harmonizations re-
quiring a lavish use of secondary triads, even to the point of blurring
the tonal center of the melody, as in Example 7-4; the beginning
sounds like F major but the middle A major or minor. Brahms's
rather somber harmonic coloring derives from his fondness for sub-

EXAMPLE 7-4. Brahms, Quartet, Op. 51, No. 1, third movement, trio.

dominant harmony, the "dark" side of the circle of fifths as opposed to the "brightness" of dominant harmony. Often when Brahms goes to the dominant side of the circle of fifths he returns via the subdominant to the tonic. The minor forms of the subdominant and the tonic are his favorite pivots for modulation, and many of his diminished-seventh chords consist of the third of the minor subdominant (B-flat in the key of D) added to an incomplete dominant harmony (C♯–E–G) and are thus functional; similarly, chords of the augmented sixth are used to reinforce the tonic or half-diminished sevenths, usually in first inversion (E–G–B♭–D, with G in the bass), as dominant preparation in cadences.

Though writers disagree as to the actual amount of thematic or psychological interrelationships there are between movements of his instrumental cycles, Brahms occasionally uses material from the opening movement in a finale, as in his skillful insertion of material from the first movement into the final variations of both the Op. 67 String Quartet and the Clarinet Quintet. The introductions to the outer movements of the First Symphony contain most of the salient thematic material. Most frequently Brahms creates cyclic links within his movements, especially by using crucial motives in transitional passages.

In his sonata-form movements Brahms follows the models of middle-period through late-period Beethoven, late Schubert (especially the sonatas), or the Chopin of the B minor and G minor sonatas. His expositions are clear-cut, with considerable contrast among the themes. When he does not indicate a repeat of the exposition (which should be observed in performance when so marked), his developments usually begin in the tonic with a restatement of the opening theme to give the effect of a repeated exposition. When this occurs, and especially if the material of the first theme has dominated the development, the recapitulation is highly truncated, in the manner of Beethoven's Quartet, Op. 95, first movement, or Chopin's mature sonatas, or may be even a sort of "mirror" recapitulation as in the first movement of the Op. 25 Piano Quartet. The slow movements, like Schubert's and, later, some of Mahler's, are modeled on the art-song rather than the aria, hymn, or romance; this is especially evident when the "accompanying" instruments open the movement with a ritornello. The form is generally ternary on a large scale, with some reprises characterized by melodic variation.

Brahms's scherzo movements are seldom of the bumptious sort; only that of the Fourth Symphony really fits that description. Sometimes the scherzo will be mysterious, deft, and fantastic, as in the Trio, Op. 87; sometimes it is a sturdy movement in 6/8 meter replete with duplets, as in the Horn Trio or the Op. 99 Cello Sonata. In the Op. 88 String Quintet and Op. 100 Violin Sonata the slow and scherzo movements are "telescoped" into one movement. But the most typical type of third movement is a contemplative intermezzo, sometimes with varying tempos and thematic transformation as in the Second Symphony, most often highly poignant as in the Op. 67 Quartet or any of the late instrumental cycles; the comparable movements in Beethoven's Op. 130 and Op. 132 Quartets are the most evident models.

Considerable variety exists among Brahms's finales. One exciting type, which Liszt liked, is the Hungarian rondo, at its most fiery in the G minor Piano Quartet and also found as a highly effective close to the Violin Concerto and the "Double" Concerto. A relaxed and expansive conclusion, often a rondo or set of variations, is characteristic of such works in B-flat major as the Op. 18 Sextet, the Op. 67 Quartet, and the Piano Concerto in B-flat. Some of the finales are contrary to the "optimistic" and "victorious" instrumental cycle by being in minor, even when the first movement is in tonic major. Most of the finales are in sonata form, but the conclusion of the Fourth Symphony freely utilizes ground-bass techniques with numerous variations, refinements, motivic play, and harmonic substitution and is unique, not only in Brahms's oeuvre but also for the century.

Brahms's sets of variations, whether movements of an instrumental cycle or independent compositions, are an important portion of his work. They derive more from J. S. Bach's "Goldberg" Variations and Beethoven's later variations than from the free variations of Schumann's *Symphonic Etudes*, and are generally called "character variations" in that each individual variation is an alteration of the "character" of the theme. To use a mathematical analogy, the "constants" are the structure of the theme (number of phrases, binary or ternary organization) and the harmony in the broadest sense, allowing for substitutions of chords especially in changes of mode; the variables are the other elements—melody, rhythm, pitch-location, and texture. Figure 7-1 shows the organization of Brahms's most familiar set of variations, the Variations on a Theme by Haydn,

Op. 56. The analysis should be regarded as a point of departure for an intensive study of the motivic development and harmonic substitution typical of the composer's other mature variations.

Brahms's achievement. It is generally thought today that Brahms's contemporaries viewed him as a pedantic musical reactionary who eschewed program music and music drama in favor of Classic-era forms, yet Wagner remarked, on hearing Brahms play his Handel Variations, that there was still life in the old forms when one knew how to handle them, and Liszt, though cool to most of Brahms's music, enjoyed his Hungarian finales. Actually, Brahms fused Baroque attitudes toward counterpoint and exploitation of all the possibilities of a musical idea and Classic techniques of musical craftsmanship with the Romantic views of musical expressiveness through harmonic and sonorous resources; he thus synthesized the best elements of the eighteenth and nineteenth centuries in music without creating stylistic incongruities or relying on antiquarian devices divorced from a living musical language. Brahms was the greatest composer of Protestant church music since J. S. Bach; his arrangements of folk or popular music, either as solo songs, in choral settings, or for piano duet, provided models for future composers; and he revived the duet sonata, the independent set of variations, and chamber music as viable artistic forms. Especially in the variation form, Brahms's influence strongly affected such twentieth-century composers as Reger, Dohnányi, and Hindemith.

The "French Musical Renaissance"

Berlioz died, broken and embittered, in 1869. In the following year Prussia crushingly defeated France, and in 1871, shortly before the victorious German armies paraded through Paris, the Société nationale de musique was founded with the slogan *Ars gallica*—French art; its founding marked a rebirth of French instrumental composition which was soon to provide musical alternatives to German symphonic thought or music drama.

The superficial impression given by the term "French Musical Renaissance" is that instrumental music finally became appreciated by Parisian audiences. In reality, quartet societies and symphony orchestras had been founded between 1850 and 1870, but the dislocations of the Franco-Prussian war and the insurrection of the Paris

VARIATION	TEMPO	METER	STRUCTURE				REMARKS
Theme	*Andante*	2/4	A 5 + 5	B 4 + 4	A 4	Coda 7	(Prolongation of tonic.)
I	*Poco più animato*	2/4	The same				Essentially the same harmony.
II	*Più vivace*	2/4	The same				5-measure phrase of A 1 + 4. Essentially the same harmony but in minor.
III	*Con moto*	2/4	A 10 + 10	B 4 + 4	A Coda 4 + 7 (repeated)		Major. Written-out repeats with changes of orchestration and pitch-location.
IV	*Andante con moto*	3/8	B 4 + 4	A 5 + 5	A 5 + 5 Coda A 4 + 7 (repeated)		Written-out repeats with second statement in invertible counterpoint at the twelfth. Minor.
V	*Vivace*	6/8	A 10 + 10	B+A 12 + 7	B+A 12 + 7	B+A 12 + 7	Diminution and distortion of theme, often using hemiola. Major.
VI	*Vivace*	2/4	A 5 + 5	B 4 + 4	A 4	Coda 4 + 3	Reversion to original structure with repeats. Theme recognizable but changes in harmony, especially at cadences.

			Structure		
VII	*Grazioso*	6/8	A B A Coda 5 + 5 8 + 4 + 7		Richer harmony; oscillation between 6/8 and 3/4, especially in section B. Major.
VIII	*Presto non troppo*	3/4	A B A Coda 10 + 5 + 5 4 + 4 + 4 + 7		Minor. Variation farthest removed from theme.
Finale	*Andante*	2/2	Five-measure ground bass derived from harmony of theme.		Bass pattern repeated eleven times; 12th time ornamented; 13th through 15th time in minor and in upper parts; 16th time as before. Concludes with statement of theme and coda.

FIGURE 7-1. Brahms: Variations on a Theme by Haydn, Op. 56.

Commune caused a temporary suspension of musical activities; after the war, instrumental organizations found it easier to resume their schedules than did opera companies. Besides Berlioz, other though lesser instrumental composers were active in France before 1870: the expatriate Englishman George Onslow (1784–1853), for example, turned out a prodigious amount of chamber music in a style resembling second-rate Weber and Mendelssohn, and both Franck and Saint-Saëns wrote instrumental music before 1870. Absolute music, furthermore, was only one facet of the activity of French composers after 1870, for all of them at least dabbled in opera and to some extent were influenced by the "new German school," especially Liszt. Wagner's influence on these composers, however, has been overstated, and the French cult of Wagner consisted of literary or even political figures rather than musicians.

The principal musical change after 1870 was that French composers were accepted in more than one field of music. Between 1750 and 1870, absolute and serious music had been regarded as chiefly a German province, from Schobert and Gluck to Meyerbeer and even Offenbach; other composers who dominated Parisian musical life were Italians such as Cherubini, Salieri, Spontini, and Rossini. Between 1780 and 1870 the proper province for the French composer was a certain kind of opera: the rescue opera, *opéra comique*, or *opéra lyrique*. During the first stage of the "French Musical Renaissance" influences from across the Rhine were strong, especially those of Beethoven, Schumann, and Liszt; furthermore, Franck was born in Belgium and Lalo was of Spanish descent.

César Franck (1822–1890) was not a prolific composer, and most of his major works date from the last decade of his life. The organ was his central instrument: this accounts for his polyphonic writing; the improvisatory nature of much of his music, especially developments and transitions; the awkwardness of his piano music; and the "registration changes" of his orchestration. In contrast to his organist-contemporary Anton Bruckner, Franck's orchestra stresses the reed- or flute- pipe sounds of the oboe, English horn, and bass clarinet.

Chromaticism and cyclic form are usually cited as the two salient characteristics of Franck's style, but like most attempts to summarize a composer's style in a few lines, such statements have resulted in oversimplified generalizations. Franck used chromaticism as a source of contrast to a diatonicism with modal undercurrents, best seen in the central movement of his *Prelude, Chorale, and Fugue* for piano; his chromaticism is often the result of melodic chromaticism in many parts rather than either a functional or coloristic harmony. Typical devices are sequences, either stepwise or by thirds; sinuous chromatic motion within a narrow melodic ambitus, often centered around the third degree of the scale; and an essentially tonal framework. Example 7-5 is a good illustration: note the third-related chords, the enharmonic use of augmented triads,

EXAMPLE 7-5. Franck, Organ Chorale in B minor.

and the irregular resolution of chords of the augmented sixth. Critics are seldom neutral about Franck's chromaticism; either it is an expressive seasoning which compensates for bland melodies and sagging rhythms, or (especially in the Piano Quintet) is an irritating mannerism.

Though Franck gave hints of his future reliance on cyclic form in his F-sharp minor Trio (1841), he did not set his ideas definitely forth until his *Grande pièce symphonique* (1860–1862) for organ. His cyclic form consists of thematic transformation and the recapitulation of salient motives or even full themes in subsequent movements; it derives from the practice of Liszt's Weimar works. Cyclic forms are most evident in *Le Chasseur maudit* (1882, his noisiest work), the Piano Quintet (1879), and the Symphony in D minor (1889), but are subtly stated in his *Prelude, Chorale, and Fugue*. Franck frequently used not one but two "germ-cells" to create a contrast and duality of expression, often with a mystic connotation of light opposed to darkness; the best examples of such usage are the Symphony and the *Variations symphoniques* (1885), in which he also contributed to the re-assessment of the solo piano as a participatory rather than the dominant instrument in a concerto. Cyclic form for Franck was an effective means of unifying an often loose, rhapsodic, and rambling musical structure, but it remained for his pupil Vincent d'Indy to carry this device to its most logical conclusion (see Ex. 9-8).

Though Franck's students called him "Pater Seraphicus," the line between the sacred and the secular elements in his music is most difficult to draw, and there are few more voluptuous compositions than the first movement of his Violin Sonata. Franck's church music stands midway between the unashamedly operatic expressiveness, sometimes bordering on sentimentality, of Gounod's *St. Cecilia Mass* and *The Seven Last Words* of the young Théodore Dubois (1837–1924) and the relative austerity of Fauré, d'Indy, and Dubois's twentieth-century works. Franck's church music, like that of his French and Victorian contemporaries, was also influenced by a kind of feminized Christianity, different from the sturdy piety of Bruckner, Brahms, and Dvořák or the rugged self-taught American "Sacred Harp" composers.[1]

---

[1] It is difficult for us properly to assess nineteenth-century church music, especially that of Catholic France, because our ideals of musical austerity as the most fitting expression of religious worship make this music sound operatic

Franck's highly individual style did not permit imitation, yet he taught a diverse group of composers, some of whom will be discussed in Chapter 9, and passed on to them a sense of high seriousness about music with patriotic and religious overtones, also a different interpretation of chromatic harmony and musical structure that contributed to the breaking-down of nineteenth-century concepts of tonality and form; this may be his most significant contribution to posterity.

Edouard Lalo (1823–1892) spent most of his life as a violinist in orchestras or chamber ensembles and was second violinist in a string quartet that introduced Wagner to Beethoven's late works in this genre. Strongly influenced by Schumann, Lalo wrote little music but it is of high quality, sound technique, and appropriate for its purpose. His Symphony in G minor (1889) is exceeded only by Brahms's C minor String Quartet as the most somber instrumental work of the century, but the soberness of the Cello Concerto (1877) is relieved in the second and third movements by delightful Spanish intermezzi, a vein Lalo had previously exploited in his best-known work, the *Symphonie espagnole* (1875) for violin and orchestra. Lalo was not successful as an operatic composer, but his best work, *Le Roi d'Ys* (1888) enjoys occasional performances and is a midpoint between Massenet's lyric operas and Debussy's *Pelléas et Mélisande*.

Camille Saint-Saëns (1835–1921) was the most prolific and universal among his contemporaries, for he wrote in virtually every musical medium. In 1871, when he was 36, he was considered the dean of French composers and became the most important founder of the Société nationale de musique. Though he wrote some significant works before 1870, especially the intimate *Oratorio de Noël* and G minor Piano Concerto, his reputation rests solely on his works of the 1870's and 1880's, since his later music was eclipsed by the new developments of the 1890's.

Among his instrumental works are four symphonic poems, modeled on Liszt's works but with a much simpler structure: *Danse macabre* (1875) is the best known. His most admired chamber work is the Septet for strings, piano, and trumpet (1881); its movements, entitled "Préambule," "Menuet," "Intermède," and "Gavotte et final," hearken back in spirit to the chamber suites of Couperin and

---

and saccharine, particularly to Protestant ears attuned to Schütz, J. S. Bach, and Vaughan Williams. The socio-cultural and theological connotations of church music are fertile fields for investigation.

Rameau rather than to the instrumental cycles of the High Classic and Romantic period. His Third Symphony (1886) is from a technical standpoint the best synthesis of the expressive resources of the "music of the future" with the ethos and techniques of absolute instrumental music, for Saint-Saëns uses thematic transformation and reminiscence as effectively as Liszt and with more technical surety than Franck, and he links the sections together with thematically connecting material, often contrapuntally treated, with almost as much finesse as Brahms. The elegance, unpretentiousness, and skillful craftsmanship characteristic of his best work may be seen in his finest concertos: the A minor Cello Concerto (1873), C minor Piano Concerto (1875), and B minor Violin Concerto (1880).

Saint-Saëns strove for years to make a reputation as an opera composer but with little success. *La Princesse jaune* (1872) has a delightful overture replete with pentatonic exoticism. *Samson and Delilah* (completed 1877) was originally conceived as an oratorio and betrays many characteristics of this genre—for one thing, static action—but the work contains much fine and idiomatic choral writing as well as voluptuous arias for the mezzo-soprano.

Saint-Saëns was one of the major forerunners of twentieth-century music, more in his attitude toward the art than in his compositions. Toward the end of his life he stated: "He who does not feel wholly satisfied with elegant lines, harmonious colors, and a fine series of chords does not understand art."[2] The subjective approach to music which had continued from the Baroque through the "*Sturm und Drang*" and culminated in nineteenth-century Romanticism ended with Saint-Saëns far more than with Brahms, whose music is full-bloodedly Romantic despite its composer's technical mastery and reliance on what Baroque composers called "invention." Saint-Saëns's music is objective: an orderly, disciplined kaleidoscope of sonorities lacking both the cosmic message of a Beethoven, a Wagner, a Franck, or a d'Indy and the sublimated personal emotions of Schumann, Liszt, or Brahms. Saint-Saëns's use of musical parody, best seen in his *Carnival of the Animals* (completed in 1886 but suppressed during his lifetime lest it damage his reputation as a serious composer) stemmed from Rossini's "secret" piano compositions but (in contrast to Beethoven's "Romantic irony") is an important transition to the anti-Romantic parody and caricature of Satie, Poulenc,

[2] *Les Idées de M. Vincent d'Indy* (Paris, 1919), cited in James Harding, *Saint-Saëns and His Circle* (London, 1965), p. 219.

and Milhaud. Saint-Saëns was a great admirer of earlier French music; he edited the music of Gluck, Rameau, and the *clavecinistes*, and incorporated their aesthetic into his works through his use of restraint and simplicity. He may be therefore considered the chief forerunner of the neo-Classic revival transmitted by his pupil Fauré to Ravel, and ultimately to others like Stravinsky and Piston.

Bibliography

Robert Haas's *Bruckner* (Potsdam, 1934), in German, is the best biography of this composer; the most satisfactory work in English is Erwin Doernberg's *The Life and Symphonies of Anton Bruckner* (London, 1960), though its analyses resemble program notes. Karl Geiringer's *Brahms: His Life and Work* (2d. ed., New York, 1947) is the standard biography in English; the monumental analyses of Brahms's works by Edwin Evans, Sr. (London, 1912–1936, 4 vols.) can be disagreed with but should not be disregarded. Martin Cooper's *French Music from the Death of Berlioz to the Death of Fauré* (London, 1951) and Paul Landormy's *La Musique française*, volume II (Paris, 1945) are the best surveys of this period of French music. James Harding's *Saint-Saëns and His Circle* (London, 1965) is anecdotal rather than critical or analytical.

8

Nineteenth-Century Nationalism in Music

Nationalism is a term which is better described than defined. It includes a feeling of political or cultural inferiority, a seeking for identity among the folk arts of the common people and especially the "unspoiled" peasants, and a search for particular national means of expression different from the cultural norms of the dominant group. Music played an important role in the cultural nationalism that swept Europe during the nineteenth century. The opposite side of musical nationalism was exoticism, a search for new effects from the folk music of other lands and peoples, generally those considered to be less spoiled by civilization; this even led to the phenomenon of Russian nationalists who proclaimed their musical independence from western European models by exploiting the exotica of the peoples of central Asia, at that moment being conquered by the Tsarist imperium.

Nationalism in the nineteenth century is first evident in western Europe. The reaction against the French literary and Italian musical culture of the eighteenth-century German courts culminated in the temporary unification of the Germanic peoples at the "Battle of the Nations" near Leipzig in 1813 against Napoleon, whose downfall was celebrated by cantatas or battle pieces by Weber and Beethoven, who at this time began to use German tempo and expression markings rather than the customary Italian indications. The male chorus (Männerchor) movement played an important role in the drive for German unification, and Wagner's writings, with their anti-Semitism and mythologizing, reflect the souring of German liberalism into a perverse nationalism after 1848.

We have already seen the important roles played by Verdi in the Italian *Risorgimento* and by nationalism in French music after the Franco-Prussian War. Yet the French more eagerly seized on exoticism, as reflected by the use of Near Eastern motives in the pastel colors of *Le Désert* and *Lalla Roukh* by Felicien David (1810–1876) or in Saint-Saëns's works of the 1890's. Spain was a favorite topic for French exoticism, from Auber's *Le Domino noir* (1839) to such masterpieces of local color as Bizet's *Carmen*, Chabrier's *España*, and Debussy's *Ibéria*. As we shall see, Hungary was a similar source of exotica for German composers. Yet nationalism was at its strongest in the countries east of Germany or in areas peripheral to the musical developments of the eighteenth century.

Not all the composers mentioned in this chapter were deliberate nationalists. Such composers as Anton Rubinstein and Horatio Parker wrote in an "international" Romantic style; Berwald, Chaikovsky, and MacDowell are unique musical figures who are included here largely for convenience's sake. Many national composers eschewed the deliberate quotation of folk-song but wrote in the melodic, harmonic, and rhythmic spirit of folk music. Furthermore, by 1900 virtually every ethnic group in Europe had developed its own "national" music. Limitations of space permit my discussing only the most significant national developments.

FIGURE 8-1. Political and Linguistic Areas of Europe, 1867–1914. From Edward Raymond Turner, *Europe Since 1870* (Garden City, 1921), p. 36. Reproduced by permission.

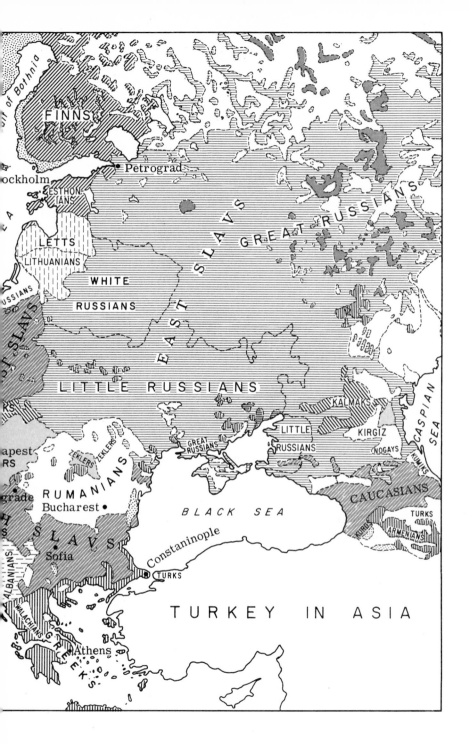

Russia

Tsar Pëtr the Great (1672–1725) opened a "window on the West" with his conquest of the eastern shores of the Baltic and the construction of his new capital, St. Petersburg, by Western architects. Throughout the eighteenth century many foreign musicians and composers came there, among them Galuppi, Paisiello, and finally Boïeldieu and John Field. Catherine the Great (1729–1796) attempted to create a "national opera" by writing opera librettos in Russian and having them set by court composers. At the opening of the nineteenth century the principal Russian composer, Dmitri Bortniansky (1751–1825), wrote Italianate operas and keyboard music, although Russian elements are present in the church music by which he is best known today. Ventures were also made at this time in utilizing Russian folksong in the context of Western tonal harmony; the best specimens are the *thèmes russes* in Beethoven's Op. 59 Quartets (see Ex. 8-2a).

In 1802 Spohr described the singing of Russian soldiers which he heard near Mitau:

> They howled frightfully, so that one would almost have to cover his ears. The songs are rehearsed by a cudgel-wielding noncom. The melodies of the songs were not bad, but were accompanied by nothing but false harmonies.[1]

Such views of native Russian music were shared by most of the local connoisseurs. It remained for Mikhail Ivanovich Glinka (1803–1856) to synthesize authentic folk idioms with the heritage of Western music.

A dilettante like most of his Russian successors, Glinka was influenced by Italian music, especially Bellini's, and loved the folk music of Spain. His output was not large; it consists chiefly of short orchestral pieces utilizing either Russian or Spanish folk and popular music, some piano pieces, and two operas, the historical *A Life for the Tsar* (1836) and the fairy-tale *Ruslan and Lyudmila* (1842). Little of his music exists in its original form.

Glinka's operas show, respectively, two of the three basic trends of east European opera during the nineteenth century (the third trend, the parody of the Meyerbeerian opera exemplified by

[1] Louis Spohr, *Selbstbiographie* (Kassel and Göttingen, 1860–61, 2 vols.), I, 36–37.

Dargomÿzhsky's *Esmeralda* and Chaikovsky's *Orleanskaya Dieva*, need not detain us here). *A Life for the Tsar* is a historical opera calculated to arouse strong national or patriotic feelings, with the peasants or popular heroes as the central figures, their music in the style of folksong and folk harmony. This harmony utilizes a large number of secondary triads, especially in the minor mode, which had led many to refer to this as "modal" harmony; Glinka often gives his folk-like melodies contrapuntal treatment, as Example 8-1 shows. The enemy are depicted by their own national music, Polish dances like the krakowiak, mazurka, and polonaise, and the opera

EXAMPLE 8-1. Glinka, *A Life for the Tsar*, Act I.

concludes with the patriotic cannon-shots-*cum*-Kremlin-bells finale epitomized in the conclusion of Chaikovsky's *1812 Overture*. *Ruslan and Lyudmila*, on the other hand, is a fairy-tale opera with brilliant orchestration and strange melodies and harmonies for fantastic episodes: Example 8-2 accompanies the cortege of the wicked magician Chernomor. Exoticism, through the use of Persian dances or the

EXAMPLE 8-2. Glinka, *Ruslan and Lyudmila*, Act IV.

Caucasian *lezginka*, plays an important role. Noteworthy in both operas are the important role of the chorus, the exotic ballets, and the use of the alto and low bass voices for principal characters. Folk idioms and intonations appear most frequently in the choruses, less in the arias for male voices, and least of all in the soprano arias, which are strongly influenced by Bellini and Donizetti. Glinka's remarkable orchestration (with which Rimski-Korsakov may have tinkered) deserves comment for its extensive use of the "primary" or unmixed colors of the orchestral palette rather than the blended sounds of the Germanic composers.

Glinka's treatment of folksong influenced composers throughout the century. He employed such techniques as changing the harmonies, placing the song in different voices, or contriving effective countermelodies, all of which gave variety to repeated melodic material. One of his favorite devices, the use of sinuous chromatic inner parts, is found also in Cherubini, Beethoven, and Auber but became a hallmark of various "national" composers' treatment of folk-like melodies, as Example 8-3 shows.

Glinka's work was continued by Aleksandr Sergeyevich Dargomÿzhsky (1813–1869), whose music contains a vein of lyricism lacking in Glinka's works and leads directly to the soaring melodies of Chaikovsky. In such "experimental" works, however, as

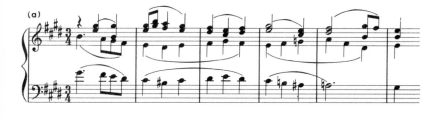

EXAMPLE 8-3. (a) Beethoven, Quartet Op. 59, No. 2, third movement; (b) Glinka, *Kamarinskaya;* (c) Grieg, Ballade, Op. 24; (Copyright 1918 by G. Schirmer, Inc. Reproduced by permission.); (d) Delius. *Appalachia.* (Copyright 1906 by Harmonie, Berlin. Copyright 1927 by Universal Edition. Reproduced by permission.)

(c) Andante espressivo

(d) Andante

EXAMPLE 8-3 continued.

the *Overture on Finnish Themes* and *The Stone Guest* (another setting of the Don Giovanni story), Dargomyzhsky intensified Glinka's
dissonances and linear writing; these and his experiments in musical
declamation led to the speech-dominated vocal writing in Musorgsky's operas and songs.

The term "Kuchka" —"Mighty Five," or simply "The Five"—
is a convenience for grouping the quite dissimilar Russian nationalist
composers of the third quarter of the nineteenth century. The music

EXAMPLE 8-4. Dargomÿzhsky, *Rusalka*, Act III.

of César Cui (1835–1918) is almost unknown today, and the music of Mily Aleksandrovich Balakirev (1837–1910), the mentor of the group, is seldom performed. Aleksandr Porfirievich Borodin (1833–1887) made an extensive use of Caucasian and central Asian local color in his music, especially in his opera *Prince Igor* (source of the "Polovetsian Dances") and his Second Symphony. Despite its brilliant orchestration, the music of Nikolai Andreyevich Rimski-Korsakov (1844–1908), who arranged, re-orchestrated, completed, and "improved" many of the works of his colleagues, has undergone a sharp decline in popularity; his best works follow Glinka's reliance on the exotic and fantastic, like his last opera *Le Coq d'Or* (1907).

The greatest composer of this group is Modest Petrovich Musorg-sky (1839–1881), the composer of operas in various states of comple-tion or revision (*Boris Godunov, Khovanchina*), some keyboard music, and a number of superb songs. Though Balakirev had some training in Western music, all these composers were essentially self-taught and were frequently engaged in other than musical occupa-tions—Cui, for example, as a lieutenant general of engineers and Bo-rodin as a research chemist.

An army officer or civil servant during most of his life, Musorg-sky deplored his lack of "polish" and "craftsmanship," yet it is pre-cisely the lack of Western-oriented training that gives his music such an uninhibited power and directness. His harmony is the most empirical of any composer since Monteverdi; one of his most inter-esting devices is the coloristic juxtaposition of chords unrelated by conventional standards but containing two common 'ones, as in Ex-ample 8-5[2], and one need only compare Beethoven's (Ex. 8-3a) and

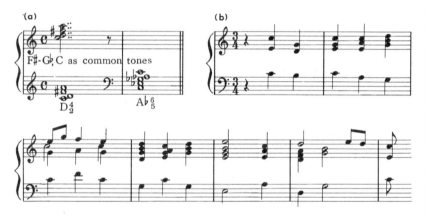

EXAMPLE 8-5. Musorgsky, *Boris Godunov*, Prologue.

Musorgsky's (Ex. 8-5) harmonizations of the same melody to be aware of the basic differences between Western and Russian har-monic practices. In *Boris Godunov* Musorgsky contrasts Western and Eastern idioms in the third (Polish) act, added to provide a love interest to the opera, and in the powerful "Revolutionary" scene, where the tonal chant of the Jesuits is opposed to the Russian hymnody of the rascally monks Missail and Varlaam. Russian folk

[2] Yet Balakirev anticipated this effect in his *King Lear* overture (1859).

or ecclesiastical music dominates the choral scenes (as it does also in *Khovanchina*) and folksong idioms characterize the scene between Boris's son Fedor and his nurse. The soloistic high points of the opera are Boris's soliloquies, the confrontation scene between Boris and Prince Shuisky, and Boris's death.

Musorgsky, building on Dargomÿzhsky's unsuccessful experiments, succeeded in creating a speech-dominated Slavic musical language much as Caccini, Schütz, Lully, and Purcell had done for Western European languages during the Baroque. The Slavic countries had lagged in achieving this kind of declamation possibly because of the widespread performance of Western operas in translation, the reluctance of singers (especially female) to try anything new, and the pervasiveness of Western melodic idioms which could not readily be adapted to Slavic or Magyar languages; other Eastern countries did not develop their own speech-dominated musical languages until the time of Janáček and Bartók early in the twentieth century. Musorgsky succeeded because he combined realistic declamation with a compelling musical expression that is declamatory rather than lyric, interjectory rather than melodically continuous, motivic rather than phrase-dominated, variable rather than symmetrical; it often relies on irregular or complex musical meters, and it is often reinforced by empirical harmonies and snatches of folk or ecclesiastical motives.

In both his operas and songs Musorgsky achieves a realism comparable to Courbet's in painting or Zola's in literature. Like his contemporary Fëdor Dostoyevsky (1821–1881), Musorgsky excels in the psychological portrayal of character and thus anticipates twentieth-century realism and expressionism. His posthumous influence was strong not only on Janáček and Bartók but also on Debussy, who spent a brief time in Russia, and who continued Musorgsky's work in using coloristic harmonies, seemingly unrelated chords in succession, and declamatory expression.

Other Russian composers turned to the West for inspiration. Anton Grigorievich Rubinstein (1829–1894), a conservative and eclectic cosmopolitan, did much to bring Western standards of musical education to Russia. Petr Ilyich Chaikovsky (1840–1893) was far more oriented toward the West than the composers of "The Five," but incorporated Russian folk music within an essentially Western framework in the first two of his six symphonies. His lyricism, inherited from Dargomyzhsky, is best seen in his symphonic slow movements and in his operas, especially *Eugene Onegin*, which is probably his finest work. He displays a strong if not always subtle harmonic sense, obtaining his effects chiefly through oscillations around the mediants (as in Ex. 8-6) or through clustered non-harmonic tones. His best instrumental music is centered around Western forms of absolute music and especially the ballet, and like Glinka, Raff, and Rimski-Korsakov he created brilliant settings of the folk or popular music of other nations, as in his *Capriccio Italien* or the musical travelogues in the ballets *Swan Lake* and *The Nut-*

EXAMPLE 8-6. Chaikovsky, *Eugene Onegin*, Act I.

cracker; Russian nationalism was only one of the many colors in his palette.

Two later Russian nationalists deserve brief mention: Aleksandr Konstantinovich Glazunov (1865–1936), who continued Chaikovsky's lyrical tradition with a vein of national color, and Reinhold Glière (1875–1956), whose Third Symphony, "Ilia Mourometz" (1911), may be regarded as an epitome of almost hysterically epigonous post-Romanticism.

Bohemia

Bohemia, the westernmost of the Czech provinces, was musically dominant in this region during the nineteenth century. During the Thirty Years' War (1618–1648) the Austrians subjugated Bohemia and overlaid its culture with Germanic influences to which the natives had to adapt. During the eighteenth century there was a great efflorescence of musical education in Bohemia, for since the Slavs were to be servants, the Austrian authorities thought that music would be a useful trade, and the products of especially the instrumental music programs of the Jesuit schools were disseminated throughout Europe, chiefly in Mannheim and Vienna; one need but mention Jan Stamic (Johann Stamitz) in Mannheim or Koželuch, Tomašek, and Vorišek in Vienna. Bohemian music remained dominant during the nineteenth century, with that of the other Czech peoples (Moravians and Slovaks) regarded as exotic rather than national products; the reason may have been that the Austrian rule over Bohemia was less restrictive than the Hungarian dominance over Moravia and Slovakia. Indeed, Moravian nationalism did not come to prominence until the music of Leoš Janáček. Tuneful homophony was characteristic of both Baroque and Classic music in Bohemia; combined with a long tradition of instrumental, especially string, performance, this gave birth to the Mannheim school and was a strong influence on Viennese composers from Haydn to Schubert. Yet not until the nineteenth century could Bohemian composers obtain recognition at home and devote themselves to a particularly national style.

František Skroup (1801–1862), the founder of Bohemian musical nationalism, wrote operas to librettos in Czech which contain some of the most technically simple music ever written. His most famous work, *Fidlovačka* (1834), includes folksong, quotations from *Der Freischütz*, and the aria "Kde domoj muj" which later became the Czech national anthem. The models for this work are evidently Rousseau's *Le Devin du village* and the simpler *Singspiele*.

Bedřich Smetana (1824–1884) founded the most viable school of Bohemian national music. His musical development was late, and his first significant compositions date from the late 1850's—tone-poems for Goteborg in Sweden, where he was musical director. One of them, *Wallenstein's Camp*, is based on a Bohemian subject and contains most of the composer's stylistic traits: passages in fast harmonic rhythm with considerable chromatic activity to create a sense of excitement; dance motives; and a triumphal conclusion. The apex of his orchestral achievement is the cycle of six symphonic poems *Má Vlast* (My Country), of which *The Moldau* is best known. His historical operas dealing with Bohemian topics (*Libuše*, *The Brandenburgers in Bohemia*) contain many striking passages but are somewhat influenced by Meyerbeer; on the other hand, his popular *Bartered Bride*, essentially (like *Fidlovačka*) an *opéra comique* transferred to a Czech village, is one of the masterpieces of national opera with its humorous intrigue, natural characters, tuneful and delightful music (in the opening chorus, authentic folk music). His best keyboard compositions, technically quite difficult, frequently utilize folk dances.

Antonín Dvořák (1841–1904) is the most important Bohemian composer of the nineteenth century. In many ways his career parallels Haydn's: humble peasant beginnings, struggling musical apprenticeship, the slow growth of an international reputation to result in great acclaim in later life, a deeply fervent religious faith, and a reputation with the mass audience based on only one creative period. Dvořák is one of the few truly "universal" composers of the century in the sense that he wrote in all existing genres; though known primarily as a symphonist, he was both active and skilled as a composer of operas, chamber music, songs, and choral works.

Though Dvořák's operas are popular in their native land they have not travelled well; the only one habitually performed outside Czechoslovakia is *Rusalka* (1901). The triptych of overtures, including the popular *Carnival*, dates from 1891; his other symphonic poems were written after his return from America and range from the prolix *Golden Spinning Wheel* to the concise *Midday Witch* (both 1896). Posthumous publication of four symphonies repudiated by the composer during his lifetime has resulted in a re-numbering of his works in that form: the old First, Second, Fourth, and Fifth are now, respectively, the Sixth, Seventh, Eighth, and Ninth. As a symphonist Dvořák was most influenced by his friend Brahms, chiefly in his choice of an intermezzo rather than a scherzo in his Fifth, Seventh, and Eighth Symphonies and in architectonic structure, though not in instrumentation. Dvořák's labored attempts to make his Ninth or "New World" Symphony a cyclic structure make this one of his weaker works, and the so-called Negro and Indian themes cannot be ascribed to indigenous American "intonations" since six-note scales and "Lombard" rhythms are also prominent characteristics of Czech folk music (Ex. 8-7).

EXAMPLE 8-7. (a) Dvořák, Symphony No. 9, first movement; (b) Czech folksong "Já ne, to ty" from Jan Seidel, ed., *Národ v Písni* (Prague, 1941), p. 175.

The chamber works from Dvořák's "American" period, the F major Quartet Op. 96 and the E-flat String Quintet Op. 99, have been overplayed to the exclusion of his finer chamber works, the Op. 81 Piano Quintet and the magnificent late quartets in A-flat, Op. 105, and G, Op. 106. As a violist, Dvořák was a skilled performer of chamber music and showed great and sympathetic understanding of the true possibilities of this medium.

If Smetana's basic dance rhythm is the slow polka, Dvořák's is the furiant, a dance based on the use of hemiola rhythm. In many furiants, Dvořák gives the impression of alternating a pattern consisting of one measure of 3/2 meter with two measures of 3/4 meter, as in Example 8-8b, but sometimes entire sections in one of the two meters (sometimes with cross-rhythms between the two) occur, as in his Slavonic Dance, Op. 42, No. 1. The two collections of Slavonic Dances (Op. 42 and Op. 72) are the most popular of his dance pieces and were originally for piano four-hands but subsequently orchestrated; in these he includes not only Bohemian but other Slavic dances. This pan-Slavism is also shown by his choral harmonizations of Slavic and even Lithuanian folksongs.

EXAMPLE 8-8. (a) Smetana, *The Moldau;* (b) Dvořák, Symphony No. 6, third movement.

With the exception of his oratorio *St. Ludmila,* Dvořák was least nationalistic in his large choral works, especially those to sacred texts. In these works the composer eschewed dance and folksong idioms and permitted his personal melodic and harmonic styles to be strongly pronounced, with a frequent use of secondary triads. The types of musical expression range from the "severe," as in the "Inflammatus" of the *Stabat Mater,* to the soulfully lyric, as in Example 8-9.

EXAMPLE 8-9. Dvořák, "Recordare" from *Requiem*, Op. 89.

Among the minor Bohemian composers of the century should be cited Zdeněk Fibich (1850–1900), chiefly an operatic composer; Dvořák's son-in-law Josef Šuk (1874–1935); and J. B. Foerster (1859–1951). The musical development of the great Moravian composer Leoš Janáček (1854–1928) was late and belongs in a study of twentieth-century music, rather than in one on the nineteenth.

Scandinavia

At the opening of the nineteenth century, the major musical figures in Scandinavian countries were German emigrants. The most important was Friedrich Kuhlau (1786–1832), who moved to Copenhagen in 1810 and became a Danish citizen in 1813. Although he is remembered today by his easy sonatinas, which have become favorite teaching pieces for beginning pianists, his sonatas for piano four-hands show Weber's brilliance, and his flute music is highly esteemed by players of that instrument.

The Swedish composer Franz Berwald (1796–1868) is one of the most original and interesting of the composers of the first half of the nineteenth century. Although he wrote chamber music and operas, his symphonies are the peak of his achievement. His style is highly original, especially in its harmonic and rhythmic aspects, and his use of rhythmic surprise and silence can be compared only with Berlioz's. As Example 8-10 shows, Berwald's music is very melodious, with a subtle and original use of harmonic colors, but the Stockholm audiences for which he wrote had to be educated even to Beethoven's style, and Berwald—too progressive for them—had to support himself chiefly as a maker of orthopedic appliances. It is quite probable that Sibelius was well acquainted with such passages in Berwald's music as the opening of the *Sinfonie singulière* and the conclusion of the *Sinfonie sérieuse*.

Though the Danish composer Niels Wilhelm Gade (1817–1890) is written about as the most important Scandinavian composer before Grieg, his music is never heard. A protegé of Mendelssohn whose music was popular in Germany and England as well as in his native Denmark, Gade devoted much of his life to developing Danish musical institutions. He is at his best in his miniatures, like the *Aquarelles* for piano, and as a musical landscape painter, as in the opening movements of his choral work *The Erl-King's Daughter*. A preference for the minor mode, often in its natural form, and a certain austerity are the chief "Nordic" elements in his music.

Edvard Hagerup Grieg (1843–1907), the major figure of nineteenth-century Scandinavian music, insisted that he was not Scandinavian but Norwegian. In his early works, like the E minor Piano Sonata or the popular A minor Piano Concerto, the influence of Schumann is pronounced. The Ballade, Op. 24, a set of variations on a Norwegian folk melody, is Grieg's most extensive solo piano work

EXAMPLE 8-10. Berwald, *Sinfonie sérieuse*, second theme of fourth movement.

and can be regarded as the first of his individual compositions, especially in its harmonic devices (see Ex. 8-3c). His most important works for piano are arrangements of Norwegian folk dances and ten books of *Lyric Pieces*, which range from simple teaching pieces to such novel "impressionistic" works as the "Klokkeklang," Op. 54, No. 6. Of his orchestral music, the two suites compiled from his incidental music to Ibsen's drama *Peer Gynt* (1874) are deservedly popular, but his fine choral music, especially his settings of psalms for baritone solo and male chorus, is virtually unknown today.

There are several facets to Grieg's musical personality: there is
Grieg the "Mendelssohn of the trolls," evident in "The Hall of the
Mountain King" from the *Peer Gynt* music and in the piano piece
"Kobold" (Op. 71, No. 3); Grieg the lyricist, seen in the A minor
Concerto and the violin sonatas; Grieg the elegiac singer, at his best
in the slow movement of the G minor Violin Sonata; Grieg the
harmonist, whose effective use of altered chords and non-harmonic
tones so strongly influenced MacDowell, Delius, and Gilbert; and
finally Grieg the folklorist, whose transcriptions of the *Slåtter* of
the Hardanger fiddle—with its major scale with a raised fourth degree, ornamentation, and drone strings—have a very "modern" sound
(Ex. 8-11). Grieg is one of the most individual composers of the
nineteenth century, and those whose knowledge of his music is

EXAMPLE 8-11. Grieg, "Bridal March from Telemark," *Slåtter*, Op. 72
(1902). Compare this example with his popular "Wedding Day at
Troldhaugen!"

based only on the song "Ich liebe dich," the *Peer Gynt* suites, or his easier *Lyric Pieces* would do well to examine his song cycle *Haugtussa* or his *Slåtter*.

Hungary

During the eighteenth and nineteenth centuries the Hungarians were the most culturally independent of the national groups of eastern Europe. Many Hungarian aristocratic families, of which the Esterházys are best known, were patrons of Viennese composers, who in turn reciprocated by using "Hungarian" motives in their works. The separation of Hungarian, Turkish, and gypsy elements in Hungarian music of the nineteenth century is a near impossible task, inasmuch as Hungary was occupied by the Turks for nearly two centuries and gypsy musicians were the chief disseminators of what became known as the Hungarian style; yet Turkish-oriented music was characterized by a greater degree of tonal instability and a more marked rhythmic emphasis, often helped by a lavish use of percussion. Example 8-12a shows tonal instability (for the period) in the introduction, a major scale with a raised fourth in the choral part, and the strongly percussive rhythm of Turkish music, whereas Example 8-12c is a characteristically languorous melody with a typical Hungarian cadence in the fourth measure.

In the middle of the eighteenth century a new type of Hungarian popular music appeared, the *verbunkos* or recruiting music, originally played by bands of gypsy string players which accompanied Austrian recruiting officers to peasant villages. This music, disseminated by gypsy orchestras and composers of light music, soon became the favorite music of the Hungarian bourgeoisie and lesser nobility and, through the works of Germanic composers from Haydn to Brahms, became known as "Hungarian" music in the West until Bartók's folksong researches in the early twentieth century. Highly ornamented slow passages, syncopations, a characteristic cadential pattern (Exx. 8-12c, 13a, 13b), and fast passages in a fiery duple meter with much instrumental fioritura are characteristic of this style.

As the Viennese school of composition declined in influence after 1820, French and Italian opera became popular in Hungary. Their influences were effectively combined with the *verbunkos* style by Ferenc Erkel (1810–1893), Hungary's most important composer of this period, whose principal achievements were grand operas based on Hungarian history. His best-known work, *Hunyádi László* (1844), utilizes a mixture of styles: the *verbunkos* in its slow aspects (the farewell duet cited as Ex. 8-13c) or in the coloratura fireworks of the "La Grange" aria of Act II for his sympathetic characters, and an "international" style, largely based on Meyerbeer's, for such unsympathetic personages as King László V. In his later operas, like *Bánk Bán* (1860) and *Dósza György* (1867), Erkel's development surprisingly parallels Verdi's in its increasing musical depth and use of harmonic and orchestral resources.

Liszt's Hungarian works are chiefly utilizations of the *verbunkos* style by a highly cosmopolitan composer, and his Hungarian Rhap-

(a) Allegro

8th-note rhythm; bass, percussion

(b) Allegro

EXAMPLE 8-12. Turkish (a) and Hungarian (b), (c) influences in Western art music. (a) Mozart, *Die Entführung aus dem Serail*, Act I; (b) Beethoven, "Eroica" Symphony, last movement; (c) Schubert, *Divertissement à l'hongroise*, D. 818.

Un poco più mosso

EXAMPLE 8-12 continued

(a)

EXAMPLE 8-13. The *Verbunkos* style in popular and art music. (a) "Saltus Hungaricus" from the Martonfi MS. (late eighteenth century),[3] (b) Márk Rószavölgyi, "First Hungarian Social Dance," 1842; (c) Ferenc Erkel, *Hunyádi László*, Act IV.

[3] Cited in P. P. Domokos, "Magyar Táncdallamok a XVIII. Századból" in B. Szabolcsi and D. Bartha, eds., *Az Opera Történetéböl* (Budapest, 1961), p. 284.

(b) Allegretto

(c) Andante

Is - ten ve - leb hát   hös baj - no - kom

e - nyém le - en - desz   túl a sí -   ron,

EXAMPLE 8-13 continued.

Is - ten ve - led hát hös baj - no - kom

e - nyém le - en - desz tól a si - ron.

EXAMPLE 8-13 continued.

sodies and book *The Gypsy in Music,* as well as the continued exploitation of the *verbunkos* style by Raff and Brahms (Hungarian gypsy music had the same influence on German composers that Spanish gypsy music had on their French colleagues), gave the West a false picture of Hungarian music. Though the *verbunkos* style degenerated into the salon piece or "Csárdás Princess" operetta during the closing years of the nineteenth century, it won a new lease on life with Kodály's popular compositions like *Háry János* and the *Galanta Dances.*

England

England's prosperity, which attracted many foreign musicians and composers during the nineteenth century, hampered the development of a native serious art music. William Sterndale Bennett (1816–1875), highly praised by Schumann, gave evidence of talent in early works like his Piano Concerto and the overture *The Naiads,* which resembles in many respects Mendelssohn's "Melusine" overture; but the choir loft, the hymnal, and the festival chorus provided the main opportunities for serious English composers during the bulk of the century. The cathedral music of Samuel Sebastian Wesley (1810–1876) and the anthems of John Goss (1800–1880) are solid and effective, the best examples of Victorian church music; the processional hymns of the time, e.g., "Holy, Holy, Holy" by

John Bacchus Dykes (1821–1876), have no rivals. But compositions in the larger vocal forms by English composers were too strongly influenced by foreign models: first Spohr and Mendelssohn, then Gounod and Dvořák, whose choral works were extremely popular in England. Perhaps England's most viable contributions during this period were its school of theorists, best represented by Ebenezer Prout (1835–1909) and Donald F. Tovey (1875–1940), and the deft operettas of Arthur Sullivan (1842–1900), who combined a fine sense of craftsmanship with the piquancy of Auber in the works he wrote in collaboration with W. S. Gilbert; the most characteristic elements are the "patter songs," which derived from the fast parlando of the comic baritone arias of Rossini, and the bouncy choruses accompanied by a thrumming accompaniment in 6/8 or 2/4 meter.

Edward Elgar (1857–1934) is remembered today chiefly through his *Pomp and Circumstance* marches, models for the ceremonial processional march at which subsequent English composers have excelled. Moods of placid contemplativeness or elegiac reflection also influenced many of his orchestral works, of which the "Enigma" Variations (1899) shows the most variety. As a composer of oratorios, of which *The Dream of Gerontius* (1900) is best known, Elgar excelled in the portrayal of a Christian heaven, musically the opposite pole from the diabolism of Berlioz and Liszt. Frederick Delius (1862–1934), another late-developing composer, spent most of his days in France and during his lifetime was most celebrated in Germany. His English nationalist music consists of genre pictures of the countryside (*Brigg Fair, On Hearing the First Cuckoo in Spring*) which can be compared with the landscape paintings of John Constable (1776–1837). His rich harmonic sense was influenced to some extent by Grieg (compare Ex. 8-3c and -3d), but his characteristic blend of lush chromatic harmony and static harmonic rhythm repels some listeners. His *Appalachia* (1902) is still the best musical portrait of the American South; it was inspired by its composer's stay in Florida and Virginia during the mid-1880's.

United States

In 1800 the concert life of the urban Eastern seaboard was a pale reflection of London's musical activities, but the opening of the continent, the rise of cities in the Midwest, and the streams of immigration provided an increased strength for American musical life. Not until the twentieth century, however, did the strains of American popular music—the "singing school" tune, the minstrel-show tune, the gospel hymn, and the martial or sentimental Civil War song—become incorporated into art music; most nineteenth-century American art music was based on European models by composers who had studied there, and American musical nationalism was based chiefly on exploring Afro-American and, to a lesser extent, Indian music.

Louis Moreau Gottschalk (1829–1869) expressed the Creole culture of the Gulf coast and the Caribbean islands rather than that of Anglo-Saxon Protestant America. His use of Louisianan, Cuban, and Puerto Rican tunes and rhythms; his unusual piano sonorities which exploit the extreme upper ranges of the instrument; and a certain piquancy of expression raise his best piano compositions above the level of the "salon piece," although his *The Dying Poet* is the epitome of Romantic sentimentality.

The most important American composer at the end of the century was Edward MacDowell (1861–1908), a pupil of Joachim Raff who was also influenced by Grieg, especially in his harmony and musical miniatures. MacDowell's "Indian" Suite for orchestra is directly in line of descent from Raff's Hungarian travelogues, and his sonatas exploit a certain vein of Celtic nationalism. MacDowell is at his best in his genre pictures of the northeastern countryside and his finely wrought songs.

When Dvořák came to America in the early 1890's he advised the local composers to turn to Negro melodies for inspiration. The chief utilizer of Afro-American melodies and rhythms was Mac-Dowell's pupil Henry F. Gilbert (1868–1928), both in his larger orchestral works like the *Dance in Place Congo* and in his collections of piano miniatures like the *Negro Dances* or *A Rag Bag*, which show the influences of the cakewalk and the new dance craze of ragtime. Although Gilbert's treatment of Negro material seems patronizing today, he was serious and sincere in trying to reconcile these popular idioms with art music. In contrast, Horatio Parker (1863–1919) is the best of the "international" American composers; his oratorio *Hora Novissima* (1900) is one of the finest works written for the English choral festivals, but the eclecticism of his operas *Mona* and *Fairyland* prevented them from surviving. Mention should be made of the Irish-born Victor Herbert (1859–

EXAMPLE 8-14. Comparative treatments of Afro-American musical material by American composers: (a) Gottschalk, *Bamboula;* (b) Gilbert, "Br'er Rabbit" from *Three American Dances*. (Copyright 1919 by The Boston Music Co. Reproduced by permission.)

1924), whose successful operettas have overshadowed his fine serious compositions, particularly his magnificent Second Concerto for violoncello.[4]

Bibliography

Only the most selective bibliography can be given. Concerning Russian music, Boris Asafiev's *Russian Music since the Beginning of the 19th Century* (tr. Alfred Swan, Ann Arbor, 1953) is clumsily written and translated; more viable are Gerald Abraham's *Studies in Russian Music* (London, 1935) and his successive volumes and articles on this topic and

[4] The reader is referred for a much more comprehensive evaluation to H. Wiley Hitchcock's *Music in the United States: A Historical Introduction* (Prentice-Hall, 1969) in this series.

R. A. Leonard, *A History of Russian Music* (London, 1956). Good English translations of primary sources dealing with Russian nationalism are Richard B. Mudge (trans.), *Mikhail Ivanovich Glinka: Memoirs* (Norman, 1963) and Jan Leyda and Sergei Bertensson, *The Musorgsky Reader* (New York, 1942). Rosa Newmarch's *The Music of Czechoslovakia* (London, 1942) is badly out of date and a new volume on this topic is needed; see also John Clapham's valuable biography of Dvořák (London, 1966). Forthcoming in the Prentice-Hall History of Music Series is a volume on Russian and Soviet Music by Boris Schwarz.

John Horton's *Scandinavian Music: A Short History* (London, 1963) is an excellent survey, and further detail may be found in Robert Layton's *Franz Berwald* (London, 1959) and Monrad Johansen's *Grieg* (Princeton, 1938). Bence Szabolcsi's *A Concise History of Hungarian Music* (English translation, London, 1964) gives fine coverage of an extensive topic; I have not been able to hear the recorded anthology of Hungarian music which he has prepared.

Histories of English music represent a reaction against the Victorian era; the best concise accounts of the music of Elgar and Delius may be found in William W. Austin's *Music in the 20th Century* (New York, 1966). Gilbert Chase's *America's Music* (2d. ed., New York, 1966) has been the standard handbook for this field; Wilfrid Mellers' *Music in a New Found Land* (New York, 1965) is an interesting view by an English critic. H. Wiley Hitchcock's *Music in the United States* (Prentice-Hall: 1969) is to appear.

9

The Twilight of Romanticism

The term "post-Romanticism" is often used to describe the music of composers born between 1850 and 1875 who adhered neither to an overtly nationalistic school (though Delius and Glière are frequently included) nor to the musical revolution accomplished by Debussy during the 1890's. Yet there are two "post-Romanticisms": that of the end of the nineteenth century and that of the beginning of the twentieth, with the point of demarcation lying between 1898 and 1905.

The post-Romanticism of the nineteenth century is that of the twilight of a musical epoch and represents consolidations of musical trends initiated by earlier composers. On the other hand, twentieth-century post-Romanticism is a separate if small epoch in itself, a unique transitional period. An expression from art history, "manner-ism," is appropriate for this period, as it is for describing the chan-sons of the late fourteenth century in France and the chromatic madrigals of Gesualdo; it indicates a period of transition, distortion, exaggeration, epigonism, and a running up musical blind alleys, al-though many splendid works were the result. A few composers worked in both kinds of post-Romantic idioms, especially Richard Strauss and Gustav Mahler; the dividing point for the former was his change in emphasis from the symphonic poem to opera, and for the latter the interval between his Fourth and Fifth symphonies.

Twentieth-century post-Romanticism, covered briefly in Eric Salzman's *Twentieth-Century Music* and in greater detail in William Austin's *Music in the 20th Century*, deserves more detailed investi-gation. However, this volume is not the place for it, for twentieth-century post-Romanticism, despite its epigonism and blind alleys, looked to the future: one need but cite the new paths for the sym-phony found by Carl Nielsen (1865–1931) and Jan Sibelius (1865–1957), the searches for ways of combining Baroque contrapuntal techniques and Classic formal structures with new expressive means made by Ferrucio Busoni (1866–1924) and Max Reger (1873–1916), or the logical progression from exaggerated hyper-Romanticism to serial music achieved by Arnold Schoenberg (1874–1951) and his disciples Anton Webern (1883–1945) and Alban Berg (1885–1935), whose early compositions were also post-Romantic.

The inescapable conclusion is that the 1890's saw not only the last works of Verdi and Brahms but also the first mature works of Debussy and Schoenberg and is therefore one of the more tangled decades of the history of music as well as one of the least explored. It is hoped that the remainder of this chapter will provide some incentive for further study of this period.

Italian opera after La Traviata

Verdi, after writing *La Traviata* in 1853, went through a crea-tive hiatus shorter than Wagner's fallow spell between *Lohengrin* and *Das Rheingold*, for he was now writing operas for France and thus came under the influence of the best elements of Meyerbeer's style—harmonic richness and appreciation of the dramatic and gestic functions of the orchestra. Verdi's first opera in this vein, *The Sicilian Vespers* (1855), has vanished from the repertoire although its overture, one of Verdi's last full-scale works in this genre, is a magnificent example of the "old war-horse" overture once a staple of outdoor band concerts. *The Masked Ball* (1859), based on the libretto Scribe wrote for Auber about the assassination of Gustav III of Sweden in 1792 but with the locale changed by censor's decree to colonial Massachusetts, looks back to the melodrama of *Rigoletto* but also ahead, in the Act II finale, to the comic genius of *Falstaff*. *Simone Boccanegra* (1857, revised 1881), is an opera reminiscent of Verdi's earlier works and is chiefly a psychological drama on the order of *Luisa Miller*. *La Forza del Destino* (1862) and *Don Carlo* (1867) are the most representative operas of this "experimental" period, which closed in 1871 with the first two acts of *Aïda*.

Several features are common to these operas. Most of them are long, and many divertissements, either unrelated to or tenuously connected with the plot, are often eliminated in performance (even the entire first act of *Don Carlo*). The plots are farfetched, though no more so than those of *Lohengrin* or the *Ring* tetralogy. The musical inspiration of these operas is uneven, and they are more appreciated by singers and connoisseurs than by the general public. Spectacle plays an important role in many of these works, and in all of them the tenor-baritone duet is a climactic moment, especially in *Don Carlo* where the "reminiscence motive" of freedom is grandiloquently proclaimed. The conclusion of the grandest soprano arias is often a magnificently soaring melody, introduced first in Act II of *La Traviata* and brought to its heights in *La Forza del Destino*, *Don Carlo*, and the first act of *Aïda*. Verdi's harmony in these operas is much richer than formerly, and the orchestra plays an important part in the musical dramaturgy instead of being confined to ritornelli, fortissimo interjections, and strumming accompaniments.

Verdi's final creative period includes not only a delightful string quartet, written during the rehearsals of *Aïda*, and the magnificent *Requiem* (1874) and other sacred choral works, but also the last two acts of *Aïda* and the two glowing sunsets of Romantic Italian opera: *Otello* (1887) for the serious style and *Falstaff* (1893) for the comic. These two operas display the quintessence of Verdi's harmonic, orchestral, and psychological development; in them his enthusiastic vulgarity, which persisted as late as the Act II finale of *Aïda*, was finally purged; and the character portrayal in *Otello* is equaled in musico-psychological insight only by Musorgsky. *Falstaff* is actually the epitome of Wagner's theories of opera, for plot and music, orchestra and singers, are on an equal footing; the demarcations between set-numbers are well dissolved; and the aria, except for Falstaff's declamatory soliloquies, is replaced by deft ensemble writing. One need but compare Falstaff's soliloquies or Iago's "Credo" in Act II of *Otello* with Example 5-4 to trace Verdi's development.

Verdi overshadowed his later contemporaries, who were chiefly "one-opera" composers. Arrigo Boito (1842–1918), the most musically imaginative of this group, made his best contributions to music by writing the librettos for *Otello* and *Falstaff;* his one major opera, *Mefistofele* (1868, revised 1875), is a grandiose and impressive work but, perhaps because it also contains too much music, is one of that triad of "magnificent failures" of nineteenth-century opera which includes also Berlioz's *Les Troyens* and Cornelius's *Barber of Bagdad.* The somberly bitter-sweet tone of the operas of Alfredo Catalani (1854–1893) have affected their popularity, though his music is the most important Italian influence on Puccini's style. The best Italianate opera by a contemporary of Verdi is *Il Guaraný* (1870) by the Brazilian A. Carlo Gomes (1836–1896), where intonations of Amazonian Indian melodies are woven into an operatic canvas comparable to that of *Don Carlo.*

Verismo (realism) is the generic term for a short-lived operatic movement which attempted to combine the musical portrayal of raw emotions, seen best previously in *Il Trovatore*, with the literary realism of such authors as Emile Zola (1840–1902) and Giovanni Verga (1840–1922). Only two Italian successes resulted: *Cavalleria Rusticana* (1890) by Pietro Mascagni (1863–1945) and *I Pagliacci* (1892) by Ruggiero Leoncavallo (1858–1919). Neither composer was able to repeat his success and the other operas of each have sunk into oblivion, though there are many beautiful portions in Mascagni's *L'Amico Fritz* (1891). The best verist work is actually Czech: Janáček's *Jenufa* (completed 1903), one of the initial masterworks of twentieth-century opera.

Since the operas of Giacomo Puccini (1858–1924) span both the nineteenth and twentieth centuries and his two masterpieces, *Gianni Schicchi* (1918) and *Turandot* (incomplete at his death), are outside the chronological confines of this volume, attention need be paid only to the genesis of his style. Except for the memorable soaring melodies often sung by soprano and tenor in unison at the climax of a love duet, Puccini's Italian model was Catalani rather than Verdi, and he was principally influenced by French *opéra lyrique*, especially in his focusing of attention on the wayward heroine and in his use of understatement and restraint. Puccini's writing for the voice and his operatic orchestration deserve detailed study by today's opera composers. His harmony is a delicately pastel synthesis of all the effective devices from Liszt through Debussy, especially an employment of augmented triads and half-diminished-seventh chords, and his "modal" harmony, which he shares with Fauré, may well stem from the organ accompaniments to Gregorian chant which became increasingly used during the nineteenth century. Puccini's fine sense for the theatre covers the essential meretriciousness of most of his music.

Central Europe

During the closing years of the nineteenth century Vienna again became a musical capital. Brahms and Bruckner were still active, Wagner had gained impressive support despite the opposition of the critic Eduard Hanslick (1825–1904), and despite the decline of the Austro-Hungarian Empire Vienna was virtually the crossroads of Europe. On the other hand, the unification of Germany after 1870, though it resulted in centralizing political and financial power in Berlin, also saw a decline in Germany's musical energies.

Hugo Wolf (1860–1903) came from a border province of the Austro-Hungarian Empire and is said to have been partially of Slavic (Slovene) descent. His reputation rests almost exclusively on his songs, though he made ventures into opera, the symphonic poem, and chamber music. His creative process consisted of short bursts of intense activity, during which he wrote as many as three songs in a single day, followed by extensive periods of fallowness; one writer has speculated that the works on which Wolf's reputation rests were the product of only eighteen months of effort spread over nine years: his first major songs date from 1888 and he became incurably insane in 1897.

More space than is available here is necessary to define what is meant by the frequent comment that Wolf set "the inner meaning" of a poem to music, but several generalizations about his musical style are possible. He showed more literary fastidiousness and judgment than any other composer, and his major works consist of a prodigious number of settings either of poems by Mörike, Eichendorff, Goethe, and lesser poets or of translations of Spanish and Italian folk poetry; virtually all these are in collections designated by the name or nationality of the poet. His songs show a great variety of mood and emotional intensity, ranging from deep pathos to ironical humor; from placid contemplativeness, seen in the songs dealing with nature, to rollicking waltzes or songs in a popular style (on the evidence of "Auftrag," Wolf could have made a fortune as a composer of light music); from deeply mystical religious ecstacy, best seen in the *Spanish Songbook*, to a realism exceeding even Musorgsky's, as in "Zur Warnung," Mörike's description of a hangover, in setting which Wolf pushed nineteenth-century tonality to its limits.

Wolf's songs are superficially thought of as being piano-dominated and filled with chromatic harmony; like all generalizations, there is some truth in this statement but also salient exceptions. One may profitably compare the songs "Peregrina I" and "Peregrina II" from the Mörike songs; the former contains one of Wolf's finest vocal melodies, supported by the piano, whereas the other is a piano-dominated song with the voice declaiming the text; both songs are linked by a common ritornel. Even as late as the *Italian Songbook* some of the songs, e.g., "Mein Liebster singt," are independent piano pieces with words attached. The most common type of song has an ostinato-like accompaniment, often subtly varied in the course of the song. Many of the songs are declamatory with a chromatic substructure, but some are quite diatonic, yet with the phrases extended to avoid square-cut writing, e.g., "Fussreise" from the Mörike songs.

Wolf's rich harmonic palette derives from that of Liszt and Wagner. His sharpest dissonance is the chord of the major seventh, chiefly associated with the more tortured aspects of religious mysticism, as in Example 9-1. Actually, most of Wolf's harmonic vocabulary and turns of expression may be found in the miniatures of MacDowell and Grieg. Though some of the songs, especially the narrative ballads, are rather long, most of the finest are extremely concentrated and show great restraint and economy of means; in structure they are through-composed but unified by the musical patterns of the accompaniment.

EXAMPLE 9-1. Wolf, "Herr, was trägt der Boden hier" from the *Spanish Songbook* (1889–1890).

Wolf is a major forerunner of the twentieth-century Viennese school. The intense concentration of many of his songs inspired the similarly condensed instrumental compositions of Schoenberg and Webern; the "progressive tonality," with many changes of key, of several of his songs contributed in no small degree to the breakdown of traditional tonality;[1] and Wolf's realism anticipates the expressionism of Schoenberg's *Erwartung* or Berg's *Wozzeck* and *Lulu*.

Gustav Mahler (1860–1911), like Wolf, came from a border province of Austria. Except for an early oratorio, Mahler limited himself to two musical genres, the song and the symphony, and described himself as a "holiday composer" since so much of his life was spent in conducting. But whereas Wolf aimed toward an increasing condensation of musical space in his songs through economy of means and a corresponding heightening of intensity, Mahler endeavored to create the "symphonic song," not only through the use of orchestral accompaniments in the *Songs of a Wayfarer* (1883–1885) and several settings of folk poems from *Des Knaben Wunderhorn* (his chief source of texts) but also in expanding the scale of the song and elaborating its accompaniment. Certain topics appealed to him: the ironic and sardonic ("St. Anthony's Sermon to the Fish," later used as the third movement of the Second Symphony), the macabre ("Reveille," 1899), or the child's pictures of Heaven in the Third and Fourth Symphonies. The culmination of Mahler's symphonic songs came in the first decade of the twentieth century with his songs to Rückert's texts, especially the moving *Kindertotenlieder*, and the most massive and symphonic of song cycles, *Das Lied von der Erde* (1907–1908), to German translations of pessimistic Chinese poems. Mahler led the art-song on a grand scale (as opposed to the ballad), originally exemplified by Schubert's "Der Zwerg" and "Ganymed," to a point from which further development was impossible.

Mahler's first four symphonies belong chronologically as well as aesthetically to the nineteenth century. They are all on a massive time-scale, though the intimacy and light orchestration of the Fourth Symphony makes it seem like a chamber work in comparison with the others. Only the First Symphony is purely orchestral; the others use voices in at least one movement. Except in the Fourth Symphony, Mahler uses a large orchestra, with quadrupled woodwinds (many doubling on piccolo, English horn, E-flat or bass clarinet), eight horns, occasional offstage brass choirs, and the heaviest artillery of the brass and percussion to emphasize his climaxes.

---

[1] One might go so far as to say that Wolf's modulations within a four-page song are as extensive, far-reaching, and significant as those within an entire act of one of Wagner's operas.

Added woodwind color is used for doubling melodic lines in high registers to provide a "military band" effect. The scores are liberally sprinkled with explicit directions to performers and the conductor and are an excellent source for the study of orchestral performance practice around 1900. Far more than Schubert or Brahms, Mahler relied on songs to provide movements for his instrumental cycles, either pre-existing songs expanded as instrumental symphonic movements or newly composed, orchestrally accompanied solo songs. To Mahler the symphony was a kaleidoscopic world, calling for a mixture of a variety of styles and often incongruous musical elements and moods.

Though Bruckner taught and befriended the young Mahler, the principal similarities between them are not their long symphonies with apocalyptic climaxes but certain harmonic devices, especially the use of shifting tonal planes (but for different reasons) and certain effects like the slow march, which Bruckner used in his Fourth Symphony and which Mahler even more extensively adopted. Mahler's symphonies are really continuations of the symphonic ideal established by Liszt in his *Dante* and *Faust* Symphonies, with reliance on thematic transformations, sharp contrasts between diatonic and chromatic writing, an expanded time-scale, rhetorical and even sensational passages for dramatic effect, and sardonically diabolic distortion of melodic materials—the last-named deriving from the finale of Berlioz' *Symphonie fantastique* and fully established in Liszt's *Totentanz* and the third movement of his *Faust Symphony*. Liszt's funeral marches, especially that of *Héroïde funèbre*, also influenced Mahler, and the climactic apotheoses of Liszt's symphonies and tone poems were further intensified by Mahler through expanded orchestration and sudden shifting of tonal planes, as in Example 9-2. As a harmonist, Mahler was more conservative than such contemporaries of his as Wolf, Grieg, or Fauré; his chromaticism consists chiefly of melodic non-harmonic tones, often accented, with the resolutions delayed and imparting an intense yearning to his lyrical melodies. He relied heavily on wide melodic leaps, especially in violin melodies, and on sudden changes of tonal plane for effect (as in Example 9-2 or in several places in the choral finale of the Second Symphony) rather than for architectonic reasons in the manner of Bruckner.

Mahler's chief influences were the tradition of the expanded symphony with more or less programmatic content, from the Third

EXAMPLE 9-2. Mahler, Symphony No. 1, finale (string and most wood-wind parts omitted). (Copyright assigned 1952 to Universal Edition (London), Ltd. Reproduced by permission.)

and Ninth Symphonies of Beethoven through the program symphonies of Berlioz and Liszt to the Fourth and Sixth Symphonies of Bruckner. With his Fifth Symphony (1901-1902), however, Mahler stepped from nineteenth-century to twentieth-century post- if not hyper-Romanticism. His time-scales become more massive; he oscillates between the huge resources demanded for his Eighth Symphony to the extremely restricted scoring (strings and harp) of the adagietto of the Fifth Symphony or the delicate opening of the Ninth Symphony; his sardonic diabolisms become more and more distorted, especially in his scherzos; and his climaxes, though ever more apocalyptic, soon peter out to be succeeded by moods of deep pessimism. He brought the expanded programmatic symphony to its fullest possible development and, as with the art song, concluded a chapter in the history of this genre.

The early development of Richard Strauss (1864–1949) is almost as astounding as those of the young Mozart or Mendelssohn. Among the magnificent works of this early period (1881–1888) are the Cello Sonata Op. 5, the Serenade for wind instruments Op. 7, the First Concerto for horn, the *Burleske* for piano and orchestra, some of his finest songs, and the concluding work of this period, the Violin Sonata. Erroneously are these works called "classical," but they are really the legitimate legacy of Schumann, Brahms, and other German composers of absolute music; it is significant that all these works were written before Brahms's "late" period, which began in 1891. They all contain a virile and sturdy expression, strong and forceful harmonies, and fine construction leavened with a vein of piquant humor, most evident in the *Burleske* and the finale of the Cello Sonata.

Strauss is said to have changed his musical style under the ence of Alexander Ritter, who introduced the young comp the works of Liszt and Wagner. In the first works where this change is evident, the symphonic fantasy *Aus Italien* (1886) and the first version of the symphonic poem *Macbeth* (1888, revised 1890), the influences seem also to include, respectively, Raff's musical travelogues and Chaikovsky's tone-poems. *Aus Italien* particularly contains harbingers of Strauss's later styles: soaring, fortissimo string melodies, brass fanfares, bubbling horns in the first movement, and intimations of *Der Rosenkavalier* in the third movement. In the finale, the popular song "Funiculi-funiculà" (in using which Strauss had some trouble with copyright laws) is contrasted with a *Meistersinger*-like second theme. *Macbeth*, on the other hand, is too influenced by Liszt's and Chaikovsky's tone poems, too experimental, and often too gloomy and lacking in contrast and variety to be viable.

The pivotal year for Strauss was 1888, for during it he not only completed the Violin Sonata but also *Don Juan*, his first successful symphonic poem; *Death and Transfiguration* was finished in the following year. Both works owe much to Liszt and something to Raff, but the influence of two other composers is evident: the organist-composer Josef Rheinberger (1839–1901), best known as the teacher of many American composers of the nineteenth-century "New England" school, and Moritz Moszkowski (1854–1925), best known for his "Spanish dances" and salon music but who also made ventures in the larger forms. *Don Juan* is written in a free but recognizable sonata form with its most striking theme (initially stated by the horns) first appearing in the development; its recapitulation is truncated and its coda is wry, a direct contrast to Liszt's optimistic conclusions. *Death and Transfiguration*, influenced by Moszkowski even to its title, is a sonata-form movement with long introduction and coda, and represents a fine continuation of Liszt's best ideas of thematic transformation (see Ex. 9-3) as well as Liszt's tendency to anticipate his apotheoses.[2] *Till Eulenspiegel's Merry Pranks*

---

[2] See my study "Schiller, Moszkowski, and Strauss: Joan of Arc's 'Death and Transfiguration,'" *Music Review*, XVIII (1967), 209–217.

EXAMPLE 9-3. Thematic transformation in Strauss's *Death and Transfiguration*.

(1895), a "scherzo in rondeau form," is a later work but in spirit and in its brevity belongs with Strauss's earlier tone poems; these three works represent the peak of his career during the nineteenth century.

The next group of tone poems, from *Also sprach Zarathustra* (1896) to the *Symphonia Domestica* (1903), show a decline in the composer's creative powers. Though each is triple the length of his earlier tone poems, they do not have an equivalent amount of the earlier verve, élan, and dash, which appear only occasionally. Strauss at this time also began a kind of "role-playing," like Berlioz more than sixty years previously, in setting himself up as a "bad boy of music." He provoked indignation by imitating, in muted brass, the bleating of sheep and even calling for a real wind machine in *Don*

Quixote (1897), à free set of variations analogous to Franck's *Variations symphoniques* in its use of a double theme; and he aroused critical wrath with *Ein Heldenleben* (1898), an autobiographical tone poem of large dimensions in which he utilized several quotations from his earlier works to make the hero's identity clear.

Comparisons have been made between Strauss's expansion of his musical and orchestral dimensions and the ethos of Germany after the accession of Kaiser Wilhelm II in 1888 and the subsequent transformation of German life into emphasis on armaments and imperialist adventures. It is more appropriate to compare Strauss's change of style and his attitude toward the orchestra with the industrialization of Germany and its concentration not only on armaments but also on precision machinery, for Strauss's orchestra relies not so much on the heavy artillery of brass and percussion, which he uses with much more restraint than Mahler, as on efficient, meticulous precision, best seen in the difficult string passages which entire sections must execute cleanly. Strauss's orchestra became a precision instrument like a Siemens dynamo or Zeiss camera, with a corresponding loss of status for the individual musician, who became a cog in a remarkably efficient mechanism. It should be added that Strauss's orchestral music must be heard in live performance to be fully appreciated.

The active inner parts in Strauss's music have been attacked as a cluttering of the texture, but this is true only in a few passages such as the introduction to *Don Quixote*, where the composer tried to create an atmosphere of confusion for deliberate effect. The function of these inner parts is either to sustain a mood of drive and excitement, through intricate string passages of a sort derived from Wagner, or to give a restful or propulsive effect, through countermelodies or active accompaniment patterns, often in involved rhythms. In the middle of *Don Juan*, for example, the quiet pattern which accompanies the yearning oboe solo is transformed into the driving transition to the exuberant horn melody. When Strauss used genuine counterpoint it was to create a mood of archaism or "learnedness," as in the fugue "Science" in *Also sprach Zarathustra*. Strauss's melodies, for the most part, are motives rather than themes, but there are many memorable examples of the latter, like the horn themes in *Don Juan* or *Till Eulenspiegel*, the apotheosis of *Death and Transfiguration*, or the conclusion of *Also sprach Zarathustra*, accompanied with parallel thirds, which can be considered a poignant farewell to the nineteenth century. Strauss's harmony seldom goes beyond that of his contemporaries; one of the most striking examples, the conflict, at the end of *Zarathustra*, between B major and C major (with an added tritone), was anticipated by Berlioz over sixty years earlier in the second movement of *Harold in Italy*.

Strauss's abandonment of nineteenth-century post-Romanticism is shown in his change of emphasis from the symphonic poem to opera. He had begun this shift of interest with *Guntram* (1887–1893), but his successes in this medium did not occur until the first decade of the twentieth century with *Salome* and *Electra*, with their monster orchestras and Grand Guignol effects; these actually are an aberration in his stylistic development (his songs, for instance, show little change in style throughout his career), for he later found the vein of a post-Romantic nostalgia in *Der Rosenkavalier* and *Ariadne auf Naxos* most congenial to his muse.

France

French music during the closing years of the nineteenth century presents a complex picture of overlapping styles. The pioneers of the "French Musical Renaissance" continued their activity—Franck until 1890 and Saint-Saëns until 1920—whereas Fauré's first major works date from the late 1870's, and Franck's best pupils, Chausson and d'Indy, wrote their first major compositions during the 1880's. The music by all these composers except Franck overlapped to some extent Debussy's revolutionary works of the 1890's; hence chronology alone is no guide to this period, for French music after 1880 moved along several different paths.

Many of the composers in France had made a pilgrimage to Bayreuth or Munich to hear Wagner's operas, and most found the program of instruction at the Paris Conservatoire to be musically stultifying since it centered around operatic composition and the acquisition of mere technical skills in performance; this did not change until Fauré became director in 1905. Composers often found alternate means of instruction: private lessons with Franck; study at the École Niedermeyer, originally a school to train organists and church musicians, which included Saint-Saëns on its faculty and Gounod and Fauré among its distinguished alumni; and even, in the case of d'Indy and his friends, the founding of a new school of music, the Schola Cantorum, which placed considerable emphasis on the history of music in its curriculum. All four of the major French post-Romantic composers discussed in this chapter were outside the prevailing musical "Establishment," which stressed opera as the highest form of musical expression; all followed different paths; and all had significant influence on twentieth-century French music.

Emmanuel Chabrier (1841–1894) was a minor bureaucrat who heard a performance of *Tristan* when he was 38 and decided to devote himself to composition. Though his reputation today rests on a single orchestral work, *España* (1883), an exciting musical travelogue, his genius is best revealed in his light, unpretentious compositions, often with touches of parody, wherein he is a significant forerunner of Satie, Milhaud, and Poulenc. Chabrier has erroneously been called a Wagnerian because of his opera *Gwendoline* (1886), but Wagner's influence is felt more in the libretto than in the music, which contains much modal writing or emphasizes the tritone. Chabrier's rhythm is quite free and supple, as *España* or the parodistic *Trois valses romantiques* for two pianos will show; his phrases are often irregular in length and thus avoid the square-cut four-measure symmetry so common during the century. An anticipator of twentieth-century pan-diatonicism, he uses lush harmonies generally in a parodistic context. In Example 9-4, quite representative of his style, he delays the tonic chord until the end of the phrase.

EXAMPLE 9-4. Chabrier, "Idylle" from *Pièces pittoresques* (1881).

Gabriel Fauré (1845–1924), Saint-Saëns's pupil, strayed the farthest of all these composers from the musical language of Romanticism, and to many writers he is no Romantic at all. He excelled in works on an intimate scale, like piano pieces, chamber music, and songs; friends or pupils scored most of his few orchestral works. As a composer of absolute instrumental music, he followed the leadership of Schumann as transmitted through Saint-Saëns, but in a very original manner, as can be seen in his two most important early works, the Violin Sonata in A major, Op. 13 (1876) and the First Piano Quartet, Op. 15 (1879); it is interesting to note that his Violin Sonata precedes Franck's by a decade and that the Piano Quartet stems from the same year as Franck's Piano Quintet. Fauré's melodic lines are as long, unsymmetrical, and unpredictable as those of Berlioz; his slow movements are derived from song, but from the French romance rather than from the German Lied; and his music has a grace, elegance, and lightness which is often mistaken for lack of depth by those oriented toward German music.

Fauré's piano writing, deriving from Chopin's, is centered around expansions of small forms with such noncommittal titles as "Barcarolle" or "Nocturne," with melodies floating above or within arpeggiated accompaniments. Among his most delightful works for piano is the suite *Dolly*, Op. 56 (1894) for piano four-hands, in which the composer showed himself as adept in portraying the child's world as Schumann, Bizet (*Jeux d'enfants*), or Debussy.

Fauré's chief achievements are his songs, and in them the contrast between the German Lied and the French song is most evident. Only in the late years of the nineteenth century did France enjoy a school of poets comparable to those between 1770 and 1850 in Germany; their poetry was evocative, hinting, suggesting, hesitant, and restrained in its declarations. Similar are Fauré's settings of these poems; they lack the exuberance of Schubert or most of Schumann, the idealized, sublimated sensuality of Brahms, or Wolf's musical "close reading" of a poem. Typical of Fauré's songs is an active yet subordinate piano accompaniment over which floats a vocal melody that sedulously avoids any suggestion of the square-cut popular song or of the strophic style; sometimes the piano participates with the voice in dialogue. The nearest German equivalents are Schumann's "Der Nussbaum" and his *Frauenliebe und Leben* songs. The French song melody is neither tuneful nor declamatory, for it characteristically moves within a fairly limited ambitus and is principally devoted to bringing out the limited vocal sonority of the French language with its diphthongs and mute "e" sounds. Not until Debussy's *Pelléas et Mélisande* was the technique of French song transferred to opera.

Fauré's restrained musical language is the antithesis of German Romanticism. Fauré eschewed *"Sturm und Drang"* tempestuousness (note the opening of the First Piano Quartet), unbridled exuberance, or obvious wrestling with knotty compositional problems, though his secure contrapuntal technique is evident in such disparate works as the *Requiem* (1887) and *Dolly*. Fauré's supple and flexible rhythm is quite different from that of Schumann or Brahms, for the latter two composers wrote "bar-line" music even though the impression of the bar-line is different from that which appears on the printed page, and the idea of a four-measure phrase in the background, to be extended or elided, is ingrained in their thinking,[3] though the suppleness of the rhythm and phrase-structure of the second acts of *Tristan* and *Parsifal* contributed, as did Berlioz's rhythmic flexibility, to the freedom of French rhythm and phrasing. One may contrast the following illustrations with Example 7-3 to see the difference between sophisticated French and German rhythm and phrase-structure.

Fauré was one of the most revolutionary harmonists of the cen-

EXAMPLE 9-5. (a) Fauré, Piano Quartet, Op. 15, second movement; (b) Chausson, Symphony in B-flat major, Op. 20, first movement.

[3] It had to be a German, Hugo Riemann (1849–1919), to postulate that the four-measure phrase was the basic building-block of music.

tury, a fact which may be surprising because of his constant under-statement which avoids the rhetorical gestures, attempts at surprise and pathos, or dramatic contrasts so characteristic of both German and nationalist composers. A major ingredient of Fauré's harmony, its modality, stems from his study of Gregorian chant accompani-ment at the École Niedermeyer and his years as organist in Parisian churches; this style of chant accompaniment, though frowned on by the purists of Solesmes, conformed to the inherent modality of the chant through using many secondary triads, especially in minor, rather than forcing it into a major-minor straitjacket. Especially in minor, Fauré's melodies are also modal, with much use of the low-ered leading tone, as is best seen in the C minor Piano Quartet or the *Requiem*.

As did Puccini to a lesser extent, Fauré discovered the effective-ness of two chords of the seventh which had been neglected dur-ing the century, perhaps because of their lack of tonal directive properties: the minor seventh (C-E♭-G-B♭) and the major seventh (C-E-G-B natural). These differ from what Suckling has called the "straitjacket of leading-note diatonicism" characteristic of German music and evident in the chords of the dominant seventh, augmented sixth, and the juicier "altered" chords in which "tendency" tones, resolved (or seeming to demand to be resolved) as if they were lead-ing tones or dominant sevenths, are prominent. With Fauré the major seventh chord is not a tortured dissonance as in Wolf's music (see Ex. 9-1) but a passing dissonance, generally in an inversion, and the minor seventh, either in root position or inverted, is flexibly used not only as a harmonization of modal melodies but also as a pivot to or from remote key centers since it lacks the "pull" of a dominant harmony with a leading tone. Fauré's tonality is very clear, but he avoids strong emphasis on dominant harmonies. The following cadence is illuminating, especially if compared with a "traditional" resolution (Ex. 9-6).

A love for Fauré's music is an acquired taste and is generally found among those with a conspicuous lack of enthusiasm for Wag-ner and Brahms. Among his pupils only Maurice Ravel (1875–1937) became a major composer, but Fauré's influence was transmitted well into the twentieth century by the teacher Nadia Boulanger (born 1887), another of his pupils, and he can be considered one of the principal sources of French neo-Classicism with its emphasis on restraint, long melodic lines, and modal-sounding harmonies.

EXAMPLE 9-6. (a) Fauré, *La bonne chanson*, Op. 61, No. 3; (b) "Traditional" resolution of the cadential augmented-sixth chord.

Ernest Chausson (1855–1899) is both one of the most derivative and one of the most progressive of this group of composers. Independently wealthy, he was not a professional composer, and his music suffers from a certain amateurishness. He is at his most derivative in such Franckian works as the *Poème* for violin and orchestra (1896), the first movement of the curiously hybrid Concerto for piano, violin, and string quartet (1889–1891), and in the cyclic structure of his best composition, the Symphony in B-flat major (1889–1890), the finale of which recapitulates material from the previous two movements in the manner of his mentor Franck's D minor Symphony. Chausson constantly wrestled with what he called "the red spectre of Wagner which does not let go of me;" this Wagnerian influence was the evocative, atmospheric mood of most of the second act of *Tristan*, the last act of *Parsifal*, and the *Siegfried Idyl*, and is chiefly evident in the symphonic poem *Vivianne* (1882, revised 1887) and the extended song-cycle, the *Poème de l'amour et de la mer* (1882–1892).

Chausson's most progressive ideas are to be seen in his use of a neo-Classic style, most evident in the delightful Sicilienne of his Violin Concerto or the *Quelques danses* (1896) for piano, of which the Sarabande is cited as an example of the progress of nineteenth-century neo-Classicism: note, in Example 9-7, the change from Raff's diatonically-oriented major harmony to Saint-Saëns's extensive use of secondary triads and Chausson's free modality. Chausson seemed on the verge of creating a highly individual style when he was killed in a bicycling accident at the age of 44.

EXAMPLE 9-7. (a) Raff, Sarabande from Suite, Op. 207 (*ca.* 1880); (b) Saint-Saëns, trio of minuet from Septuor, Op. 65 (1881); (c) Chausson, Sarabande from *Quelques danses*, Op. 26 (1896).

Vincent d'Indy (1851–1931) made the best synthesis of French and Germanic musical styles in creating works of strong originality and masterly workmanship. Though in his later works he used such Debussyesque devices as whole-tone scales and unrelated parallel fifths or triads, chiefly for coloristic effects, as in his *Sept chants de terroir* (1918), in spirit he was of all French composers the most antithetical to Debussy's music and the newer French trends; yet his influence extended into the twentieth century in the larger works of Albert Roussel (1869–1937) and Arthur Honegger (1892–1955) as well as in the French version of *Gebrauchsmusik*, the Paris Conservatoire contest solo. An ardent and contentious polemicist not only for his musical ideals but also for a conservatively ultramontane Catholicism and a chauvinistic nationalism, as a literary figure he may be compared with Wagner. D'Indy's logical, systematic, intellectual view of music was expressed not only in his compositions but also in his gifts as a teacher and his monumental *Cours de composition musicale* (1903–1933).

One of the few "universal" composers of the century, d'Indy wrote in many different media. His atmospherically Wagnerian operas belong to the twentieth century, and his choral works include not only much church music (which increased in austerity during the course of his career) but also an early statement of his artistic credo in *Le Chant de la cloche* (1885), in which he overlaid Schiller's poem with a sturdily uncompromising Catholicism and the artistic ideals expressed by Wagner in *Die Meistersinger*. D'Indy's absolute instrumental music is strongly influenced by the architectonic principles of cyclic form and the melodic styles of Gregorian chant and French folksong; his chamber music includes not only string quartets (the E major Quartet is based on a chant motive) but also chamber music with winds.

D'Indy began his career as an orchestral composer with symphonic poems, of which the best known is the trilogy based on Schiller's *Wallenstein* (1874–1880). The *Symphony on a French Mountain Air* (1887), his most frequently performed work, follows the example of Franck's *Variations symphoniques* in having the solo piano prominent yet subordinate to the orchestra and contains ingenious thematic transformation. *Istar* (1897), based on an Assyrian legend in which Istar is gradually unclothed as she passes through the various portals of the temple, is a reversal of the standard variation form in that the theme, in a most effective orchestral unison, is stated toward the end of the composition.

D'Indy's crowning orchestral achievement is his Second Symphony in B-flat (1904); as the following examples illustrate, the composer declined to add the term "major" or "minor" because of the ambiguity of the opening germ-motive. This symphony represents the culmination of the art of thematic transformation, for the germ motives, especially motive "A," permeate each movement, especially in transitional passages, and many of the themes that do not derive from the germ motives can nevertheless be combined with them. This work is the greatest French symphony since Berlioz's *Symphonie fantastique* and forms an effective musical conclusion to a study of nineteenth-century Romanticism in music.

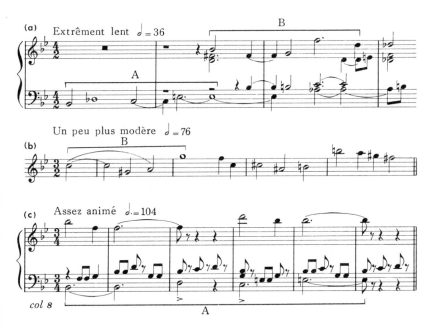

EXAMPLE 9-8. Selected cyclic interrelationships in d'Indy's Symphony No. 2 in B-flat, Op. 57. (a) First movement, introduction; (b) First movement, second theme; (c) Coda of first movement: combination of motive A with (1) transitional theme between first- and second theme-groups and (2) transformation of first theme; (d) Second movement, second theme with oboe countermelody; (e) Fourth movement, fugue subject; (f) Fourth movement, chorale in coda (inner voices omitted). (Permission for reprint granted by Durand and Cie, Copyright Owners of Paris, France; Elkan-Vogel Co., Inc., Philadelphia, Pa., Sole Agents.)

EXAMPLE 9-8 continued.

Bibliography

Barbara Tuchman's *The Proud Tower* (New York, 1966) purports
to give a synoptic view of this period but is so full of bias and, in the
musical sections, outright error, that it is suspect as a source of solid
information. One can get a better picture of this period by reading the
novels of Joris-Karl Huysmans and Marcel Proust.

Grout's *Short History of Opera* is the best survey of the Italian
opera of this period; Mosco Carner's *Puccini: A Critical Biography*
(London, 1958) is the best study of this composer's music.

Frank Walker has written a good biography of Hugo Wolf (London, 1952); Eric Sams's *The Songs of Hugo Wolf* (London, 1961) is a
detailed investigation. Neville Cardus's *Gustav Mahler: His Mind and
His Music* (Vol. I, 1965) may be the definitive study of this composer
when completed. There are serviceable biographies of Richard Strauss by
Norman Del Mar (London, 1962) and (from a Marxist viewpoint)
Ernst Krause (English translation, London, 1964); Strauss's nineteenth-
century works deserve more study.

The books by Cooper and Landormy cited in the bibliography for
Chapter 7 give the best overview of late nineteenth-century French

music. Chabrier has yet to receive a study in English, and d'Indy is not well served either by the appreciation of his pupil Daniel Gregory Mason in *Contemporary Composers* (New York, 1929), pp. 153–228, or by Norman Demuth's defensive biography (London, 1951). Norman Suckling's *Fauré* (London, 1951) points out many interesting contrasts between French and German music, and Fauré's pupil Charles Koechlin has written a biography of his mentor (English translation, London, 1946). *Ernest Chausson* by Jean-Pierre Barricelli and Leo Weinstein (Norman, 1955) is a solid study of this neglected composer's music.

IO

Nineteenth-Century Musical Romanticism in Music

At no time in history has music existed in a vacuum. Even during the individualistic nineteenth century, music and the relationship of composer and performer to their audience were affected by extra-artistic trends. These should be at least briefly examined if the music of this period is to be understood in its context. This chapter is also the best place to discuss the performance practice of Romantic music in hope that more detailed investigations of this neglected topic will be made.

Sociology of musical romanticism

One of the most striking differences between the Classic and Romantic periods is the change in the social function of the musician and his music. Most eighteenth-century composers were under some form of patronage, sometimes ecclesiastical but usually courtly, but the growing secularization of society and the increasing demands by the bourgeois classes for a constitutional government that would limit the arbitrary expenditure of revenues caused a sharp decline in the private patronage of music. The few composers of the nineteenth century who were under some form of courtly patronage during their careers, like Hummel, Spohr, or Wagner, bitterly resented it as demeaning.[1]

Composers and musicians became free artists, much as Handel was in eighteenth-century London. A few, like Mozart and Schubert, suffered from this new social arrangement. Much has been written about the exploitation of composers by unscrupulous publishers, but one must remember that copyright laws were not really enforced until the closing years of the century, that publishers had to depend for their income on exclusive relationships with composers and on rentals of performing materials, and that the less than scrupulous dealings of Beethoven or Wagner with publishers would not be tolerated today.

The musician, no longer under patronage, enjoyed a rise in social status but suffered from a corresponding drop in security. Whereas in the eighteenth century most musicians outside of Italy were trained under a system of apprenticeship, with the neophyte taken into a court orchestra under the watchful eye of his teacher, nineteenth-century musicians were generally trained in conservatories, institutions which originally began in Italy to teach orphans a trade but which received universal impetus after the founding of the Paris Conservatoire in 1795. These newer conservatories accepted children at an early age and their administration was characterized by frequent examinations, low tuition charges, governmental or philanthropic support, and a vocational type of instruction. A large number of positions were available for trained instrumentalists or singers, from military bands and light music ensembles to symphony orchestras and opera companies; rewards for leading singers and virtuosos were great, but many opportunities (more than at present!) existed for the humble musician. As in previous centuries,

---

[1] For a study of the effects of the breakdown of the patronage system in Germany, see my "Musical Portraits in 'Sturm und Drang' Drama," *Music and Letters* XLVI (1965), 39–49. I discuss musical instruction as a means of achieving social mobility in "Music at the 'Hohe Karlsschule,' 1770–1794," *Journal of Research in Music Education* XII (1964), 123–133.

music was an effective means for achieving upward social mobility; though a musician's duties were arduous and he was more subject to exploitation than at present, his life was considerably better than that of a coal miner or factory hand. The century also saw the rise of the musical entrepreneur, often a promoter in the manner of P. T. Barnum; though many of them were not exactly savory characters, we must acknowledge their importance in bringing music to a much wider audience. Composers and singers of opera, and touring virtuosos, were the chief beneficiaries of—or sufferers from— these entrepreneurs.

Composers were writing for a new audience. The Industrial Revolution and the improved transportation of the steamboat and railroad brought about a rapid growth of cities and distributed wealth among a wider segment of the population. Art music became an urban phenomenon, for mass audiences were needed to support resident opera companies and symphony orchestras or to attend the concerts of the virtuosos. Books on how to understand music, musical journalism and criticism, and private musical instruction to provide an "accomplishment" for the daughters of the bourgeoisie flourished. The creation of salon and "entertainment" music became an industry in itself, with such specialists as Johann Strauss, jr. and the Dane Hans Christian Lumbye (1810–1874) creating its masterpieces; analogous are the simple, sentimental, and beloved songs of Friedrich Silcher (1789–1860) in Germany, Stephen Collins Foster (1826–1864) in America, and Paolo Tosti (1846–1916) in Italy.

More people than before participated in the making of music. Under the influence of such pedagogical reformers as Rousseau, Johann Heinrich Pestalozzi (1746–1827), and Lowell Mason (1792– 1872), musical education was no longer limited to future professionals but spread through those segments of society fortunate enough to attend school. Tonic sol-fa, a form of solfège based on "movable do," made choral music easier to sing and, with the price of music constantly decreasing thanks to innovations in printing, brought about an efflorescence of choral societies and musical festivals. Through the improvements in technology and metallurgy brought about by the Industrial Revolution, musical instruments became both easier to make and cheaper, thus accessible to more people. The development of the concert grand and upright pianos and the addition of valves to brass instruments, more keys to woodwind instruments, and chin-rests or end-pins to stringed instruments made them easier to play although it significantly altered their timbres. Composers were not unduly hesitant to take advantage of these innovations.

The resultant growth in both orchestras and choral groups meant that by 1900 an essential manifestation of civic and national pride was the support of a resident symphony orchestra, choral society, music festival, and even of such luxuries as an opera company or musicological investigation and publication of the works of important bygone composers, often from public funds. This replaced the princely support of music, especially in continental Europe, though it often meant that the frustrations of Wagner with courtly protocol were replaced by Berlioz's impatience with bureaucratic delay, and often such privately sponsored groups as the Société national de musique, École Niedermeyer, or Schola Cantorum were needed to create alternatives to officially controlled musical establishments.

Romantically or politically inclined biographers have emphasized the alienation of the artist from society during the nineteenth century. Most composers at some time felt a conflict between the demands of a Philistine public and the ideas, originally fostered by Goethe and Schiller and continued by Beethoven and Wagner, of art as equal to religion and of the composer as a superior being. Yet the composer willing to come to terms with the lowest common tastes of his public, like Meyerbeer and Puccini, was lavishly rewarded, and some were able to enjoy both general acclaim and a large measure of artistic integrity, like Mendelssohn, Verdi, and Richard Strauss. It is true that a few composers, like Schubert and Berwald, were grossly neglected or abused during their lifetimes; and Nicolas Slonimsky's *Lexicon of Musical Invective* (New York, 1953) is a fascinating chrestomathy of attacks on famous composers and their music, but the whole concept of the general lack of public or critical appreciation for the major composers of the century has been exaggerated.[2] The gap between composer and audience was not to become a yawning chasm until the twentieth century, and the blame for this does not rest exclusively on the musically-inclined public.

[2] John H. Mueller's "The Aesthetic Gap Between Consumer and Composer," *Journal of Research in Music Education* XV (1967), 151–158, effectively explodes the legend of Beethoven's being "unappreciated" during his lifetime, and establishes a methodology whereby similar studies of the reception of other composers' works can be made.

Romantic performance practice

The study of the performance practice of nineteenth-century music has been neglected, since priority has been given to examining the manifold problems of the correct interpretation of even earlier musics; "tradition," it has been felt, is a sufficient guide to today's performers of the "standard repertoire." Yet much needs to be done to obtain reasonably correct interpretation of the musical literature between Beethoven and Fauré.

One salient problem is the existence of so many corrupt musical texts. Though most of the errors consist of erroneous dynamic, phrasing, and interpretative markings or inconsistent reproductions of variant versions of given passages, even wrong notes have crept in, and the policies of several publishing houses have led to the re-peated reissuing of defective scores.[3] It is further noteworthy that although among the once-definitive complete editions being redone are those of Schubert's and Berlioz's music, nevertheless the eighteenth and nineteenth centuries suffer most from the absence of scholarly complete collected editions of the works of many major composers, from C. P. E. Bach to Fauré.

The changes in instrumental and orchestral sonorities between Beethoven's time and the present have seldom been considered, especially by conductors. Of the instruments that Beethoven used in his Ninth Symphony, the trombones and cymbals are the only ones whose tone-colors have not undergone radical changes. Techniques of performance have undergone alterations of similar scope. The addition of chin-rests or end-pins to stringed instruments made it possible to produce a wider and more constant vibrato without tiring; the addition of valves to brass instuments and more keys to woodwind instruments made these instruments easier to play and more secure in intonation, but much of the original tone-color was lost, especially with the French horn. Characteristic of most nine-teenth-century string playing was a frequent use of audible shifts of position on the string, heard at its most exaggerated in the glissandos of the gypsy fiddle and at its best in the old 78 rpm recordings of

---

[3] See, for example, Eva Badura-Skoda, "Textual Problems in Masterpieces of the 18th and 19th Centuries," *Musical Quarterly* LI (1965), 301–317, and "In Verdi Veritas," *Newsweek*, XXXI (December 1962), 54; Emmanuel Winternitz, *Musical Autographs from Monteverdi to Hindemith* (Princeton, 1955, 2 vols.).

the Lener, Pro Arte, and original Budapest quartets. However, the Russian-Jewish school of violin playing headed by Leopold Auer (1845–1930), dominant in the twentieth century, emphasizes a continuous bowstroke which conceals the difference between up-bow and down-bow and suppresses audible shifts of position. Orchestral seating plans of the nineteenth century varied, but Spontini's dictum "My left eye, first violins; my right eye, second violins" was prevalent through this period, and antiphonal writing for the two violin sections occurs as late as Bruckner and Chaikovsky; the effect is lost if, as is now customary, all the violins are grouped together. Cellos and basses should face the audience, and the brass and percussion should be grouped together, not spatially separated. It is possible to secure reasonable approximation of the sound of a nineteenth-century orchestral performance by following these suggestions—and no one would miss the sloppy technical execution, insecure intonation, and almost hysterically subjective "interpretations" by conductors or soloists that were the negative features of much nineteenth-century playing.

The topic of Romantic ornamentation is still not wholly clear, yet many of the rules for eighteenth-century performance, particularly the playing of ornaments on instead of before the beat, hold true, even in the case of the compound appoggiaturas of Hummel and Chopin. Whether the trills are to begin with the main note or to follow the earlier practice of starting on the beat with the upper auxiliary is subject to dispute; Beethoven was as careless as Chopin was meticulous in indicating preparations for his trills, but it is most likely that chains of trills, such as those typical of Beethoven's last sonatas and quartets, were begun on the main note.

works as Schiller's *Kabale und Liebe* and Balzac's *Le Cousin Pons*. Albert Lavignac's *Musical Education* (English trans., New York, 1902) is a good survey of trends in the education of the professional musician, but a history of general musical éducation remains to be written.

Romantic performance practice is touched on at various points in Thurston Dart's *The Interpretation of Music* (London, 1954) and Robert Donington's *The Interpretation of Early Music* (2d ed., New York, 1966), but much more work with primary sources, tutors, and such documents as early phonograph records needs to be done.

Index

Abraham, Gerald, 91
Adam, Adolphe, 88
Albinoni, Tomaso, 10
Albrechtsberger, Johann Georg, 15, 20
Alkan (Morhange), Charles-Valentin, 57, *128*
Auber, Daniel François Esprit, 78, 85, 86, 100, 155, 161, 180, 186
Auer, Leopold, 213
Austin, William, 185

Bach, Anna Magdalena, 135
Bach, Carl Philipp Emanuel, *11–12*, 108, 114, 212

Bach, Johann Christoph Friedrich, 4
Bach, Johann Sebastian, 2, 3, 6, 11–12, 18, 33, 37, 56, 60, 61, 63, 66, 68, 73, 89, 95, 97, 107, 113, 121, 135, 139, 142, 144, 145
Bach, Wilhelm Friedemann, 11, 94
Balakirev, Mily Aleksandrovich, 163, 164
Balzac, Honoré de, 7
Barnum, Phineas T., 210
Baroque, 1, 8, 10–11, 37, 61, 145, 152, 165, 167, 185
Bartók, Béla, 91, 104, 114, 165, 175
Barzun, Jacques, 99, 100
Baudelaire, Charles, 6
Beethoven, Karl van, 28

Beethoven, Ludwig van, 3, 4, 5, 6, 7, 9, *10–34*, 37, 38, 40, 42, 44, 45, fn. 49, 55, 59, 60, 61, 63, 66, 68, 69, 70, 72, 73, 74, 77, 78, 89, 95, 96, 97, 98, 99, 103, 107, 109, 116, 119, 120, 121, 123, 126, 127, 131, 133, 134, 139, 140, 142, 143, 144, 148, 151, 152, 155, 158, 161, 162, 164, 172, 176, 193, 209, 211, 212, 213
Bellini, Vincenzo, *79*, 80, 88, 158, 160
Bennett, William Sterndale, 179
Berg, Alban, 120, 185, 191
Berlioz, Hector, 3, 6, 7, 33, 40, 43, 57, 70, 72, 74, 85, 86, *94–100*, 101, 102, 103, 106, 107, 109, 112, 120, 121, 127, 130, 131, 139, 145, 148, 153, 180, 187, 192, 193, 195, 197, 199, 200, 205, 211, 212, 213
Berwald, Franz, 155, *172*, 173, 211
Beyle, Henri (Stendhal), 7, 78
Bizet, Georges, 128, 155, 199
Boieldieu, François Adrien, 78, 85, 88, 158
Boito, Arrigo, 187
Borodin, Aleksandr Porfirievich, 131, 163, 164
Bortniansky, Dmitri, 158
Bouilly, Jean-Nicolas, 25
Boulanger, Nadia, 201
Bourbon, French royal family, 78
Brahms, Johannes, 2, 8, 13, 30, 33, 57, 61, 64, 70, 73, 74, 75, 89, 91, 104, 109, *135–45*, 150, 151, 152, 153, 169, 175, 179, 185, 188, 192, 193, 199, 200, 201
Brown, Maurice J. E., 60
Bruch, Max, 131
Bruckner, Anton, 2, 8, 33, 48, 54, 109, *131–35*, 148, 150, 153, 188, 192, 193, 213
Burns, Robert, 71
Busoni, Ferruccio, 185
Byron, George Gordon, Lord, 73, 96, 97

Caccini, Giulio, 165
Casanova, Giovanni Battista, 3
Catalani, Alfredo, 187, 188
Catherine II, Tsarina of Russia, 158
Catholicism, 50, 96, 113, 135, 150, fn. 150–51, 204

Chabrier, Emmanuel, 155, *198*, 207
Chaikovsky, Pëtr Ilyich, 8, 74, 131, 155, 159, 160, 161, *165–67*, 194, 213
Chateaubriand, François René, 7
Chausson, Ernest, 197, 200, *202–03*, 207
Cherubini, Luigi, 13, 31, 77, 85, 119, 120, 148, 161
Chopin, Fryderyk, 2, 3, 4, 33, 39, 43, 55, 56, 57, 68, 70, *88–94*, 95, 99. 100–01, 102, 103, 106, 107, 108, 114, 118, 123, 143, 199, 213
Chromaticism, 37, 39, 41, 91–93, 118, 123, 149–50, 152, 161
Ciurlionis, Mikolajus, 6, 8, 93
Classic, Classicism, 1, 2, 3, 4, 11, 48, 49, 50, 56, 68, 95, 130, 145, 152, 167, 185, 193, 201, 202–03, 208–09
Clementi, Muzio, *15–17*, 18, 19, 23, 34, 39, 56
Colbran, Isabella, 77
Collin, Heinrich Joseph von, 26
Constable, John, 180
Cornelius, Peter, *128–29*, 187
Couperin, François, 151
Courbet, Gustave, 165
Cui, César, 163, 164
Cyclic Forms, 22–23, 33, 61, 69–70, 72, 99, 107–112, 121–22, 143, 150, 169, 202–06

Dalayrac, Nicolas, 85
Dargomÿzhsky, Aleksandr Sergeyevich, 159, *161–62*, 165
David, Félicien, 87, 155
Debussy, Claude, 3, 114, 127, 128, 135, 151, 155, 165, 185, 188, 197, 199, 200, 204
Délibes, Léo, 88
Delius, Frederick, 4, 162, 174, *180*, 184
Des Prez, Josquin, 29
Deutsch, Otto Erich, 60
Diabelli, Anton, 29, 30
D'Indy, Vincent, 3, 7, 8, 84, 112, 135, 150, 152, 197, *204–06*, 207
Dohnányi, Ernö, 145
Donizetti, Gaetano, 2, *79–80*, 100, 160
Dostoyevsky, Fëdor, 165
Draeseke, Felix, 129
Dubois, Théodore, *150*
Dunstable, John, 114

Dussek (Dušek), Jan Ladislas, 55, 58, 66, 90
Dvořák, Antonin, 8, fn. 49, 64, 136, 150, *168–71*, 180, 181
Dykes, John Bacchus, 179–80

Eddy, Mary Baker, 2
Eichendorff, Josef von, 51, 71, 189
Einstein, Alfred, 66
Elgar, Edward, 3, 4, *180*
Encyclopédie, 4
Erkel, Ferenc, 121, *176–77*
Esterházy, family, 12, 45, 55, 175

Fauré, Gabriel, 74, 128, 150, 153, 188, 192, 197, *199–202*, 207, 212
Fibich, Zdeněk, 171
Field, John, 39, *56–57*, 58, 61, 89, 90, 158
Flotow, Friedrich von, 116
Foerster, Jozef Bohuslav, 171
Förster, Emanuel Aloys, 15, *18–19*
Foster, Stephen Collins, 210
Franck, César, 109, 128, 134, *148–51*, 152, 196, 197, 199, 202, 204
Franklin, Benjamin, 3
Franz, Robert, 74
Frederick the Great, 55
Fricken, Ernestine von, 68, 69

Gade, Niels Wilhelm, 64, *172*
Galuppi, Baldassare, 158
Gautier, Théophile, 3, 7, 88
Gaveaux, Pierre, 25
Geiringer, Karl, 11, 30, 135
Gellert, Christian Fürchtegott, 26
George IV, King of England, 78
Gesualdo da Venosa, Carlo, 94, 185
Gilbert, Henry F., 136, 174, *181–82*
Gilbert, William S., 180
Glazunov, Aleksandr Konstantinovich, 167
Glière, Reinhold, 167, 184
Glinka, Mikhail Ivanovich, 4, 57, *158–61*, 163, 166, 213
Gluck, Christoph Willibald von, 3, 5, 11, 13, 40, 84, 85, 88, 94, 95, 104, 119, 148, 153

Goethe, Johann Wolfgang von, 4, 5, 9, 21, 26, 37, 51, 52, 64, 74, 88, 95, 97, 112, 119, 189, 211
Gomes, A. Carlo, 187
Goss, John, 179
Gottschalk, Louis Moreau, 57, *181–82*
Gounod, Charles, 43, 87, 88, 150, 180, 197
Grand Opera, 85–87, 103, 158–59, 186
Grétry, André Ernest Modeste, 40
Grieg, Edvard Hagerup, 4, 74, 89, 114, 135, 136, 162, *172–75*, 180, 181, 189, 192
Grillparzer, Franz, 119

Haeckel, Ernst, 2
Handel, George Frideric, 4, 29, 30–31, 33, 37, 63, 64, 95, 136, 138, 140, 145, 209
Hanslick, Eduard, 95, 188
Haslinger, Tobias, fn. 52
Hasse, Johann Adolf, 3
Haydn, Joseph, 3, 5, 6, 7, 11, 12, 13, 15, 18, 19, 20, 22, 23, 24, 31, 36, 37, 45, 136, 142, 144, 146–47, 167, 168, 175
Haydn, Michael, 50
Hegel, Georg Wilhelm Friedrich, 84
Heine, Heinrich, 51, 52, 71, 88
Heinse, Johann Jacob Wilhelm, 5, 7, 9
Herbert, Victor, *181–82*
Herder, Johann Gottfried, 4–5, 9
Herold, Ferdinand, 78, 85, 86, 98
Herz, Henri, 57
Hiller, Ferdinand, 97
Hindemith, Paul, 40, fn. 49, 134, 145
Hoffmann, Ernst Theodor Amadeus, 3, *5–6*, 7, 9, 13
Hölderlin, Johann Christian Friedrich, 51, 139
Hölty, Ludwig Christoph Heinrich, 51
Holzbauer, Ignaz, 13
Honegger, Arthur, 204
Hugo, Victor, 2, 8, 63
Hummel, Johann Nepomuk, 12–13, 44, *55–56*, 57, 58, 89, 209, 213
Humperdinck, Engelbert, *127–28*
Hünten, Franz, 57

Ibsen, Henrik, 4, 173
Indy, see d'Indy

Ippolitov-Ivanòv, Mikhail Mikhailo-
vich, 129
Isouard, Niccolò, 85

Janáček, Leoš, 94, 131, 165, 171, 187
Jean Paul, see Richter, J. P. F.
Jensen, Adolf, 74
Joseph II, Emperor of Austria, 13–14,
15, 50

Kabalevsky, Dmitri, 57
Kalkbrenner, Friedrich, 57
Kleist, Heinrich von, 6
Klinger, Maximilian, 4
Klopstock, Friedrich Gottlieb, 51
Knepler, Georg, 67
Kodály, Zoltán, 179
Koželuch, Leopold, 15, 17–18, 167
Kreutzer, Rodolphe, 21
Krufft, Nikolaus Freiherr von, 51, 52
Kuhlau, Friedrich, 172

Lalo, Edouard, 148, 151
Lamennais, Félicité Robert de, 113
Lanner, Josef, 45
Lenau (Nikolaus Niembsch von Streh-
lenau), 71
Leoncavallo, Ruggiero, 187
Lesueur, Jean François, 95, 96, 97
Lippmann, Edward Arthur, 67
Liszt, Ferenc, 37, 55, 57, 59, 63, 70, 74–
75, 90, 91, 93, 101, 102, 103, 104–
115, 116, 118, 121, 123, 126, 128,
129, 130, 131, 136, 142, 144, 145,
148, 150, 151, 152, 180, 188, 189,
192, 193, 194
Lortzing, Albert, 116
Louis Ferdinand, Prince of Prussia, 55
Louis Philippe, King of France, 77
Lovejoy, Arthur, 1
Ludwig II, King of Bavaria, 116–17
Lully, Jean-Baptiste, 84, 165
Lumbye, Hans Christian, 210
Luther, Martin, 63, 86

MacDowell, Edward, 4, 114, 135, 155,
174, 181, 189

Mahler, Gustav, 3, 33, 109, 114, 135,
143, 185, 191–93, 196, 206
Marcello, Alessandro, 10
Marcello, Benedetto, 10
Marschner, Heinrich, 116
Mary Stuart, Queen of Scots, 71
Mascagni, Pietro, 187
Mason, Lowell, 210
Massenet, Jules, 87–88, 151
Matthisson, Friedrich von, 51
Mayrhofer, Johann, 51
Mendelssohn-Bartholdy, Felix, 7, 39,
43, 51, 57, 60–66, 72, 74, 75, 98,
103, 109, 116, 138, 148, 174, 179,
180, 193, 211
Mercadante, Saverio, 80
Metternich, Clemens Wenzel von, 78
Meyerbeer, Giacomo (Jakob Beer), 7,
63, 77, 84, 86–87, 95, 103, 104, 113,
118, 119, 120, 148, 158, 168, 176,
185, 211
Mickiewicz, Adam, 3–4
Milhaud, Darius, 4, 153, 198
Modality, 29, 91, 114, 148, 158, 164–65,
188, 201, 203
Monpou, Hippolyte, 7
Monteverdi, Claudio, 2, 10, 84, 126,
135, 164
Moore, Thomas, 73
Mörike, Eduard, 189
Moscheles, Ignaz, 61, 93, 103
Moszkowski, Moritz, 136, 194
Mozart, Wolfgang Amadeus, 3, 5, 6,
11, 12, 13, 14, 15, 17, 18, 21, 22, 23,
24, 34, 35, 37, 40, 45, fn. 49, 55, 60,
88, 119, 135, 140, 176, 193, 209
Musorgsky, Modest Petrovich, 25, 114,
163, 164–65, 187, 189
Musset, Alfred de, 7

Napoleon Bonaparte, 41, 76, 155
Napoleon III, Emperor of France, 88
Neefe, Christoph Gottlob, 14
Newman, William S., 26
Nicolai, Otto, 116
Niedermeyer, Louis, 197, 201, 211
Nielsen, Carl, 131, 185

Offenbach, Jacques, 2, 88, 101, 106, 148
Onslow, George, 148

Opéra comique, *84–86*, 103, 148, 168
Opéra lyrique, *87–88*, 103, 148, 150, 188
Operetta, 41, 88

Paër, Ferdinando, 25
Paganini, Niccolò, *57*, 58, 68, 73, 103, 106, 136
Paisiello, Giovanni, 158
Palacký, František, 4
Palestrina, Giovanni Pierluigi da, 6
Parker, Horatio, 155, 181
Pestalozzi, Johann Heinrich, 210
Pëtr I, Tsar of Russia, 158
Petrarch (Francesco Petrarca), 112
Pisendel, Johann Georg, 11
Piston, Walter, 153
Pius IX, Pope, 2, 113
Plato, 2
Platti, Giovanni Battista, 11
Pleyel, Ignaz Joseph, 3
Plutarch, 20
Poulenc, Francis, 152, 198
Prokofiev, Sergei, 106, 109, 114
Protestantism, 39, 60, 66, 74, 145, 179–80
Prout, Ebenezer, 180
Puccini, Giacomo, *187–88*, 201, 206, 211
Purcell, Henry, 165
Pushkin, Aleksandr Sergeyevich, 3

Raff, Joachim, *129*, 139, *166*, 179, 181, 194, 203
Rakhmaninov, Sergei, 57, 74
Rameau, Jean Philippe, 84, 152, 153
Raphael Santi, 88
Ravel, Maurice, 114, 135, 153, 201
Razumovsky, Andrei Kyrillovich, 25
Reger, Max, 145, 185
Reichardt, Johann Friedrich, 5, 6, 7, 26, 50–51, 52
Reinecke, Carl, *131*, 139
Rescue opera, 22, 37, 85
Respighi, Ottorino, 135
Rheinberger, Josef, 194
Richter, Jean Paul Friedrich, 5–6, 68
Riemann, Hugo, fn. 200
Righini, Vincenzo, 13, 14
Rimski-Korsakov, Nikolai Andreyevich, 114, 160, 163, 166

Risorgimento, 76, 82, 155
Ritter, Alexander, 194
Rode, Pierre, 23
Romantic Irony, *31–32*, 152
Romanticism, literary, *4–9*, 51
Romberg, Andreas, 64
Rossini, Gioacchino, 3, 7, 25, 26, 48, 76–79, 84, 85, 100, 148, 152, 180
Rousseau, Jean Jacques, 4, 7, 8, 168, 210
Roussel, Albert, 204
Rószavölgyi, Márk, 177–78
Rubinstein, Anton Grigorievich, 155, 165
Rückert (Raimar), Friedrich, 51, 71, 191

Sacred Harp, 150
St. Paul, 2
Saint-Foix, Georges, 12
Saint-Saëns, Camille, 8, 74, 148, *151–53*, 155, 197, 199, 203
Salieri, Antonio, 15, 85, 148
Salzman, Eric, 185
Satie, Eric, 152, 198
Sayn-Wittgenstein, Carolyne de, 109, 113
Scarlatti, Domenico, 15
Schiller, Friedrich von, 4, 5, 9, 30, 50, 51, 86, 116, 119, 139, fn. 194, 204, 211
Schlegel, August Wilhelm von, 51
Schlegel, Friedrich von, 51
Schober, Franz, 51
Schobert, Johann, 148
Schoenberg, Arnold, 3, 52, 72, 114, 120, 127, 128, 137, 185, 190–91
Schubart, Christian Daniel Friedrich, 5, 7
Schubert, Franz, 4, 5, 7, 26, 27, 33, 37, 40, *43–54*, 55, 56, 58, 59, 60, 61, 64, 65, 68, 73, 78, 103, 107, 108, 133, 143, 167, 177, 191, 192, 199, 209, 211, 212
Schütz, Heinrich, 165
Schumann, Clara Wieck, 66, 68, 71
Schumann, Robert, 6, 7, 17, 30, 33, 48, 57, 59, 60, 64, *66–75*, 89, 90, 93, 102, 103, 106, 107, 108, 112, 116, 121, 123, 131, 136, 139, 142, 144, 148, 151, 152, 172, 193, 199, 200

Scott, Walter, 51, 86
Scribe, Augustin Eugène, 86, 185
Sechter, Simon, 54
Shakespeare, William, 26, 51, 63, 87, 96, 97
Shaw, George Bernard, 95
Shostakovich, Dmitri, 106
Sibelius, Jan, 26, 33, 72, 74, 172, 185
Silcher, Friedrich, 210
Singspiel, 5, 25, 40, 168
Škroup, František, *167–68*
Skryabin, Aleksandr Nikolayevich, 6, 93, 112
Slonimsky, Nicolas, 211
Smetana, Bedřich, 4, *168*, 169, 170
Smith, Joseph, 2
Sociology of Music, 7, 9, 33, 208–11, 213–14
Sonnleithner, Leopold von, 52
Sousa, John Philip, 2
Speaks, Oley, 74
Spengler, Oswald, 6
Spohr, Dorette, 36
Spohr, Louis (Ludwig), 8, 11, 13, 30, *36–39*, 41, 55, 57–58, 63, 77, 78, 90, 103, 109, 116, 118, 127, 135, 158, 180, 209, 213
Spontini, Gasparo, 37, 85, 86, 95, 97, 103, 116, 117, 148, 213
Stamic (Stamitz), Jan, 167
Stendhal, see Beyle, Henri
Strauss, Johann, Sr., 45
Strauss, Johann, Jr., 45, 102, 210
Strauss, Richard, 4, 109, 114, 120, 127, 128, 129, 185, *193–97*, 206, 211
Stravinsky, Igor Fëdorovich, 3, 4, 70, 104, 109, 113, 114, 128, 153
Sturm und Drang, 4, 11, 12, 63, 85, 152, 200
Suckling, Norman, 201
Šuk, Josef, 171
Sullivan, Arthur, 180
Swieten, Gottfried Bernhard van, 12
Synaesthesia, 6–8
Szabolcsi, Bence, 113, 114

Tchaikovsky, see Chaikovsky
Thalberg, Sigismond, 57
Thomas, Ambroise, 43, 85–86, 87, 88
Tieck, Ludwig, 5–6, 7, 138

Tomašek, Jan Vaclav, 44, 167
Tosti, Paolo, 210
Tovey, Donald F., 180

Varèse, Edgard, 94
Verbunkos, 175–79
Verdi, Giuseppe, 79, *80–84*, 87, 96, 100, 103, 121, 155, 176, *185–87*, 188, 211, fn. 212
Verga, Giovanni, 187
Verlaine, Paul, 6
Victorianism, 60, 66, 150, 179–80
Viotti, Giovanni Battista, 23
Vivaldi, Antonio, 10–11
Volkmann, Robert, *131*, 137
Voltaire, 3
Voříšek, Jan Hugo, 44, 168

Wackenroder, Wilhelm Heinrich, 5
Wagner, Wilhelm Richard, 7, 9, 11, 36, 37, 39, 41, 43, 52, 55, 59, 70, 73, 74, 75, 78, 84, 85, 87, 90, 93, 98, 102, 103, 107, 109, 113, 114, *116–128*, 129, 130, 131, 136, 145, 148, 151, 152, 155, 185, 186, 188, 189, 191, 194, 196, 197, 198, 200, 201, 202, 204, 209, 211, 213
Waldstein, Ferdinand Ernst Gabriel, 24
Weber, Carl Maria von, 7, 11, 37, *39–43*, 44, 58, 59, 60, 61, 68, 89, 94, 95, 103, 116, 117, 148, 155
Webern, Anton von, 4, 52, 185, 190
Weingartner, Felix, 23, 40
Wesley, Samuel Sebastian, 179
Wieland, Christoph Martin, 4
Wilhelm II, Kaiser of Germany, 196
Williams, Ralph Vaughan, 112
Wolf, Hugo, 52, 112, 128, 129, *188–190*, 192, 199, 201, 206
Wyzewa (Wyzewski), Théodor de, 12

Zelter, Carl Friedrich, 5, 51, 64
Zingarelli, Nicola, 79
Zola, Émile, 187
Zumsteeg, Johann Rudolf, 51